# TRIUMPH

## OF A

## TIME LORD

### REGENERATING *DOCTOR WHO*
### IN THE TWENTY-FIRST CENTURY

MATT HILLS

I.B. TAURIS

LONDON · NEW YORK

Published in 2010 by I.B.Tauris & Co Ltd
6 Salem Road, London W2 4BU
175 Fifth Avenue, New York NY 10010
www.ibtauris.com

Distributed in the United States and Canada Exclusively
by Palgrave Macmillan
175 Fifth Avenue, New York NY 10010

ISBN: 978 1 84855 032 3

A full CIP record for this book is available from the British Library
A full CIP record is available from the Library of Congress

Library of Congress Catalog Card Number: available

Typeset in ITC Stone Sans by Sara Millington, Editorial and
    Design Services
Printed and bound in India  by Thomson Press India Ltd

# CONTENTS

# FOREWORD

Brilliant fan-producer (Russell T. Davies) meets brilliant fan-academic (Matt Hills) across the 'fan-tastic' new series of *Doctor Who*. Here, Time Lords Eccleston and Tennant meet the lords and ladies of Cultural Theory as Davies/Foucault co-deal in the time travel of the 'de-materialising auteur'. New *Who*'s branded format engages with the genre function (Foucault, via Mittell), production fan 'gamekeepers' watch warily the watching fan 'poachers' (de Certeau, via Jenkins), and the oscillation of producers between fan and media production identities works systematically to reduce the semiotic density of the new *Who* text (Elam, via Tulloch and Alvarado). *Triumph of a Time Lord* is a wittily written study, with brilliant extended forays on Rose's 'intimate epic', celebrity-history as quasi-brand, and the reconfiguration of *Who*'s 'unfolding text'. This book is all about the agency of production reflexivity, fans' shifting pleasure since the show went off-air and – especially important – the greater branding requirements of promotion and marketing.

Hills succeeds brilliantly in his epic quest to show how 'genre discourses are ... embedded in production decisions and textual structures'. Likewise, he convinces with his analysis of the 'text-function' (again elaborating Foucault) via production play between 'mainstreaming' and 'cult', and musical scoring that brands the show beyond sci-fi identifications, all the while approved by the 'powerless duality' of fans (no longer a 'powerless elite') who are figured both in the *Who* text and outside it by its fan-producers. I predict you will read this book several times, and it will get better each time.

**John Tulloch, Brunel University, co-author of**
***Doctor Who: The Unfolding Text* and *Science Fiction
Audiences: Watching Doctor Who and Star Trek.***

# ACKNOWLEDGEMENTS

I would like to thank my colleagues in the School of Journalism, Media and Cultural Studies, and especially Gill Branston, Sara Gwenllian Jones, Justin Lewis, and Karin Wahl-Jorgensen for their support. The ideas in this book have developed through my lecturing, particularly on the 'Quality TV' module, so my thanks to all the BA students who attended that in its first year.

In the wider world of academia my thanks go to Mark Bould, David Butler, Glen Creeber, Jon Gray, Henry Jenkins, Catherine Johnson, Matthew Kilburn, Geoff King, Annette Kuhn, David Lavery, Alan McKee, Nickianne Moody, Cornel Sandvoss, Jeff Sconce, Jamie Sexton, Steve Spittle, Lyn Thomas, John Tulloch, Tim Wall and Milly Williamson.

Thanks also to Ross Garner and Tim Robins for many a *Doctor Who*-related chat, and to Beccy Harris for tipping me off about 'The Sound of Drums' location filming. I make apologies to all my PhD students, who have had to tolerate my fandom, and greetings to the David Tennant fans led by Rebecca Williams. And along with Rebecca, many thanks to my other co-authors in recent years: Bertha Chin and Amy Luther.

Outpost Gallifrey-as-was (now succeeded by Gallifrey Base) has been a constant source of interesting, intelligent commentary on *Doctor Who*, so my thanks to the many posters there who have genuinely changed how I think about the programme. Online fan crit may sometimes get a bad press but the sheer brilliance of much fan commentary should not be overlooked (*contra* Davies and Cook, 2008). A few people whose postings I have especially appreciated are cited herein (from fanzines and blogs), including Jack Graham, Simon Kinnear,

Joe McKee and Lance Parkin. Fan commentary is frequently as illuminating as published academic critique, if not more so (hence also my frequent references to the work of Lawrence Miles and Tat Wood, whether or not Lawrence would describe himself as a *Doctor Who* fan).

Thanks also to the BBC Wales production team, of course. I did once manage to mention this project to Russell T. Davies; though he thought 'official' production interviews would be impossible to arrange, he was encouraging and positive about the idea of a new *Unfolding Text*-type book for new times.[1]

With regard to life outside my personal worlds of academia and fandom (though they seem to permeate almost everything), thanks and love go to my friends and family. To Paul and Helen for suggesting I needed a project manager; to Sibylle for helping; to Ben for cards and encouragement; to Stuart and Teresa for visits and care; to Emma for looking out for me; to Ace for being ace; and to Mum and Dad for everything – especially for taking me to Longleat in 1983.

Matt Hills
Cardiff University

**NOTES**

1    John Tulloch and Manuel Alvarado (1983) Doctor Who: *The Unfolding Text*, Macmillan, London.

# INTRODUCTION

## BRINGING BACK A TV ICON

There may be a little longer between this series and the next than usual.

Peter Cregeen, BBC Head of Series in Radio Times
25 November–1 December 1989.[1]

*D*octor Who's return to the UK's TV screens on 26 March 2005 has already been documented both officially and unofficially,[2] an unsurprising fact given that there has allegedly 'been more intellectual dissection of this programme than of any other that's now classified as "cult"'.[3] Indeed, Andrew Cartmel, former script editor on the series, even goes so far as to entitle his 'Introduction' to *Through Time*, 'Another Book About *Doctor Who*'.[4] But if that volume from 2005 was an 'affectionate ... insider's account of a cultural phenomenon',[5] then *Triumph of a Time Lord* might be described as an affectionate-yet-critical outsider's account. I am writing as a life-long fan of *Doctor Who* as well as an academic in the field of cultural studies – one of the 'many ... academics in the later generations of *Doctor Who* fans' to have been inspired by the programme.[6] By happy coincidence, I lecture at Cardiff University, lodged between the Temple of Peace and the Glamorgan Building, locations from 'End of the World' (1.2) and 'Boom Town' (1.11) respectively, amongst other episodes.

Combining the roles of academic and fanboy makes me a kind of 'scholar-fan',[7] bringing to this book an awareness of very different debates within fandom *and* professional academia. Mind you, the series I have loved all my life has had an ambivalent time within the groves of academe. Piers Britton and Simon J. Barker suggested, just a few short years before its regeneration by BBC Wales, that:

> *Doctor Who* ... remains beyond the critical pale: scholarly treatments such as John Tulloch's ... study of audience responses ... belong to that class of book that are the target of journalists' ongoing scorn for cultural studies as a discipline. *Doctor Who* can make no sustainable claims to possessing intellectual respectability.[8]

However, perhaps the newfound success, cultural omnipresence and massive merchandising of *Doctor Who* have finally changed all that:

> The return of the series in 2005 seems to have finally triggered explicit recognition ... In fact I believe that [executive producer and lead writer, Russell T.] Davies has even invited academic attention by having the Doctor not only interact with literary figures and important people in history, but also hav[ing] characters make much more explicit references to politics and contemporary culture. [W]hy else would the second episode of the first new season involve characters called 'The Adherents of the Repeated Meme'? ... What academic can resist bait like that?[9]

Kim De Vries goes on to note that 'in the next few years I imagine we'll be seeing more of the Doctor at conferences and in catalogs of scholarly publishers'.[10] As Paul Magrs has argued, we may be 'at the start of *Doctor Who* Studies',[11] or at a moment in its renewal, given the presence of a few venerable forerunners.[12]

Bringing back the TV icon of *Doctor Who*, and retooling it for the twenty-first century, finally appears to have rendered the show an appropriate object for study. However, the 'scorn for cultural studies' lamented by Britton and Barker has not yet entirely dematerialised. It lurks within certain types of academic work just as much as in journalistic arenas. The author of the otherwise excellent *Inside the TARDIS*, James Chapman, states that 'popular culture can be taken seriously without recourse to the ... language of high theory. The Doctor may have conquered Daleks, Cybermen, and Ice Warriors, but would he survive an encounter with Foucault, Derrida, or Deleuze?'[13]

The surnames cited are those of philosophers influential in cultural theory: Michel Foucault, Jacques Derrida and Gilles Deleuze. Yet it seems unhelpful to assume, from the very outset, that media and cultural theory represent a kind of evil, akin to the world-shattering ambitions of Daleks or Cybermen. 'Theory' does not seek to 'exterminate' or 'delete' the TV programmes it discusses, though you might sometimes imagine, from the resistance shown to it in certain quarters, that 'theory' represents The Enemy.[14]

Fortunately, there has always been a subset of *Who* fandom which, as Paul Cornell has observed, thrives by 'applying critical techniques to the thing it loves'.[15] This tradition can be illustrated today by discussion threads on the Gallifrey Base Forum (*http://gallifreybase.com/forum/*), as well as by a range of fanzines, e-zines and blogs. Making use of media theory does not have to mean using masses of jargon, even though one person's 'jargon' is another's useful vocabulary, and even if fandom is often as guilty of this as academia. The word 'squee' probably doesn't mean much to non-fans, just as the word 'signifier' won't mean much to those who aren't already media students.[16] So-called jargon is, in reality, just another cultural group's language that we don't want to spend time getting to grips with. But we all have our own 'jargons' that seem to be straightforward ways of understanding television, mainly because we have already invested time in them.

I hope that others who care about *Doctor Who* might enjoy the adventure of thinking a little differently about their favourite TV series. And I hope that cultural studies might be seen as a source of additional knowledge by interested readers, rather than as an evil, alien force. In his review of *Inside the TARDIS* for the *Independent*, journalist-fan Matthew Sweet reverses the polarity of James Chapman's metaphor. Rather than cultural theory being the monster, Sweet playfully depicts *Doctor Who* itself in monstrous terms:

> Its concepts and metaphors have invaded our language. It has colonised the British consciousness more effectively than any race of rubber-skinned aliens. It is a monstrous, unstoppable, ever-growing discourse. So what would happen if, on some time-trip to the Left Bank in the 1970s, Deleuze, Derrida and Foucault encountered *Doctor Who*? That's easy. It would simply slide on top of them like a giant green blancmange with a four-foot phallus.[17]

Referring to a less-than-successful design creation from the classic *Who* story 'The Creature from the Pit' (1979), Sweet depicts theory as being overwhelmed by *Doctor Who*'s prodigious productivity and fecundity. The programme may always have 'left behind a trail of words', encouraging viewers' literacy,[18] but today it is the source of thousands and thousands of words every day, whether online or off, in print or in everyday chat. *Who* has become more than just an 'unfolding' text, instead aspiring to the status of a multiplatform, multilayered mega-text from which fans and academics can only ever consume a cross-section.[19]

With that in mind, my focus here resolutely is on televised *Doctor Who* from 2005 onwards, with reference to Doctors one to eight only when relevant. Readers hoping for analyses of new *Who's* tie-in novels, or *Doctor Who Magazine* comic strips, or fan fiction, will be disappointed. However, this is just my personal choice of subject matter and focus. *Doctor Who's* tie-ins and spin-offs undoubtedly deserve to be scrutinised in other academic texts of their own.[20] Furthermore, it could be argued that *Doctor Who* (2005–9) is a continuation of the same series that ran from 1963 to 1989, not just in name, but also in terms of diegesis. However, I shall distinguish between 'new' *Who* (sometimes dubbed 'Nu-Who' by the fan press) and the 'classic' series on the basis that these were produced in radically different industrial and cultural contexts, as well as therefore exhibiting significant textual differences.[21]

Scholar-fandom means bringing together different ways of interpreting *Doctor Who*. Whereas fans generally display a tendency to read the series *intratextually* – in relation to itself and its own histories[22] – academics frequently read it *intertextually* via specific theoretical frameworks.[23] Scholar-fans also draw on their fan knowledge and passion, sometimes criticising other academics for being too quick to dump a specific, favoured theory wholesale on *Doctor Who*, without considering whether it really fits.[24] The question posed by the rise of scholar-fandom, and by the 'many ... academics in the later generations of *Doctor Who* fans'[25] is this: what can being a *Doctor Who* fan add to academic analysis of the programme? And, along the same lines, what might being a paid academic add to being a fan of the show? We should refrain from assuming that this hybrid identity somehow detracts from 'innocent' enjoyment of the TV series, or that it is some sort of 'spoiling' activity, as expressed in the common-sense, anti-intellectual notion of 'over-analysis'. For, much like accusations of theoretical jargon, allegations of 'over-analysis' tend simply to mean 'analysis using theoretical intertexts' rather than 'analysis using *Doctor Who's* intratextual history'. Yet both are forms of analysis which turn to surrounding texts for their evidence and understanding – whether these are *Doctor Who* or

Michel Foucault's *oeuvre*[26] – and both are valuable and important ways of thinking through *Who*. To order these hierarchically as 'over' (or 'under') analysis merely blocks any productive relationship between them. And it is this relationship that I want to consider next, before introducing the chapter-by-chapter contents of *Triumph of a Time Lord*.

## Essence and Experience
## Or, What *Who* Fandom Can Learn From Academia
## (and Vice Versa)

Combining 'intra' with 'inter' approaches can allow *Doctor Who* fandom to sidestep one of its bugbears: the issue of what counts as 'authentic' *Who*. This argument is never far away in 'intra' debates and comparisons between different stories or eras of the programme, for by praising or condemning certain moments of the show, fans assert their model for 'proper' *Doctor Who*. The Doctor isn't in it (enough); it isn't serious (enough); it isn't science fictional (enough); it isn't British (enough); it doesn't have enough story; it has too much story; it assumes too much knowledge of continuity; it violates established continuity; and so on. Fan criticisms involve shaping an image of 'ideal' *Who*, a kind of Platonic essence of the series (which may never have been realised fully in any one story).

The establishment of 'authentic' *Doctor Who* places the show behind the same barriers that arise from any idealisation. 'Perfect' *Doctor Who* becomes the fantasy, the mirage, that sustains its own pursuit. A projected Platonic essence of the series – not always the same thing for different fans – means that *Who* is always striving for the unattainable. The idea that *Doctor Who* may have at some point 'jumped the shark' – i.e., surrendered whatever qualities made it great TV – is part of this idealisation. By accusing classic *Doctor Who* of 'jumping the shark', Kim Newman indicates the shape taken by his own personal Platonic essence of *Who*. For him, the series should be adult and scary in tone; not simply science-fictional, but also indebted to the horror genre. What it must not be is childish.[27]

Newman's 'essence' of *Who* almost fits particular stories of the old and new series, but it never quite fits anywhere perfectly. And this gothic *Who* is not necessarily the same Platonic essence identified by other fans. For example, Lawrence Miles provocatively argues that:

> If *Doctor Who* has been about one thing ... then it's been about this: outside ... *Doctor Who* is about the outside world, in a way that very few programmes ever have been. Certainly not space operas in the *Star Trek* mould, which are almost without exception about ... staying inside your own wholesome, well-furnished environment and making speeches about the greatness of the American-human spirit.[28]

Miles suggests that 'coming to terms with the unfamiliar' has been at the heart of *Doctor Who*'s format since 1963. This pervasive 'xenophilia' may not be an easy argument to sustain: *Who* has also had its fair share of repulsive, irredeemable aliens. As with all essence-claiming arguments, Miles uses his own model of what-*Who*-really-should-be to challenge versions of the programme that don't make his grade. He polemically denies textual authenticity to the new series:

> The one thing which actually made the programme *Doctor Who* ... is no longer there. This cuts at the most basic philosophy of the series, in a way that no amount of posh CGI [computer generated imagery] ever could ... This is no longer a programme about the outside.[29]

For Miles, the new series has been made smaller by its focus on Earth-bound stories. It is a time-travel show about the present day; a universe-hopping format about London, sometimes Cardiff or Leeds. Even whilst denying authenticity to the new series – 'this is not *Doctor Who*, at least not in any way I recognise it' – Miles does still find political ambiguities to cherish in the BBC Wales production.[30] But his carefully defined Platonic doctrine of *Doctor Who* nevertheless puts up a barrier: the new series is not politically radical enough, or subversive enough, or about the 'outside' enough. What both Kim Newman and Lawrence Miles' 'critical readings' highlight more than anything is a gnawing feeling of disappointment. This is idealisation's defining emotion. Seemingly paradoxically, being a fan means being disappointed by the object of fandom as much as it means appreciating it.[31] The *Doctor Who* Appreciation Society (DWAS) was potentially misnamed; it could just as well have been called the *Doctor Who* Disappointment Society.

Miles' assertion that the show's format can be organised into one basic quality, xenophilia, is a relatively unusual interpretation, even if it does have an echo in Newman's closing cadence that *Doctor Who* is really about the 'somewhere else'.[32] The problem with essence-based arguments is that they always exclude parts of the whole: some

*Doctor Who* is less 'proper' than other examples, whether it is anything broadcast after the introduction of K-9 in 1977, or seemingly anything after 2005.

A more conventional fan claim is that *Doctor Who*'s essence lies in the very fact that its format cannot be pinned down generically. As Matt Jones once suggested in his 'Fluid Links' column for *Doctor Who Magazine*:

> the Doctor appears to pop in and out of different realities ... This allows the programme to play with any genre, any style ... [I]n the middle of all of this innovation and unpredictability, the Doctor ... remains ... [T]he Doctor's strategies of non-violent resistance and the use of intelligence and cunning to succeed over brute force are somehow universally relevant and appropriate.[33]

Jones may argue for the genre-hopping quality of the show's format, but this fails to explore its generic limits. For example, the reinvented BBC Wales series tends to focus on extraordinary threats (aliens and monsters) rather than on 'ordinary threats' (humanity's inhumanity, real-world political injustices, prejudices and repressive regimes). Even where the perspective of 'ordinary bloke' Elton Pope (Marc Warren) is made central to the show in the unusual episode 'Love & Monsters' (2.10), it is the presence of a *Blue Peter*-competition-winning alien that brings this episode into line with the current format. It was not always so: the classic series, in its earlier days, was unafraid of 'straight' historicals – i.e., time-travel stories exploring Earth's past in which there were no monsters. When new *Who* explores the past, it does so not only via 'names' of Western history and culture – Charles Dickens, Queen Victoria, Shakespeare – but also via ghostly Gelth or werewolves. And where the past is explored outside of celebrity-driven dramas then monsters such as Reapers, nanogenes, and Pyroviles make their presence felt.

Science fiction and horror predominate as generic roots for the BBC Wales series. What of the political drama, the spy thriller, personal/societal parables, or even crime fiction? New *Who* has yet to attempt its own takes on *State of Play* (BBC, 2003), *GBH* (C4, 1991), *Our Friends in the North* (BBC, 1996), or *Cracker* (ITV/Granada, 1993–6, 2006). The televised Doctor has yet to cross swords with MI5, has yet to bring down a corrupt council leader and his all-too-human thugs, has yet to follow the lives of a group of friends across decades, shaping or breaking their destinies, and has yet to apprehend a human serial killer. Although the programme's premise may offer the possibility of endless innovation, in practice there are strict genre-based limits to its BBC Wales format: 'Doctor Who ... might be under pressure to stay the same for a while ... in order not to alienate the new audience the new programme has found.'[34]

Nevertheless what fandom could, I think, take from academia is the idea of exploring new Who without getting hung up on its 'essence' and on whether a given episode is 'really' Doctor Who. Viewed from the perspective of television studies, Doctor Who has no Platonic essence. It does not need to be validated as 'uniquely flexible', or championed for 'loving the alien'. But more importantly than that, it does not have to be a disappointment, because the relationship between audience and programme is not one of prescribing an ideal. Unlike fandom, media theory is anti-essentialist. Shattering one's Platonic template means refusing the idea that Doctor Who cannot, or should not, do comedy, soap opera, sentimentality, camp, nostalgia, crime fiction, the puerile, the political, or the romantic. Letting go of the 'essence' problem actually opens up a whole new world of Who where all of these tones and qualities can be analysed rather than celebrated/condemned, and where the format's generic diversity and limitations can be addressed. Oddly enough, taking a few cues from media theory might allow a more appreciative approach to Doctor Who than sometimes occurs within fandom.

This exchange cannot be one-way traffic, however. The 'fan' versus 'academic' gridlock of false binaries also needs to be tackled from the other side; academia also has much to learn from Doctor Who fandom. For instance, something that scholarship could take from fandom is its powerful emphasis on experiencing the show. For fans, every new episode is greatly anticipated. Even whilst stories are in production, many fans like to discover and read 'spoilers'. These are snippets of information about a forthcoming episode which might conceivably 'spoil' its enjoyment by giving away important plot twists and surprises. The pursuit of spoilers is not necessarily shared by all fans; some aim to remain spoiler-free in the run-up to a new episode. As a result, when posting online, 'Net etiquette requires the posting of spoiler warnings ... allowing viewers to make a rational choice between their desire for mastery over the program universe and the immediacy of a first viewing.'[35] The Gallifrey Base Forum has sought to protect fans from unwanted narrative information by clearly labelling specific 'spoiler' sections.

Although scholars are aware of the issue of spoilers, again often because they are fans themselves,[36] academic work is typically produced without any regard for whether or not it will 'spoil' fans' enjoyment of the TV episodes under discussion.[37] Television Studies arguably pays little or no attention to spoiler warnings because audience emotions and narrative pleasures are not generally prioritised.[38] For scholars, analysis requires the assumption that a programme is already highly familiar, with its 'text' then being cognitively 'read' in a detailed way.

For fans, each episode of *Doctor Who* is something anticipated, speculated-over, looked-forward to, and then picked apart: it exists in a special kind of fan chronology that stretches from long before broadcast (usually from an initial press/publicity announcement) through to immediate post-episode debate, and then onwards into years of evaluation and re-evaluation. Fans treat *Doctor Who*'s texts as 'thick' creations, seeking to trace their production histories, developments, and variant edits.[39] By contrast, much academic textual analysis occupies a very different chronology, condensing a television episode down to the moment of broadcast, or the duration of playback. Dealt with as a finished, fixed and bounded object, the text can then (supposedly) be authoritatively theorised.

Television Studies thus goes awry. It likens TV to bits of literature, which can be contained within a book's cover and treated as fixed or finished. At the same time, it downplays the emotional experience of a 'first viewing' – in which the narrative twists and turns, and the ending of an episode are not entirely known – in favour of displaying cognitive mastery. And though fans sometimes like to display their own versions of this mastery – episode guides, reviews and production histories testify to that – they rarely lose sight of the experience of first watching a new episode of *Doctor Who*. As fan-historian Stephen James Walker has written:

> For me, an essential part of the series' original appeal was always the week's gap between episodes. Seven days in which to savour and re-live in my mind the amazing events of the previous instalment. Seven days in which to speculate on what would happen next. Seven days in which to anticipate with increasing impatience the continuation of the story ...[40]

Walker's celebration of 'first viewing' contrasts *Doctor Who* as a 'current' series to its status as an 'archive' one, which is what it became from May 1996 through to March 2005, existing then via video releases.[41] His suggestion is that, in the absence of new broadcast *Who*, fans started to behave rather like academics, with 'episodes being taken completely out of their original context' and watched 'with so much foreknowledge ... [that] the sense of the series as a gradually unfolding narrative [was] ... largely lost'.[42] It is against this kind of programme consumption – asserting mastery rather than being surprised – that Walker argues for the value of fans' experience of not-knowing.

The possibility of this mode of fan reading, with the thrill of not-knowing, has returned with the return of the series. And it is an experience that the BBC Wales production team has been keen to preserve, taking steps to safeguard the twists and turns of new series' stories – such as water-marking pages of shooting scripts with their recipients' names; editing-out the cliffhanger ending of 'Army of Ghosts' (2.12) in advance DVDs sent out to press reviewers (fading to black with the caption 'Final scene withheld until transmission'); and even leaving Billie Piper's scene out of the advance press screening for 'Partners in Crime' (4.1).[43] These are just moments in what has amounted to a kind of informational war between the show's producers and paparazzi photographers at location filming, as well as between producers and fans intent on gathering and posting 'spoilers' online. As Tat Wood acerbically notes, a generation of *Who* fans have moved into professional journalism along with TV production, meaning that 'BBC Wales is finding it hard to police the [programme's] PR distribution' and prevent spoilers from reaching online fandom.[44] And though the production team generally has maintained a dignified silence with regards to the informational control that they seek to exert, series producer Phil Collinson gave an extraordinary interview to *Death Ray* magazine in which he described one fan who had leaked series four production details online as a 'wanker':

> I'm sure you must have heard that someone – some *wanker*, quite frankly – got wind that our costumier was making something for us, snuck into his workshop, and read emails and took pictures of a costume that was being made, then stuck them on the internet ... On the one hand, I love the fact that this show has such a strong and passion-

ate fanbase ... But when one of them does something like that I think it's an absolutely appalling way of behaving.[45]

It may seem strange for a media professional to attack a fan verbally in this way. Symptomatic of the producer-versus-fan info-war – sometimes won by fandom, sometimes by the *Doctor Who* production team – this nevertheless indicates the intense emotional value ascribed by fandom to experiencing *Who*, whether ahead of broadcast (for 'spoiled' fans) or during transmission (for the 'unspoiled'). It is by shocking, surprising and moving audiences that the programme comes alive affectively. Treated academically as something finished, completed and fixed under analysis, *Doctor Who* is instead decontextualised, cut adrift from the temporal cut-and-thrust of the informational economy circulating around it, as well as from viewers' emotions. Scholars such as Sue Turnbull have sought to avoid this loss of context, championing fans' experiences of television whilst also engaging in scholarly debate:

> There is a word for this ... desire to transform the lived experience of a work of art into a description couched in words. The Greeks called it *ekphrasis* ... 'the verbal representation of a visual representation' ... In other words ... I am engaging in exactly the same activity as non-academic fans who write about their own relationship with the show ... What all of us are doing ... whether this be an academic conference paper or a website bulletin board, is a kind of 'ekphrasis': an endeavour to recover in language the effect which a particular performance, moment or TV series may have had on us.[46]

It is the emotional power of televisual moments that producers of *Doctor Who* are seeking to safeguard when they engage in info-war with fans and the press. Of course, fans may not use, nor want to use, terms like *ekphrasis*. But that does not mean they are not doing it: Stephen James Walker's entire *Doctor Who Magazine* article on the value and the impact of surprise is an exercise in *ekphrasis*.[47] Academia could, I think, do with more of this kind of study and fannish self-expression, testifying to how television drama is experienced by engaged audiences. And I must acknowledge that a 'spoiler warning' very definitely applies across this study for anyone who has not yet seen all of BBC Wales' *Doctor Who* series one through to four. This proviso takes me on to the matter of exactly what I will be arguing in the rest of the book.

## The Throw-Forward: Coming Soon ...

My aim, then, is to analyse BBC Wales' *Doctor Who* through the lenses of media and cultural theory. To this end, the specific work of Michel Foucault on authorship (1979) makes an appearance in Chapter 1,[48] whilst Chapter 2 revisits both Henry Jenkins' influential (1992) theory of fan 'poachers',[49] and what is probably the single most infamous theoretical statement from the history of *Doctor Who*: discussion of the 'semiotic thickness' of the series.[50] The first two chapters, which make up Part I ('Fans and Producers'), therefore focus on relationships between fandom and official production.

In Chapter 1, I argue that particular 'fan discourses', such as an emphasis on multi-authorship, have been embraced by the latest version of *Who*, at one and the same time that showrunner Russell T. Davies has developed an 'agenda' reflecting his own auteurist explorations of queer identity. For Davies, however, the point of this agenda appears to be that it should remain unremarkable and textually incidental rather than constituting an 'issue' (as it has for reactionary sections of fandom and the UK press). Theorising *Doctor Who*'s production also means considering the organisational and institutional contexts in which it has been brought back. I therefore focus briefly on the 'authorship' of BBC Wales. Though *Doctor Who* has enabled the BBC to publicise its drive toward increased production outside London, the series has somewhat paradoxically remained textually and extra-textually London-centric, as well as drawing on 'discourses of tourism'[51] problematically in series one.

Chapter 2 then explores specifically what impact official fan-producers have had on the continuity and consistency of new *Who*. The programme is unusual in that its post-2005 production has involved, at the most senior levels, a generation of fans-turned-media-professionals, Phil Collinson included. But this rise in fan 'gamekeepers' evidently has not entirely done away with previous ways of thinking about fans as 'poachers' whose activities are opposed to the interests of producers, with empowered and disempowered modes of fandom instead uneasily coexisting. Ongoing conflict between online fandom and fans-turned-official-producers has often been less focused on the show's content *per se,* and more concerned with gaining access to 'spoiler' information. This development has made sections of fandom 'pre-textual poachers' of information that producers would prefer to keep under PR control ahead of TV transmission.

After focusing on fans and producers in Chapters 1 and 2 – which means thinking about fans *as* official producers rather than only contrasting these groups within a restrictive binary opposition – I then move on to questions of generic categorisation in Part II ('Genre and Format'). Though *Doctor Who* may be distinctive by virtue of featuring a hero whose home is effectively a time machine, the show's use of time travel is articulated with a wide range of genre codes rather than being purely science-fictional.

In Chapter 3, I consider this multi-generic status. I argue that BBC Wales' *Doctor Who* is more generically flexible and multiple than its predecessors, particularly drawing on TV industry developments and tendencies toward what has been called 'soap drama',[52] though within specific limitations. Chapter 4 examines the importance of monsters within the 'Russell T. Davies era', using influential theories of monstrosity drawn from studies of the horror genre.[53] Here, I suggest that as a type of 'television horror', new *Who* tends to represent monstrosity critically, challenging and complicating assumptions of the 'deviant' or threatening monster, and bringing into question how monstrosity can be defined and identified.

Finally, in what amounts to a three-parter, I turn my attention to the wider extra-textual classifications of *Doctor Who* rather than its generic hybridities. How has the series been positioned industrially in terms of binaries such as 'quality' versus 'popular' and 'mainstream' versus 'cult' television? In Chapter 5, I argue that production discourses have sought consistently to contextualise the regenerated programme as 'quality TV', using the 'quality debate' in TV studies,[54] particularly focusing on the casting of the Doctor. Chapter 6 then seeks to integrate fan discourses into scholarship by refuting purely narrative and visual analyses of textual representation, and focusing on the sound and music of new *Who*. I suggest that Murray Gold's contributions to *Doctor Who* have been hugely significant in terms of positioning the programme as fantasy-adventure TV, working sonically against science-fictional connotations and effectively 'regenrifying' the show for a 'mainstream' audience imagined as anti-science fiction. I argue that Gold's work has successfully unified *Who*'s texts as part of a readily identifiable and consistent 'brand'. This adds to the series' pursuit of textual consistency, analysed in Chapter 2 as part of the critique made by fan 'gamekeepers' of the classic series (which was frequently marked by inconsistency and tonal variation).

Chapter 7 concludes *Triumph of a Time Lord* by returning to some of the themes of Part I. Looping back to fandom, my interest lies in the less than harmonious relationship between production discourses aimed at refuting the textual classification of 'cult', and fan discourses that have embraced – and anxiously questioned – *Doctor Who*'s status as cult television. I argue that, as a result of the show's cancellation in 1989, fandom takes an ambivalent approach to the cult label, though production and publicity discourses have been even stronger in attempting to symbolically detach *Who* from cult identifications. However, just as fan 'gamekeepers' have formed part of a generational deconstruction of fan-versus-producer binaries, so too has BBC Wales' *Doctor Who* potentially rewritten the cult-versus-mainstream binary identified by academic writings.[55] I therefore end by identifying ways in which the 'Russell T. Davies era' has successfully united 'cult' and 'mainstream' imagined audiences around Saturday night, prime-time BBC1 TV.

My approach throughout can be best described as *discursive*. That is, I am interested in how a range of different discourses – production, fan, generic, quality – circulate around the text of BBC Wales' *Doctor Who*. There are useful precedents for this kind of work. For example, Catherine Johnson's BFI book *Telefantasy* argues that:

> [Prior] studies [D'Acci 1994; Born 2000] are concerned with examining the experience of producing television programmes ... directly observing the production process. By contrast, this book is less concerned with the actual process of production than with the broader *discourses* within which this process takes place.[56]

The same might be said of *Triumph of a Time Lord*. I have not had access to the actual process of production (something prohibited by *Doctor Who*'s contemporary practices of brand management). Nonetheless, I am interested in studying the discourses that have underpinned new *Who*'s regeneration and cultural reception.

'Discourse' is a term often linked to one post-structuralist thinker, Michel Foucault.[57] The target of James Chapman's anti-theoretical ire, and Matthew Sweet's more pro-theoretical stance, Foucault argues that discourses enable and constrain cultural meanings, constituting objects of understanding.[58] Discourses are 'ways of making sense of the world' linked to specific communities and institutions,[59] which is why we can analyse specifically 'production discourse' or 'conventional fan discourse'.[60]

Though my focus is a singular text – *Doctor Who* – studying this necessarily involves analysing a range of different discourses. As Mary Talbot has argued:

> Discourses may not be as obviously tangible as individual texts, but in an important sense they are far more durable. Foucault maintains, plausibly, that the physical unity a single actual text has ... is weaker than the 'discursive unity of which it is the support' (2002:25) ... What comes through clearly here is the constitutive, productive character of discourse.[61]

Though a text like *Doctor Who* may seem to have obvious 'frontiers' in space and time,[62] such as the bounded minutes of its broadcast, or its sell-through existence as a DVD, in Foucault's terms the text of *Who* is inevitably 'caught up in a system of references to other ... texts ... it is a node within a network ... It indicates itself, constructs itself, only on the basis of a complex field of discourse.'[63] This field does not merely link, or disarticulate, *Doctor Who*'s fans and producers. 'Public discourse' surrounding a TV show can also take in PR strategies of promotion and publicity, as Paul Rixon argues in his study of the *Radio Times'* coverage of *Star Trek: The Original Series*:

> While ... critics use the airwaves, magazines and newspapers, and now the Web, to articulate their views, broadcasters use trailers, advertising and their own listings magazines to create an official view or framing of the program or series in question ... The broadcasting industry is eager to engage in such a public discourse as it tries to construct and maintain an image beneficial for the program.[64]

And as Jason Mittell has suggested, again adopting a broadly Foucauldian approach, '[g]enres do not run through texts, but also operate within the practices of critics, audiences and industries'.[65] Mittell therefore argues that 'discursive practices concerning genres' are another important area for work in TV studies, an argument I follow here.[66]

It is thus as a 'node within a network' of discourses that I will think about *Doctor Who*. Nor can the different types of discourse referred to above (production, fan, public, genre) be thought of as hermetically sealed and always wholly separable. As I will argue in Part I, specific 'fan discourses' have been carried through into 'production discourse' by fan-producers, though fan and production discourse have also been strongly opposed via the issue of pre-transmission access to narrative information. Discursive struggles have marked the relationship between *Doctor Who*'s production team and sections of fandom. This fact has been evidenced by Phil Collinson's description of a spoiler-gathering fan as a 'wanker', as well as Russell T. Davies' decision to give a one-word title to the chapter of *The Writer's Tale* tackling online fan criticism: 'Bastards'.[67] Fan practices have sometimes clearly been judged unruly, failing to correspond to producers' expectations of 'good' fan behaviour, and calling into being (counter-)insults and attempts at disciplining 'proper' fandom.[68]

Production discourses have also carried over into areas that might be thought of as belonging to 'fandom', such as the official discourses of *Doctor Who Magazine* (see Chapter 7). And it cannot be assumed that any discourse (whether fan or production) is wholly singular. For instance, in relation to many issues confronting fandom – such as spoilerphobes/spoilerphiles, or professionalised codes of referencing fanwork (in fan publishing) versus personalised codes of permission-granting (as within LiveJournal) – there are both powerful discourses and counter-discourses.[69] And production discourses, such as on 'quality TV', also tend to be multiple and open to counter-discursive conflict (see Chapter 5).

In any case, it is the emphasis on *Doctor Who*'s many discursive lives that sustains my tripartite structure. Though production and fan discourse, introduced in Part I, continue to be relevant, Part II adds generic discourse to the mix. And Part III ('Quality and Mainstream TV') examines discursive practices circulating around and through new *Who* that are not strictly 'generic', but instead concern higher-level textual classifications (such as 'quality TV'). Part I explores issues related to the Foucaudian 'author-function',[70] that is, discourses of (fan) authorship, whilst Part II focuses more on the Foucault-inspired 'generic function'.[71] And Part III picks up on what I have termed elsewhere, in a further extrapolation from Foucault's work, the 'text-function': textual classifications such as 'cult' or 'mainstream' that are not directly concerned with authors or genres, but which nevertheless continue to frame how a programme like *Doctor Who* is interpreted and industrially or culturally positioned.[72]

The diverse approaches taken here to *Doctor Who* as a 'node' belie the basic theoretical unity of my discursive framework. And as Bruce Isaacs has recently observed, taking me back to the topic of academia and fandom: 'the notion of discursivity ... is necessary to traverse the gulf that separates theory *about* popular culture and the consumption experience of *partaking* of that culture'.[73] By considering how BBC Wales' *Doctor Who* is discursively framed and enacted, it is possible to account for a wide variety of fan and academic responses without judging any one set of statements to be 'true' and others 'false'. Fan and academic discourse can thus be treated equally (within a scholarly mode of writing, obviously) rather than hierarchically or even morally (e.g. 'academics good, fans bad', or the reverse).

Finally, one intertextuality will not have escaped many readers: my title deliberately echoes 'The Trial of a Time Lord' (1986), when *Doctor Who* returned to BBC1 after an 18-month 'hiatus', but it does so by inverting it. In 2005, the TV icon of *Doctor Who* was brought back in a very different manner. No longer on trial for its life, it offered audiences the 'trip of a lifetime'. And, as I will go on to suggest in the following chapter, the 'Russell T. Davies era' brought art discourses of the TV *auteur* to *Doctor Who* for the first time in its cultural career. Fandom's move into official production arguably had been prefigured by Philip Segal's executive producer role on the 1996 TV Movie,[74] but *Doctor Who* as 'authored' TV was a wholly new direction for the series.


## NOTES

1    Available online at *http://www.cuttingsarchive.org.uk/radiotim/cs-s24-26/ season26/letters.htm*, accessed 4 October 2008.

2    Official publications have included the likes of Gary Russell (2006) Doctor Who: *The Inside Story*, BBC Books, London, and three volumes from Andew Pixley (2006) Doctor Who *Magazine Special Edition: The* Doctor Who Companion – Series Two, Panini Comics, Tunbridge Wells (2007) Doctor Who *Magazine Special Edition: The* Doctor Who Companion – Series Three, Panini Comics, Tunbridge Wells, and (2008) Doctor Who *Magazine Special Edition: The* Doctor Who Companion – Series Four, Panini Comics, Tunbridge Wells. Unofficially, the first series has been explored in J. Shaun Lyon (2005) *Back to the Vortex*, Telos Press, Tolworth.

3    See Tat Wood and Lawrence Miles (2006) *About Time 1: 1963–66*, Mad Norwegian Press, Des Moines, IA, p.143.

4    In Andrew Cartmel (2005) *Through Time: An Unauthorised and Unofficial History of* Doctor Who, Continuum, New York and London, p.xi.

5    Ibid., p.xii.

6    Wood and Miles: *About Time 1*, p.145.

7    For more on this term and associated debates, see Matt Hills (2002) *Fan Cultures*, Routledge, London and New York.

8    Piers D. Britton and Simon J. Barker (2003) *Reading Between Designs: Visual Imagery and the Generation of Meaning in* The Avengers, The Prisoner, *and* Doctor Who, University of Texas Press, Austin, p.132.

9     Kim De Vries (2007) 'The scholarship of *Doctor Who*, or, how cult TV gained street cred in the academy', available online at *http://www.sequentialart.com/article.php?id=527*, 1 June, accessed 12 July 2007.

10    Ibid.

11    Paul Magrs (2007) 'Afterword: my adventures', in David Butler (ed.) *Time and Relative Dissertations in Space*, Manchester University Press, Manchester and New York, p.308.

12    See, for example, John Tulloch and Manuel Alvarado (1983) Doctor Who: *The Unfolding Text*, Macmillan, London, and John Tulloch and Henry Jenkins (1995) *Science Fiction Audiences: Watching* Doctor Who *and* Star Trek, Routledge, London and New York. *Doctor Who* also appears briefly in the academic text Glen Creeber (ed.) (2004) *Fifty Key Television Programmes*, Arnold, London (see Matt Hills' chapter '*Doctor Who*', pp.75–9 of Creeber's volume) and in varying cultural and critical histories, such as James Chapman (2006) *Inside the TARDIS: The Worlds of* Doctor Who, I.B.Tauris, London and New York, and John Kenneth Muir (1999) *A Critical History of* Doctor Who *on Television*, McFarland, Jefferson and London.

13    Chapman: *Inside the TARDIS*, p.viii.

14    As I argue in Matt Hills (2005) *How to Do Things with Cultural Theory*, Hodder-Arnold, London, cultural theory can be about trying to make a positive difference in the world, highlighting power imbalances and challenging forms of oppression or prejudice. These sets of ideals are, in fact, not so far away from the progressive narrative role given frequently to the Doctor.

15    Paul Cornell (ed.) (1997) *Licence Denied: Rumblings from the* Doctor Who *Underground*, Virgin Books, London, p.127.

16    'Squee' is an exclamation of gleeful delight amongst fans; a 'signifier' is the material component of a 'sign', for instance the sound or the printed shape of a word.

17    Matthew Sweet (2006) 'Inside the TARDIS, by James Chapman' in the *Independent*, available online at *http://www.independent.co.uk/arts-entertainment/books/reviews/inside-the-tardis-by-james-chapman-480122.html*, 28 May, accessed 1 June 2006.

18    See the argument in Wood and Miles: *About Time 1*, p.143.

19    See Sweet: 'Inside the TARDIS', and Cornel Sandvoss (2005) *Fans: The Mirror of Consumption*, Polity Press, Cambridge.

20    See, for example, Matt Hills (2007) 'Televisuality without television? The Big Finish audios and discourses of "tele-centric" *Doctor Who*', in David Butler (ed.) *Time and Relative Dissertations in Space*, Manchester University Press, Manchester and New York, pp.280–95, and Dale Smith (2007) 'Broader and deeper: the lineage and impact of the Timewyrm series', in David Butler (ed.): *Time and Relative Dissertations in Space*, pp.263–79.

21    All classic series episodes are given with their year of initial broadcast. Episodes of BBC Wales' *Doctor Who* are given with series and episode numbers as per transmission order, e.g. 'Rose' is 1.1, meaning series one, episode one. Series one to four were first broadcast from 2005 to 2008. Christmas specials up to and including 2007 are coded with the number of the series they preceded followed by the suffix 'X', making 'The Christmas Invasion' story 2.X, for example, since its first transmission preceded

series two by several months. However, the 2008 Christmas special is given as 4.14, in line with its unusual production code.

22 With reference to the arguments and evidence of Tulloch and Jenkins: *Science Fiction Audiences*, p.136, and Nicholas Abercrombie and Brian Longhurst (1998) *Audiences*, Sage, London, p.145.

23 See structuralism in John Fiske (1984) 'Popularity and ideology: a structuralist reading of *Doctor Who*', in William. D. Rowland and Bruce Watkins (eds) *Interpreting Television: Current Research Perspectives*, Sage, Beverly Hills, pp.58–73; semiotics in Tulloch and Alvarado: *The Unfolding Text*; and reading formation theory in Tulloch and Jenkins: *Science Fiction Audiences*.

24 As in McKee's dismissal of Fiske's (1984) reading of classic series' story 'The Creature from the Pit', in Alan McKee (2004) 'Is *Doctor Who* political?', *European Journal of Cultural Studies* vii/2, pp.201–17.

25 See n. 6.

26 Michel Foucault was an influential post-structuralist thinker whose work informs my own approach in this book. Foucault emphasised that our views of the world are always informed and constructed through discourse, or structured patterns of meaning, if you like, which we usually take for granted. I discuss this in more detail later in this Introduction.

27 See Kim Newman (2005) *BFI TV Classics: Doctor Who*, BFI Publishing, London, p.92.

28 Lawrence Miles (2005) '*Doctor Who*, season X-1: "Rose": a review of the series, and the twenty-first century, so far', available online at *http://www. beasthouse.fsnet.co.uk/who01.htm*, accessed 2 September 2008.

29 Ibid.

30 Ibid.

31 See Barry Richards (1994) *Disciplines of Delight: The Psychoanalysis of Popular Culture*, Free Association Press, London, pp.42–3.

32 Newman: *BFI TV Classics*, p.118.

33 Matthew Jones (1996) 'Fluid links: that's what I like', *Doctor Who Magazine* 238, Marvel Comics, London, p.20.

34 Newman: *BFI TV Classics*, p.117.

35 Henry Jenkins (1995) '"Do you enjoy making the rest of us feel stupid?": alt.tv.twinpeaks, the trickster author and viewer mastery', in David Lavery (ed.) *Full of Secrets: Critical Approaches to* Twin Peaks, Wayne State University Press, Detroit, p.59.

36 See also Henry Jenkins (2006) *Convergence Culture*, New York University Press, New York and London.

37 Matt Hills (2005) *The Pleasures of Horror*, Continuum, London and New York, p.43.

38 On this, see the useful arguments of Kristyn Gorton (2006) 'A sentimental journey: television, meaning and emotion', *Journal of British Cinema and Television* iii/1, pp.72–81.

39 Roz Kaveney (2005) *From Alien to the Matrix: Reading Science Fiction Film*, I.B.Tauris, London and New York, p.5.

40 Stephen James Walker (1999) 'Surprised? You should be...', in *Doctor Who Magazine* 277, Marvel Comics, London, p.8.

41 Ibid., p.7.

42    Ibid., pp.10– 11.
43    See the accounts of Pixley: Doctor Who *Companion – Series Two*, p.100, and Doctor Who *Companion – Series Four*, p.36.
44    Tat Wood (2007) *About Time 6: The Unauthorized Guide to* Doctor Who *1985–1989*, Mad Norwegian Press, Des Moines, IA, p.217.
45    Phil Collinson, quoted in Matt Bielby (2008) 'Fly, lonely angel', *Death Ray* 12, Blackfish, Bath, pp.46–7.
46    Sue Turnbull (2005) 'Moments of inspiration: performing Spike', *European Journal of Cultural Studies* viii/3, p.368.
47    See Walker: 'Surprised? You should be...'.
48    See Michel Foucault (1979) 'What is an author?', *Screen* xx/1, pp.13–33.
49    See Henry Jenkins (1992) *Textual Poachers*, Routledge, New York and London.
50    In Tulloch and Alvarado: *The Unfolding Text*, p.249.
51    See Steve Blandford (2005) 'BBC drama at the margins: the contrasting fortunes of Northern Irish, Scottish and Welsh television drama in the 1990s', in Jonathan Bignell and Stephen Lacey (eds) *Popular Television Drama: Critical Perspectives*, Manchester University Press, Manchester and New York, p.173.
52    Glen Creeber (2004) *Serial Television: Big Drama on the Small Screen*, BFI Publishing, London, p.115.
53    See Noel Carroll (1990) *The Philosophy of Horror*, Routledge, New York and London, and Robin Wood (1986) *Hollywood from Vietnam to Reagan*, Columbia University Press, New York.
54    See, for example, Charlotte Brunsdon (1997) *Screen Tastes*, Routledge, London and New York, and Jane Feuer (2007) 'HBO and the concept of quality TV', in Janet McCabe and Kim Akass (eds) *Quality TV: Contemporary American Television and Beyond*, I.B.Tauris, London and New York, pp.145–57.
55    See, for example, Mark Jancovich and Nathan Hunt (2004) 'The mainstream, distinction, and cult TV', in Sara Gwenllian-Jones and Roberta E. Pearson (eds) *Cult Television*, University of Minnesota Press, Minneapolis, pp.27–44.
56    Catherine Johnson (2005) *Telefantasy*, BFI Publishing, London, p.15.
57    See, for example, Michel Foucault (1979) *Discipline and Punish: The Birth of the Prison*, Penguin, Harmondsworth, and his (2002) *The Archaeology of Knowledge*, Routledge, London and New York.
58    See John Storey (2006) *Cultural Theory and Popular Culture: An Introduction*, 4th edn, Pearson, Harlow, p.101; Mary Talbot (2007) *Media Discourse*, Edinburgh University Press, Edinburgh, p.11; and Michael O'Shaughnessy (1999) *Media and Society*, Oxford University Press, Oxford and New York, p.157– 8.
59    Alan McKee (2003) *Textual Analysis: A Beginner's Guide*, Sage, London, p.101.
60    See Daniel O'Mahony (2007) '"Now how is that wolf able to impersonate a grandmother?" History, pseudo-history and genre in *Doctor Who*', in David Butler (ed.) *Time and Relative Dissertations in Space: Critical Perspectives on* Doctor Who, Manchester University Press, Manchester and New York, p.65, referring to *Doctor Who* fandom. By contrast, Michele Pierson

(2002) *Special Effects: Still In Search of Wonder*, Columbia University Press, New York, p.112, refers to 'fan discourse' more generally, as a way of understanding and interpreting special effects that is shared across different fantasy/SF/action film fandoms. My use of the term 'fan discourse' throughout this book is, like O'Mahony, meant specifically in relation to *Who* fan culture(s).

61  Talbot: *Media Discourse*, p.12; see also Myra Macdonald (2003) *Exploring Media Discourse*, Arnold, London, p.19.

62  Foucault: *Archaeology of Knowledge*, p.25.

63  Ibid., pp.25– 6.

64  Paul Rixon (2008) '*Star Trek*: popular discourses – the role of broadcasters and critics', in Lincoln Geraghty (ed.) *The Influence of* Star Trek *on Television, Film and Culture*, McFarland, Jefferson and London, p.154.

65  Jason Mittell (2004) *Genre and Television*, Routledge, New York and London, p.13.

66  Ibid.

67  See Russell T. Davies and Benjamin Cook (2008) *The Writer's Tale*, BBC Books, London, pp.63, 76–7, though the chapter also discusses whether those who succeed in the TV industry have to behave like 'bastards'.

68  See Derek Johnson (2007) 'Inviting audiences in: the spatial reorganization of production and consumption in "TVIII"', *New Review of Film and Television Studies* v/1, pp.61–80, and his (2007) 'Fan-tagonism: factions, institutions, and constitutive hegemonies of fandom', in Jonathan Gray, Cornel Sandvoss and C. Lee Harrington (eds) *Fandom: Identities and Communities in a Mediated World*, New York University, New York and London, pp.285–300.

69  For a useful introduction to scholarship on LiveJournal and fandom, see Karen Hellekson and Kristina Busse (eds) (2006) *Fan Fiction and Fan Communities in the Age of the Internet*, McFarland, Jefferson and London. LiveJournal is found at *http://www.livejournal.com* and is a forum for online discussion including blogging and social networking features.

70  Foucault: 'What is an author?', p.21.

71  Mittell: *Genre and Television*, p.15.

72  Matt Hills (2007) 'From the box in the corner to the box set on the shelf: "TV III" and the cultural/textual valorisations of DVD', *New Review of Film and Television Studies* v/1, pp.46–7. My broadly Foucauldian approach here thus differs significantly from that in Marc Schuster and Tom Powers (2007) *The Greatest Show in the Galaxy: The Discerning Fan's Guide to Doctor Who*, McFarland, Jefferson and London, p.89, which seeks to apply Foucault to the characters and diegesis of classic *Doctor Who*. My interest, by contrast, lies in the range of discourses that frame and flow through the texts of new *Who*, not in whether specific character actions or narrative events can be said to somehow mirror Foucauldian theory.

73  Bruce Isaacs (2008) *Toward a New Film Aesthetic*, Continuum, New York and London, p.107.

74  See Alan McKee (2004) 'How to tell the difference between production and consumption: a case study in *Doctor Who* fandom', in Sara Gwenllian Jones and Roberta E. Pearson (eds) *Cult Television*, University of Minnesota Press, Minneapolis and London, p.174.

# PART I

# FANS AND PRODUCERS

[T]his 'author-function' ... is not formed spontaneously through the simple attribution of a discourse to an individual. It results from a complex operation whose purpose is to construct the rational entity we call an author. Undoubtedly, this construction is assigned a 'realistic' dimension as we speak of an individual's 'profundity' or 'creative' power, his intentions or the original inspiration manifested in writing. Nevertheless, these aspects of an individual ... are projections ... of our way of handling texts: in the comparisons we make, the traits we extract as pertinent, the continuities we assign, or the exclusions we practice.

Michel Foucault (1979) 'What is an author?', Screen xx/1, p.21.

# 1

# 'THE RUSSELL T. DAVIES ERA':

# AUTHORSHIP AND ORGANISATION

BC Wales' reimagining of *Doctor Who* is not distinguished from its predecessors merely by virtue of a new production team offering new creative input. Unlike prior incarnations, this regeneration is strongly linked to discourses of authorship, as Kim Newman points out:

> ... previous eras within the history of *Doctor Who* ... were defined by who played the Doctor, with only fan scholars paying attention to the comings and goings of script editors, producers, and BBC regimes ... *Doctor Who* (2005– ) was from the first seen, even outside fan circles, as *authored*.[1]

In this chapter I want to analyse the consequences and distinctions of 'authored' *Doctor Who*. It is showrunner Russell T. Davies – re-creator, executive producer, lead writer and BAFTA Dennis Potter Award winner (2006) – who has taken on the mantle of *auteur*. This has potentially placed new *Who* within a body of work including children's serials such as *Dark Season* (BBC, 1991) and *Century Falls* (BBC, 1993), celebrated drama *Queer as Folk* (C4, 1999–2000) and controversial telefantasy, *The Second Coming* (ITV, 2003). Davies' multi-generic output has also taken in writing for *Coronation Street* (ITV, 1960– ), melodrama *The Grand* (ITV, 1997–8) and the playful, anachronistic 'period drama' *Casanova* (BBC, 2005). Davies has further explored contemporary, naturalistic settings in work such as *Bob & Rose* (ITV, 2001), and the comedy-drama *Mine All Mine* (ITV, 2004).

I have placed the 'Russell T. Davies era' in scare quotes for a specific reason. In the next section, I will argue that *Doctor Who* has been interpreted within fandom as multi-authored, rather than being articulated with any one creative 'vision' or authority figure. In line with fan discourses, Davies has sought not to adopt the role of singular authority, and the programme has been promoted as multi-authored, in line with egalitarian fan discourses (Davies himself also being a long-term fan of the show). The very concept of an authorial 'era' is thus an unstable artefact, winking in and out of existence like a TARDIS. Davies is a (de)materialising *auteur* – present and absent, simultaneously displaced in favour of other production team members, and solidified via specific, queered meanings and readings. Having first stressed the series' approach to multi-authorship, I will then materialise Davies' authorship by reading his work on *Doctor Who* through the intertexts of his other screenwriting – most notably *Queer as Folk*, but also *The Grand*, which tends not to be viewed as an important precursor of *Doctor Who*,[2] but which I will suggest can be read in this light. Finally, I will conclude by opening out questions of authorship into organisational, institutional issues. This new version of *Doctor Who* is 'authored' by the corporate entity of BBC Wales as much as by Russell T. Davies. What has arriving in Cardiff meant for the show's identity, and for debates over BBC Wales' provision of networked BBC television?[3] First, though, I will focus on the intertwining of fan and production discourses of authorship.

## The Many Faces of Authorship: 'The Phil Collinson Years'

Russell T. Davies' cultural and industrial positioning as *Who auteur* has been viewed differently by a number of TV scholars. James Chapman sees it as a successful attempt to emulate 'American Quality TV', which has its own secure pantheon of *auteurs* including the likes of Chris Carter and Joss Whedon.[4] By contrast, Dave Rolinson suggests that:

> Davies has an unprecedented degree of control within the 'hierarchy' of 'creative power relations' ... [new *Who* being described in *SFX* as] 'almost auteur television'. As this implies, Davies's highly distinguished pre-*Who* career creates new fissures in the attribution of agency, because *Doctor Who* is simultaneously a continuing series with a 'generically coded format' and an artefact from a writer in the 'artist' tradition.[5]

Here, the 'generic' status of the show, and its nature as an ongoing series rather than a discrete serial or one-off teleplay, appear to call Davies' authorial position into question: the programme is 'almost *auteur*' TV, with Davies himself representing matter out of place – an 'artist' working in 'genre' TV rather than in the more rarefied realm of 'drama'. Davies has evidently encountered this TV industry prejudice: 'There are some sniffy people in the TV industry who have asked, archly, why I'm now writing genre, instead of drama. Obviously they've never watched a single episode of *Doctor Who*.'[6]

These two differing takes on Davies' authorship can be characterised as 'cult TV' versus 'television-as-culture' discourses. The former sees authorship as legitimately extending into the realm of genre/series TV; though Chapman uses the label 'American Quality TV',[7] his exemplars are nevertheless writer-creator-directors from *The X-Files* (Fox, 1993–2002) and *Buffy the Vampire Slayer* (WB, 1997–2001; UPN, 2001–3). The latter position, meanwhile, restricts authorship to TV 'drama' conceptualised as a kind of genre-plus television, which supposedly transcends genre and attains the status of capital-C 'Culture'.[8]

New *Who* may deny strenuously its 'cult' credentials (see Chapter 7), but by fusing 'genre' and 'authorship' it falls squarely into the domain of 'authored' cult telefantasy.[9] This approach to authorship and value is one shared by *Doctor Who*'s long-term fandom, which has consistently interpreted the classic series as 'authored' as part of its textual revaluing and cultification. The work of writers such as Robert Holmes and Douglas Adams has been celebrated within fandom, with this authorial approach to old *Who* – interpreting it as multi-authored by isolating out the 'signatures' of different directors, writers and script-editors – carrying over into work from scholar-fans.[10] This tendency to read TV as multi-authored is prevalent in other cult fandoms.[11]

An emphasis on multi-authorship extends to the interpretation of producers' work. For instance, it has been argued that 1980's '[producer John] Nathan-Turner's "signature" is less creative than ad-ministrative',[12] that is, he successfully 'got the money on-screen' in his first series. Russell T. Davies himself has sought to extend discourses of authorship in relation to new *Who*, noting of series producer Phil Collinson that:

> [2005–08] should be known forever as the Phil Collinson Years ... you get far too much of me, me, me in *DWM* ... And sometimes, when I read the stuff back, it sounds as though Phil's job is purely technical ... And while that's a creative job in itself ... it doesn't allow for the mas-sive input Phil has had into the scripts and ideas ... of this bonkers old show.[13]

Davies details Collinson's input on series four, particularly singling out the idea for 'The Unicorn and the Wasp' (4.7), and the botanical *mise-en-scene* at the end of 'The Doctor's Daughter' (4.6) as examples of his creative work.[14] New *Who* hence shares an emphasis on multi-authored readings of the text with the show's established cult fandom. This particular integration of fan and production discourses may be unsurprising given that Davies and Collinson are both themselves fans of the programme. It does, however, contrast the series with some of its US SF TV contemporaries, such as the re-imagined *Battlestar Galac-tica* (Sci-Fi, 2003–9), which has a more monotheistic approach to the 'author-as-God', or at least the author-as-military-leader. As Suzanne Scott has argued of the Sci-Fi Channel's *BSG* podcasts, typically featur-ing showrunner Ronald D. Moore:

> fans' consumption of the podcasts is intimately bound up with the acceptance of Moore's word as law ... That Moore's podcasts open up dialogue not limited to the textual content of the show, but to the cre-ative process that generates it, is surely a boon to enunciative modes of fan productivity such as online forums. In terms of fans' textual pro-ductivity, the degree to which Moore's commentary puts these prac-tices 'to bed' along with each episode is still up for debate.[15]

Moore's podcasting may give fans access to behind-the-scenes de-tail, but it also tends to reinforce a specific way of reading the text.[16] By contrast, *Doctor Who*'s podcasts have not reproduced such an empha-sis on Davies as the show's singular *auteur*. Instead, they have repeat-edly involved a wide range of production team members, including actors, directors, writers, executive producers, special effects techni-cians and sound engineers. These podcasts have clearly been planned and designed as episode-specific, with Dalek operator Barnaby Edwards and voice of the Daleks, Nick Briggs, featuring on 'The Stolen Earth' (4.12), whilst sound recordist Julian Howarth and supervising sound editor Paul McFadden are included on 'Midnight' (4.10).[17]

As a podcaster, Russell T. Davies has adopted a playful persona, welcoming listeners with the greeting 'Hello, faithful viewer', which gestures towards fandom whilst exnominating the term itself. The 'faithful viewer' as a hailed, interpellated audience identity need not be a self-proclaimed 'fan', thus enabling the greeting's polysemic openness to address new and old fans, and to welcome the curious general audience as much as established cult fans. Davies' emphasis on faithful *viewing* also positions *Doctor Who* podcasts as supplements to the TV texts, remaining resolutely TV-centric, and hence seamlessly aligning the showrunner's enunciative bonhomie with BBC policy on new media add-ons. This dictates that online or other textual supplements must not be essential to the consumption and understanding of broadcast TV texts.[18] However, unlike Ron Moore on *BSG*'s podcasts, Davies is rarely positioned as a singular voice of authorial 'authority'. *Who*'s podcasts frequently resemble social events and performances of convivial friendship as much as behind-the-scenes commentaries – David Tennant, Russell T. Davies and Steven Moffat's contributions to 'Forest of the Dead' (4. 9) being one notable example of this digressive and zoo-radio-like approach.

Multi-authorship discourses derived from fandom are thus woven into the new media strategies of new *Who*. The monotheistic 'author-God' of 'literary' and 'television-as-Culture' discourses is decentred, even whilst authorship discourses continue to be mobilised. Poststructuralist theorist Michel Foucault has famously argued that 'in our culture, the name of an author is a variable that accompanies only certain texts to the exclusion of others ... the function of an author is to characterize the existence, circulation, and operation of certain discourses within a society'.[19] Foremost amongst these discourses is that of 'art'; where the author-function is invoked then notions of artistic, literary worth tend to be articulated. In television, this means seeing texts as singularly envisioned, as with a 'Dennis Potter serial', for example, even though an entire creative team will have been involved in realising this 'vision'.

However, it is not the case that all 'cult' TV can be contrasted to all 'television-as-Culture'; some cult shows have indeed utilised powerful, singular author-functions – for example the original *Star Trek* (NBC, 1966–9) as the 'vision' of Gene Roddenberry. It is telling that in a study of classic *Doctor Who* and *Star Trek*, the only analysis of the Foucauldian 'author-function' occurs in relation to the latter.[20] It is argued that Roddenberry's name acted as a typical 'author-function', serving as a principle of classification for *Star Trek*'s texts, as a principle of explanation (e.g. via Roddenberry's philosophy and vision for the programme), and as a sign of value.[21] Classic *Doctor Who*, on the other hand, was never industrially positioned in such a way. If it ever had any overarching 'author-function' then this was perhaps, rather more amorphously, 'the BBC' as a public service institution and an emblem of 'Britishness' through which the show could be read as articulating a 'British' identity.

New *Who* carries a fan–cultural, egalitarian approach to authorship back into its official discourses. It represents an industrial consecration of fan approaches to multiple authorship, and a refusal to limit authorship to the singular vision (and author-ity) typical of US and UK traditions of quality TV 'drama'". Seemingly contradicting this – and akin to James Chapman's argument that new *Who* seeks equivalence with 'American Quality TV' by nominating Russell T. Davies as its sole *auteur* – is Andy Murray's reading of *Guardian* article 'Have a Russell T. Davies TV festival'.[22]

This newspaper article involved Davies' selection of 'classic' TV, which Murray interprets as follows:

> Davies nominated ... [producer Philip Hinchcliffe and writer Robert Holmes' classic 1975 *Who* story] 'The Ark in Space' – alongside the luminary likes of *Pennies from Heaven* [BBC, 1978] ... *Twin Peaks* [ABC, 1990–1] ... and *The Sopranos* [HBO, 1999–2007] ... – as an all-time television highlight.[23]

Upon closer inspection, however, Davies' 'TV festival' of supposed 'Greats' actually is an attack on totemic US and UK 'quality' TV, and an argument in favour of the overlooked brilliance of both *Doctor Who* and British soap *Coronation Street* (not mentioned by Murray since it rather undermines his interpretation). Rather than simply re-contextualising *Doctor Who* in the 'quality' company of *The Sopranos* and *Pennies from Heaven*, Davies takes the opportunity to point out that:

> I'm not recommending ... [*The Sopranos*] because it's the best TV drama ever made. I wouldn't know – it's only on the list because I've never

seen a single episode. It seems to be shameful to admit it. I've even lied my way through conversations ... Bluffing is easy, just read the billings. I was bought the Season One box set three years ago ... Can someone watch it for me? ... Am I also allowed to say that I find *The Singing Detective* a bit boring?[24]

Critiquing these totems of 'quality' TV, Davies champions *Coronation Street* instead: 'In one whipcrack of an [opening] episode, Tony Warren establishes ... a style of television writing that still dominates the ratings, and the culture, 45 years later.'[25] And whilst Davies does indeed lionise 'The Ark in Space', by virtue of being placed alongside *Corrie* this reads less as a fan-producer's strategy for revaluing *Who* as 'quality' and more as a defence of popular genre TV that hasn't ever been rendered fully canonical by critical/academic celebration, despite the love, care and criticism of generations of soap and cult TV fans. If Davies is utilising any 'author-function' here, it is not the contextualising of *Doctor Who* as 'quality', but is instead a fan-like emphasis on what gets shamefully left out, and othered, in TV critics' and scholars' lists of 'Great TV'. 'Drama' should not be the be-all and end-all of 'television-as-Culture'; ordinary, popular, genre TV can be brilliant too, or so Davies chides *Guardian* readers. Again, the voice of the fan, seeking a more egalitarian stance on TV creativity, can be discerned.

*Doctor Who's* fan culture has also taken synchronic and diachronic approaches to multiple authorship, that is, focusing on different 'signatures' of writers, producers, script editors and directors working on the show at the same time, and comparing different production teams over time. Where synchronic multiple authorship is concerned, fans read for the collision of different 'signatures', seeking to isolate out the impact of script editors, the concerns of writers, and the guiding principles of producers. For example, though Russell T. Davies may be the identifiable 'showrunner' on new *Who* (2005–9), Steven Moffat's Hugo and BAFTA-winning scripts have nonetheless also been read by fans as involving 'signature' devices. Commercial fan magazine *Death Ray* says of Moffat's episodes 'Silence in the Library'/'Forest of the Dead' (4.8–4.9):

You might call this a checklist of everything Moffat's tried and tested previously – 'everybody lives!', hints at the Doctor's sex-life, timey-wimeyness, demented technology ... but if Moffat's arsenal of tools is becoming familiar, it's also true to say he's perfecting his use of them. One of the reasons these stories are all fan favourites is that Moffat is a card-carrying *Who*phile himself – the DVD extras business in 'Blink' [3.10] and the finger-wagging talk of 'spoilers' here are the kind of things the devoted get anxious about. Moffat knows this well, and plays with fandom all the time.[26]

As this indicates, Moffat's scripts are highly self-referential, referring to his earlier contributions as well as to *Doctor Who* fandom. Alongside citing his own dialogue, Moffat has developed a characteristic approach to dialogue-as-special-effect, introducing 'catchphrases' for his monsters such as 'Are you my mummy?' and 'Hey, who turned out the lights?' His series four scripts display a logic of intensification, with 'Silence in the Library' (4.8) ending on a cliffhanger made up of not one but two such catchphrases, the data ghost's 'Who turned out the lights?' and the library node's 'Donna Noble has left the library; Donna Noble has been saved.' Moffat's screenplays have also recurrently avoided cliched 'evil' monsters in favour of representing technology gone awry (the nanogenes; Clockwork Droids; the library's data core), and his work has focused repeatedly on the time travel aspects of *Doctor Who*, featuring the Doctor meeting Sally Sparrow and River Song out of linear, temporal sequence, as well as stepping into different moments along Madame de Pompadour's personal timeline.[27]

Time travel might create problems for the Doctor, but the passing of time, and different phases of diachronic authorship, have also created an identity problem for fandom: (how) can the many different versions of *Doctor Who* be reconciled as the same show, other than via title alone?[28] This disciplining of multiple authorship, and the attempt to produce an essence of '*Doctor Who*-ness', has manifested itself in various ways. For example, it is evident in fan magazine *SFX*'s staged meeting between the programme's first producer, Verity Lambert, and Russell T. Davies:

*Verity, can you see a throughline from your* Doctor Who *to Russell's?*

[Verity Lambert:] What you've managed to do is extract the essence of what was there, and at the same time bring it into 2006.

[Russell T. Davies:] We've really taken it back to the 60s. All the structures that were put up in between are gone – the Time Lords and all that pompery ... when you look at what you were doing in 1963, it was just so open.[29]

A similar attempt at textual smoothing-out in pursuit of some imputed textual 'essence' appears in an article in newspaper *The*

*Stage*.[30] Here, Philip Hinchcliffe – producer of one of the programme's 'Golden Ages' in fan consensus[31] – watches 'Planet of the Ood' (4.3) and comments on the BBC Wales series. Despite identifying technical differences, such as in the creation of monster masks, Hinchcliffe predominantly equates 'his' 1970s *Who* with the 2008 incarnation, symbolically downplaying differences in favour of an essential *Who*-ness.[32] Through these staged encounters between different authorial figures, and through the contested clashing of author-functions, a resolution of sorts is constructed for the show's enduring fandom. Multiple authorship over time is brought dialogically into alignment, and paradoxically centred on the author(ity) function of *Doctor Who* itself as a textual 'essence'.[33] The programme's narrative universe threatens to become a kind of 'living textuality', in Umberto Eco's terms,[34] to which different authors can, in fact, all be subordinated. Fidelity to intention is removed to the *n*th degree here,[35] as the work of the current production team is read through all previous 'eras' of the show, back through Hinchcliffe's producership, and all the way to Lambert's.

Though Foucault's work on the 'author-function' is useful for thinking about what kinds of television are culturally positioned as 'authored' ('drama' and cult TV), and what sorts of TV are precisely denied this articulation with discourses of 'art' (soap, reality TV), it has its limitations. As film scholar Janet Staiger has argued, analysing 'the author as a site of discourses' is potentially a slight 'dodge',[36] downplaying authorial agency. What authors actually do and say – the specific meanings repeatedly constructed through their work – are marginalised in favour of the 'author' as a construction of specific interpretative communities (e.g. inside fan circles, or in industry publicity). Against this, and referring to the title of Foucault's infamous article on the author-function, 'What is an author?[37], Staiger asserts: '[w]hat an author *is*, is the repetition of statements'.[38] Not fully discounting the Foucauldian 'author-function', this nevertheless directs us to think about the textual and extra-textual statements that perform and display 'authorship'. Such an approach does not make the author an 'authorising' centre to 'their' texts,[39] but stresses authorial intertexts as a way to discern similarities and differences across a body of work. With this in mind, in the next section I want to turn to Russell T. Davies' non-*Who* work, analysing new *Who* through these intertexts.

## Authorship as a Non-Agenda Agenda:
### 'I'll say what I want. That's what good writers do'

Davies' career has been interpreted by critics and fans alike as following specific agendas – or, in Staiger's terms, as repeatedly making
statements with a distinct cultural politics. Davies has been a progressive champion of queer identities, challenging right-wing prejudice
as well as left-wing clichés ('the burden of representation'), and consistently aiming for a naturalistic representation of social and cultural
equality. For Davies, characters' sexual identities should not constitute
narrative 'issues'. As such, he has sought to normalise queer identities, which even in the 1970s and 1980s were frequently still linked to
'queer monster' storylines on television,[40] as well as typically being
demonised in popular genres such as fantasy-horror.[41]

The most obvious instance in Davies' career of this normalisation
is *Queer as Folk*, but his authorship has been performatively realised
through iterated statements of ordinary queering:

> There is another gay teenager – like Nathan Maloney, also 15 years old
> – in *Mine All Mine* ... And with *Doctor Who* and its subsequent spin-off,
> *Torchwood* (CBC/BBC, 2006– ), Davies introduced the character of Cap-
> tain Jack, a pansexual time-traveller from the 51st century ... Certainly,
> Davies' contributions to 'gay television' over the last decade – since
> the appearance of Clive the barman [in *The Grand*], in fact – have been
> considerable.[42]

This authorial 'agenda' has been referred to jokingly by Davies,
describing *Torchwood* as 'the next stage of my plan to make everyone on TV gay'.[43] The notion of a 'gay agenda' has also entered the
lexicon of online *Doctor Who* fandom, occasionally being opposed in
a reactionary manner not far from the *Sun*'s journalistic response of
27 September 2003: 'Duckie *Who*: Time Lord has gay show writer'.[44]
Writing in *Death Ray* magazine, Thom Hutchinson and Matt Bielby
point out that there 'are few topics upon which more vinegar and vit-
riol are spent than the so-called gay agenda; just check out the news-
groups'.[45] These journalist-fans argue that new *Who* does have such
an agenda, but what distinguishes it is a kind of 'casual candidness'.
The term 'agenda' suggests an outmoded approach to sexuality as an
'issue'. By contrast, Davies' *Doctor Who* screenwriting renders characters' sexuality an almost throwaway, unimportant point. Ordinary

queer is what distinctively threads together many of Davies' invented societies:

> lesbian grannies, Sky Sylvestry ... the preponderance of characters casually candid about their queer orientation, while high, isn't over-whelming. But nor is it accidental ... sometimes, as with Jack, it's a de-liberately radical step for a television show ... *Doctor Who* has probably already done more for gay rights – especially rights in the playground – than *Queer as Folk* ever did ... The best thing about the agenda is that it's at most a minor ingredient of a multi-flavoured show, as good as irrelevant, and that's its greatest gift.[46]

The reactionary fan label 'gay agenda' appears to be rooted dis-cursively in conservative and right-wing furore, as well as in a restric-tive view that sexuality should perhaps not be written about at all in *Doctor Who*. Given that Davies' approach to equality is premised on sexuality being a non-issue, this strand of his work might better be de-scribed as a 'non-agenda agenda', aiming to make sexuality resolutely unremarkable rather than a focus for celebration or condemnation. Davies' cultural politics have brought him into conflict with conserva-tive voices in the media previously. Interviewed by Alan McKee for the journal *Continuum*, Davies argued that particular newspapers didn't take up a position against *Queer as Folk*, but columnists certainly did.[47] And it was a columnist on the *Daily Mail*, Quentin Letts, who went on to attack Davies' work on *Doctor Who* in terms eerily similar to reac-tionary press responses in the wake of *Queer as Folk*: 'Tennant's Doctor ... was not helped by the programme's scriptwriter Russell T Davies, an irksome little man with ... a tendency to proselytise for gay rights at any opportunity.'[48]

Davies promptly responded to this in the *Guardian*, noting that the inclusion of Captain Jack in *Doctor Who* had entirely escaped the *Daily Mail*'s attention:

> 'There was not really a whisper about that,' he says of the inclusion of the bisexual Captain Jack Harkness ... He adds, for good measure, that there were 'actually a low number of gay characters compared with heterosexual characters'. He sounds triumphant when he says: 'The *Daily Mail* didn't complain, and there weren't any other official complaints' ... He makes no apology for what the *Mail* sees as his proselytising for homosexuality ... '[T]hey can't stop me,' he chuckles scornfully, about those he regards as inhabiting the 'dark corners of the internet'.[49]

Interviewed in *Attitude*, John Barrowman described Captain Jack's bisexuality as a 'press label', noting that in terms of *Who*'s diegesis, he is 'omnisexual. He comes from an era where people don't put people into categories.'[50] This hints at why Captain Jack may have evaded censure from the likes of Letts and *Daily Mail* columnists: the character's bisexuality is very much subtextual rather than textual, being coded in science-fictional terms as a vision of futuristic pansexuality or 'omnisexuality'. The description of Jack as bisexual does, indeed, occur in extra-textual press coverage, but it doesn't leak back into the text of *Doctor Who*. This may be unsurprising, given the show's time-slot and child audience. Jack's sexuality is represented visually and verbally, but in symbolically contained ways. Visually, it exists on-screen via his kissing the Doctor and Rose in 'The Parting of the Ways' (1.13), as well as Ianto Jones and Gwen Cooper in 'The Stolen Earth' (4.12). In each case, however, these moments are coded as desexualised and as nondesiring: Jack is saying farewell to his compatriots, perhaps forever, in the first instance, and appears to be comforting Torchwood members facing mortal peril in the latter. His kisses are melancholic farewells rather than passionate clinches. Verbally, Jack's sexuality is conveyed through witty dialogue and repeated flirting with male, female, human and non-human characters, again leaving the precise question of his sexual identity firmly off-screen and subtextual. However, Davies criticises those who might want to position Captain Jack as part of an authorial 'gay agenda':

> To get hung up on it is almost too sad for words, frankly. It seems odd that anyone would criticise a writer for following their own agenda. I'll say what I want. That's what good writers do ... To get rid of those so-called agendas, you've got to get rid of me. It's never didactic. It's the opposite of didactic. They're little grace notes throughout the whole thing.[51]

Davies' rejection of reactionary 'gay agenda' fan/press readings is underscored by his reference to 'so-called agendas'. Whilst defending his authorship as a matter of repeated statements, Davies nevertheless reinforces a sense that Jack's sexuality should be read progressively as a non-issue. The stress on non-didacticism opposes Davies' situated agency to 'burden of representation' approaches, where images of sexuality are thought of as *having* to counter societal prejudice. It also positions Davies as an *auteur* of 'non-agenda agenda' television drama in which queer identity resists being a central 'issue'.

In 'The sex lives of cult TV characters', Sara Gwenllian Jones poses a question that resonates with Davies' repeated deployments of tele-fantasy: 'Is fantastic genre cult television perhaps inherently queer?'[52] Her answer is a strong affirmative:

> As social practice, [heterosexuality] ... assumes a narrative form of its own, with plot points of courtship, marriage, domesticity, reproduction, child-rearing, provision for the family. Heterosexuality's narrative form is, arguably, the most embedded and pervasive foundational structure of ordinary reality ... As social practice, heterosexuality is antithetical to the exoticism and adventure that characterize the fictional worlds of cult television series.[53]

For Gwenllian Jones, cult TV's 'imperatives are fantasy, adventure and the ... exotic fictional world – imperatives that make heterosexuality problematic because the narrativised social process it invokes threatens the cult fiction's anti-realism'.[54] Cult telefantasy is hence constantly required to disrupt character relationships that could take the series in the direction of heterosexual social practice. Its heroes must remain alone, with the greatest narrative threat seemingly being a cosy home life: 'failures of heterosexual romances in cult television series ... position the audience to find queer pleasures in cult ... texts ... [A]ctive heterosexuality must continually be reined in if it is not to effect a collapse of the exotic-fantastic into suburban domesticity.'[55]

This type of narrative evasion is, indeed, strongly present in new and old *Who*. The BBC Wales' incarnation is only able to countenance the tenth Doctor and Rose living out a life together off-screen via the device of a doppelganger Doctor. Though the twenty-first century Doctor may 'dance' (subtextually: have sexual relationships), his romances are ill-fated, occurring out of sequence and with unhappy consequences. 'The Impossible Planet' and 'The Satan Pit' (2.8 and 2.9) make comedically clear the Doctor's displeasure at the concept of getting a mortgage, whilst the ninth Doctor asserts matter-of-factly that he doesn't 'do family' in 'Aliens of London' (1.4). As an ongoing narrative, new *Who* is premised on an avoidance of normative heterosexual 'social practice' such as settling down or child-rearing. When the tenth Doctor has a daughter, she emerges fully grown as a science-fictional and 'exotic' conceit rather than serving to re-contextualise series four directly as a 'family drama'. Following Gwenllian Jones' argument suggests that *Doctor Who* is, by virtue of its telefantasy format rather than any *auteurist* 'vision', quintessentially queered TV.

Nevertheless, this potentially queer format plays into Davies' authorial repetitions and iterated statements, since calling for obstacles to heterosexual union generates not just scenarios of romantic loss but also the alternative narrative device of unrequited love. This has been a staple of Davies' screenwriting career,[56] occurring in the likes of *Queer as Folk*, *Bob & Rose* and *Casanova*. Indeed, Russell T. Davies has offered a self-interpretation of his work that links *Queer as Folk* and *Doctor Who* as tales of unrequited love:

> The theme of this year [series three] has, I suppose, been unrequited love ... It's one of my favourite stories. It's what ... *Queer as Folk* was about, and a lot of ... *Bob & Rose* was about ... I just realised what a trap ... [Martha] was in, and actually how I was still writing the story of *Queer as Folk*. The only way out of this story is to end it.[57]

The resolution in this case – another strategy for preventing heterosexual union – was to temporarily remove the character of Martha Jones (Freema Agyeman) from *Doctor Who*. Davies is evidently highly conscious of not wanting to 'repeat' himself excessively: 'it's hard not to repeat. I'm a good script editor of my own stuff in that sense – I can feel when I'm repeating.'[58]

Davies' characteristic iterations have been analysed in fanzines such as *Time Space Visualiser*[59] and *In Vision*.[60] Tim Robins argues that *Queer as Folk* does more than normalise gay identities, also challenging stereotyped and pathologised representations of *Doctor Who* fans through the character of Vince Tyler.[61] Somewhat playfully, Neil Lambess reads *Doctor Who* as a reworking of *Queer as Folk*, with the Doctor being a version of Stuart Jones (emotionally detached; having multiple companions; challenging authority; enjoying life to the full). Similarly, Rose Tyler is interpreted as a stand-in for Vince Tyler (a common surname; working in a shop; being a fan of the Doctor).[62] Though Lambess' fan reading is only partly serious, it makes the same point as Davies himself, that his screenwriting revisits particular themes, not as a matter of 'policy',[63] but because he cares about representing quotidian experience:

> That's what makes a great writer, someone who isn't afraid to revisit themes and subplots or characters both minor and major as they evolve over time, and present the author's world view as that itself changes ... In fact Russell T. Davies' first season of *Doctor Who* is a far better continuation of some of the themes of *Queer as Folk* [than] ... the American version of *Queer as Folk*.[64]

If Davies has focused frequently on the 'gay cliché' of 'splendid mothers'[65] in *Century Falls*, *Queer as Folk*, *Bob & Rose*, and *Doctor Who*, then he has also recurrently been drawn back to the media, and television specifically, as subject matter. *Mine All Mine* involves a TV station being set up; *Doctor Who* features futuristic reality TV; even *The Grand* – despite being set in the 1920s – involves a storyline (in 2.2) featuring a quest for music-hall fame that self-reflexively mirrors contemporary media culture. And *Casanova* anachronistically violates the norms of period drama by referencing contemporary advertising (e.g. 'You've got to be in it to win it', a National Lottery slogan). Davies has unashamedly projected TV culture backward and forward in his different diegetic time frames, from eighteenth-century Venice through to the year 200,100 in 'Bad Wolf' (1.12), as well as infamously depicting Vince's *Doctor Who* fandom in *Queer as Folk*.[66]

Although online fandom has accused Davies' scripts of falling back on alleged '*deus ex machina*' ('God in the machine') resolutions – where characters suddenly gain miraculous powers without any foreshadowing – his work actually displays a tendency towards what might be dubbed '*persona ex machina*' denouements. It is a 'character in the machine' that aids narrative resolution in *Dark Season* (1991), as schoolteacher Miss Maitland drives a bulldozer into a 'barricade of water pipes'[67] in order to flood the Behemoth computer. And in Davies' original *Doctor Who* novel, *Damaged Goods* (1996), the Doctor is rescued by companion Chris Cwej, driving, again, a bulldozer.[68] Within new *Who*, Rose is able to rescue the ninth Doctor in Davies' 'The Parting of the Ways' (1.13) thanks only to a lorry that pulls open the TARDIS console. And Kylie Minogue, playing Astrid Peth, defeats Max Capricorn in 'Voyage of the Damned' (4.X) by driving a forklift truck at him. 'Turn Left' (4.11) also involves Donna Noble righting a timeline by throwing herself deliberately in front of oncoming traffic. Though Davies' *Doctor Who* narratives involve characters taking on 'magical' powers, they also recurrently feature ordinary machines and vehicles as objects of narrative resolution. Such literal plot machinery works to ground Davies' telefantasy as the collision of ordinary, everyday technology with fantastical science-fictional powers. The extension of human agency occurs just as much in our everyday lives – by driving a car, JCB, or lorry – as in 'other-wordly' fantasy, and Davies' writing displays a tendency to collapse together these magical and concrete (generic and naturalistic) augmentations of characters' capabilities. SF devices are lent plausibility by being jammed together with mundane technology, just as present-day technologies are given an air of exoticism (e.g. Rose's mobile phone in 'The End of the World', 1.2).

Russell T. Davies' authorship is also displayed literally through statements – through the striking dialogue he gives to characters. Series two of *Queer as Folk* includes a litany of slang insults for homosexuality, delivered by Stuart Jones, which Glyn Davis reads as follows:

> Although it is possible to interpret Stuart's speech as indicative of his tendency to excess, his predilection for the spectacular, it also serves as a moment of authorial rupture, a scene when Russell T. Davies's voice as the writer of the series can be heard over Stuart's own.[69]

This dual coding – dialogue that can be read both narratively and as a performative authorial flourish – also occurs notably in *The Grand* and *Doctor Who*:

> Monica Jones: You can go up to the roof of this place and look down. We go there sometimes, me and the girls, to see the guests arriving. And it can be midnight, but there's all this light. And you look across the city, and it's all lights and people as far as the eye can see. *You can see the curve of the world and feel it turn* (beat). And all I've got is that thin bed downstairs. It's lights out by eleven and up at six. And that's not fair. (from *The Grand* (1.2); my emphasis)

> The Doctor: It's like when you're a kid, the first time they tell you that the world is turning. And you just can't believe it, 'cos everything looks like it's standing still. *I can feel it ... The turn of the Earth.* The ground beneath our feet is spinning at a thousand miles an hour, the entire planet is hurtling round the sun at 67,000 miles an hour, and I can feel it. (from 'Rose' (1.1); my emphasis)

The ninth Doctor's poetic words share much with those uttered by the character of Monica Jones (Jane Danson), a maid in *The Grand*. Although it may be possible to interpret the Earth-turning speech as a bid for a quotable moment of *Doctor Who*,[70] the sequence also self-consciously advertised the series' 'authored' status, being used heavily in the publicity for *Doctor Who*'s return to BBC1.[71]

The words Davies gives to Monica Jones and the Doctor articulate a shared sense of longing, and a desire for transcendence. Monica yearns for an escape from the restrictions of her ordinary life as a hotel maid, and it is the image of her feeling the turn of the world that suggests she may yet escape the shackles of service. Such cosmic imagery is lyrical in *The Grand*, becoming literalised in *Doctor Who*. The Doctor, we assume, really does feel the world turning, his language infusing the cosmological with a scientific bent, alluding to 'the Earth' rather than the world, and including speeds of rotation.

Monica's words introduce one of the overarching storylines of *The Grand*: will she be able to learn from her mentor, Esme Harkness (Susan Hampshire), and potentially overcome the barriers that 1920s society has placed on her as a working-class woman? In this series, Davies linked the desire for transcendence – moving above and outside social restrictions – to the dialogue and character of a young female. In 'Rose' (1.1), he gives very similar dialogue to the mentor figure of the Doctor rather than to Rose Tyler herself. This shifts the emotional and narrative balance from one where an outsider is entreated to help – *The Grand*'s Esme Harkness is a former prostitute who, despite her wealth and social standing, is not accepted by the moral guardians of the upper classes – to one where an outsider, the Doctor, proffers the promise of transcendence to Rose.

The key storylines of mentoring and longing characteristic of *The Grand* and *Doctor Who* also diverge in instructive ways. In the former, Davies pulls no punches by presenting a tragic conclusion to Monica Jones' story. She is hanged for the murder of Jackson Tyler, a miscarriage of justice suggesting that society's patriarchal and class powers – systematically favouring upper-class male versions of the world over a working-class female one – have done their brutal, prejudiced work. By marked contrast, Rose Tyler's longing for transcendence in *Doctor Who* is significantly rewarded: she takes on God-like powers of life and death, her family are reunited across universes, and ultimately she gets to spend her life with a human facsimile of the tenth Doctor. Rose's story remains more uplifting and hopeful than the tragedy of Monica Jones' tale. Rose Tyler really does escape from the Earth; Monica's world ultimately remains painfully small.

One final, important aspect of the Foucauldian 'author-function' is that it directs readers to interpret specific texts through their attributed authors. So, although a Russell T. Davies-credited screenplay might be interpreted as reflecting specific concerns and cultural politics, where the empirical, flesh-and-blood individual Davies has produced elements of a piece of work uncredited – perhaps revising a screenplay attributed to another writer – it will tend to be read through that other writer's biography, circumstances, and intertextual body of work, despite actually having been at least partly written by Davies. The 'author-function' intensifies any disjunction between who it is that actually writes, and who is then credited and positioned discursively as 'the author'. In *The Writer's Tale* (2008), Davies reflects on the fact that much of his work on *Doctor Who* effectively goes uncredited:

> [After 'Human Nature' (3.8) went out] I had a whole Sunday of people saying 'That was so brilliant', and specifically, 'What a brilliant script. Paul Cornell is a genius.' Which he is. But I'm thinking, if only you knew how much of that I wrote! ... People know that I polish stuff, but they think that polishing means adding a gag or an epigram, not writing half the script.[72]

Discourses of authorship mean that fan readings, and *Who* scholarship for that matter, can fail to correlate with real, flesh-and-blood authorship, contrasting work attributed to Davies with that attributed to others, despite the fact that these may be false binaries in some instances.[73] And although *Doctor Who*'s re-imagining can be analysed in relation to both the 'author-function' and the iterated authorial statements of Russell T. Davies, it has also been placed within other contexts of 'authorship'. Specifically, what has it meant for the programme to be produced in-house by BBC Wales?

## Made by BBC Wales:
## 'Building Production Outside London'

If *Doctor Who*'s triumphant success in 2005 could never have been predicted just a few years earlier, then likewise the production base responsible for this feat would not have been guessed. Nothing in the history of the classic series prepared fans for news that *Doctor Who* would be made by BBC Wales. The BBC's 2005–6 Annual Report makes clear one rationale for this commission, made before a single word had been written.[74] The series was part of a Charter-period pledge to increase BBC production outside London.[75] As the BBC Annual Report put it under the 'Nations and Regions' heading:

> *Dr Who*, starring David Tennant and Billie Piper, is made in Cardiff. The BBC is committed to increasing programme production outside the M25 ... BBC Cymru Wales has been notably successful in supplying the

network with memorable programming across a range of genres. Drama has been particularly strong and includes some of the high points of BBC One, such as *Doctor Who* and *Life on Mars*.[76]

The impression given here is that new *Who* was part of a slate of successful networked dramas, that is, dramas supplied to the BBC for nationwide broadcast. However, although *Life on Mars* (BBC, 2006–7) was commissioned through BBC Wales and its head of drama, Julie Gardner, the series was not produced by BBC Wales, nor filmed in Wales. Its inclusion alongside *Doctor Who* in the BBC's Annual Report, whilst technically accurate, is somewhat misleading given the programme's lack of connection to Wales and Welsh TV production. In fact, immediately prior to *Doctor Who*'s return, BBC Wales supplied no in-house drama to the BBC network:

> While the drama departments in Northern Ireland and Scotland scored major successes with *Ballykissangel* (1996–2001) and *Monarch of the Glen* (2000–2005), uncontroversial dramas that packaged stereotypical ... identities in terms of heritage culture and London's sense of the British national identity and audience, BBC Wales failed to produce a drama series deemed to have national appeal ... That changed with the recommissioning of *Doctor Who*.[77]

As Mark Bould points out above, the success of BBC Northern Ireland and BBC Scotland hinged on representing their national identities in particular, reactionary ways. Addressing this question, Steve Blandford has argued that BBC Wales failed to achieve a 1990s BBC network presence because it tended to produce content such as *Belonging* (1999–2009), which displayed 'both ... strong local roots and at least a passing acquaintance with economic realities that has excluded it from any serious consideration for the BBC network'.[78] Unlike other BBC drama departments outside England, BBC Wales refused to shape representations of Welsh national identity in line with English preconceptions, rejecting 'an attitude to place that undoubtedly owes more to discourses of tourism than drama'.[79] A clutch of BBC Wales' series networked in 1996 (*Drover's Gold*, *Mortimer's Law* and *Tiger Bay*) were not recommissioned, and Blandford comments that

> unlike *Hamish Macbeth* [BBC Scotland, 1995–7] or *Ballykissangel*, *Tiger Bay* made few concessions to the idea of popular television as being part of a total package that would also see increased sales of Shirley Bassey dolls and tourist buses pointing out ... location[s].[80]

*Doctor Who's* commission rectified this absence, and did not appear to be in any way premised on the problematic 'heritage' packaging of Welshness. However, it was not a project originated or driven by BBC Wales. Rather, it was in effect allocated to the 'nations and regions' by the BBC in London. James Chapman implies that the BBC wanted to work with Russell T. Davies, and saw the commission as a way of cementing this deal.[81] However, in spite of Davies' birthplace and Welsh identity, his role in the *Who* 'package' is unlikely to have been enough to allocate the drama to BBC Wales. Other pieces were also falling into place, such as Julie Gardner's application for the head of drama job at BBC Wales, for example:

> It's very important, the talent you take with you ... When I went for my job interview with Jane Tranter, I pitched *Casanova* to her ... When I took the BBC Wales job, I didn't know that I'd also be making *Doctor Who* ... That came about ... when I went to my first formal meeting with Jane Tranter, in the first week of September 2003 ... And then Jane just came out with the most extraordinary sentence, which was, 'Do you want to make *Doctor Who*?' ... And when they did mention Russell, I laughed ... because I knew that we'd spent the last 18 months talking about ... *Buffy* and how much we love sci-fi.[82]

Interviewed in *Doctor Who Magazine*, Gardner gives a strangely guarded answer to the question of whether she was hired at BBC Wales before or after *Doctor Who's* re-commissioning was in the air:

> As far as I know, the two things were separate ... but I've never actually asked Jane Tranter, the Controller of Drama Commissioning, at what stage ... she ... talked seriously about bringing [it] back ... I know that they always wanted Russell to be the lead writer on it.[83]

The question evaded by this politician's riposte is whether or not Gardner's appointment at BBC Wales could have formed part of a strategy to draw Davies to the *Doctor Who* project. In any case, following Gardner's appointment, BBC Wales had a head of drama known to have already worked effectively alongside Davies. And, viewed in that context, the show's allocation to BBC Wales – though it could certainly be rationalised and publicised as a matter of non-London production – appears to resemble a pragmatic decision based on having relevant staff in post. Far from being an autonomous BBC Wales decision, the show was passed over to them seemingly via centralised contingencies of BBC deal-brokering.

John Geraint, writing in the *Media Wales Journal*, has analysed the financial impact of this commission, noting that in the financial year from April 2005 to March 2006, 'BBC Wales delivered 158 hours of network television at a total cost of £49.24 million', a tally that had risen from '£30.33 million and 115 hours the previous year'.[84] Geraint points out, however, that the 'BBC's total spend on network television outside the M25 corridor during this same period was £300 million (i.e. BBC Wales received a sixth) ... the phenomenon that is *Doctor Who* was responsible for a fair chunk of the income'.[85] On the face of it, this shows a highly positive picture for BBC Wales:

> Since the National Assembly's arrival there has been growth in mass media in Wales ... Sustained growth ... is apparent in broadcasting ... There have been considerable successes such as BBC Wales's reinvention of *Doctor Who* and its spin-offs, *Torchwood* and *The Sarah Jane Adventures* [2007– ] which have not only drawn huge ratings and critical acclaim but have also proven to be a fillip to Welsh production.[86]

Nevertheless, doubts and difficulties that have plagued BBC Wales are present beneath the surface. In their survey of the media in Wales, David Barlow, Philip Mitchell and Tom O'Malley argue that the 'evolution of a Welsh system within the general system could be viewed as a form of co-option by the centre of critical voices from the periphery',[87] and Welsh media scholar Kevin Williams has likewise argued that there continues to be 'too much control of BBC Wales from London'.[88]

*Doctor Who* may be celebrated in the BBC's 2005–6 Annual Report for '[b]uilding production outside London',[89] but the programme nevertheless represents continued and centralised BBC London agenda-setting for BBC Wales, as well as largely failing to represent contemporary life in Wales. As telefantasy, it can be argued that this is not the generic remit of the show and that, furthermore, it does at least evade the touristic marketing of stereotypical Welshness. However, the tendency for commissions from the 'nations and regions' to symbolically draw on discourses of tourism has played a role in new *Who*, especially in the 2005 series:

> I wanted to use Cardiff as a location from the very moment that *Doctor Who* became a BBC Wales Production ... if you're using a town and its facilities and its population, and its goodwill, I think it's right and proper to put that place on screen, especially when so much UK drama is

based around London and Manchester. If you show Cardiff on screen, and demonstrate how beautiful it can look ... then you're going to encourage other film and TV-makers to come to the area.[90]

Russell T. Davies was very careful in extra-textual publicity to position the series as a kind of advert for the beauty of Cardiff. 'Boom Town' (1.11) eventually served this function. The episode even features Mickey Smith (Noel Clarke) arriving at Cardiff station and confronting signs in English and Welsh like a tourist disembarking in the city for the first time. The Wales Millennium Centre also figures in the story, its inscribed frontage being revealed by the TARDIS' final dematerialisation in a carefully framed aesthetic of place.

Given generic and narrative difficulties for *Doctor Who* to go on depicting contemporary Cardiff plausibly, it was spin-off *Torchwood* that shouldered the 'burden of Welsh representation' after series one. *Who*'s second run acted effectively as a gigantic advert not for Cardiff but for this new TV brand that could showcase Wales-as-Wales and further boost Welsh TV production.[91] *Torchwood* Exec Producer Julie Gardner states:

> I love ... *Smallville* [WB, 2001–6; CW, 2006– ] and *Buffy The Vampire Slayer.* I wanted to see if it was possible to make that type of investigative action series in Cardiff. I think it's a great city, and I wanted to put contemporary Cardiff on screen.[92]

The same touristic, symbolic affirmation of Wales – and Cardiff specifically – that had underpinned 'Boom Town' (1.11) was hence transferred to *Torchwood*. Along with *Doctor Who*'s emphasis on 'modern, global Britain',[93] as imaged through the Swiss Re Tower ('The Christmas Invasion', 2.X) and the London Eye ('Rose', 1.1), Cardiff was also represented through its Bay regeneration and iconic architecture in series one. The episode title 'Boom Town' ironically gestured at a diegetic, monstrous plan to destroy Cardiff as well as referencing the actual city's recent redevelopment and growth. This representational strategy – Cardiff-as-modernity – also carries over into *Torchwood*, the HQ of which is based underground adjacent to the Wales Millennium Centre, seemingly for little or no reason other than that this neatly integrates the show's dramatic 'hub' with discourses of tourism. Any promotion of Cardiff as a modern city thus becomes either explicitly or implicitly a promotion of *Torchwood*, and vice versa.

There has been some anxiety over the fact that BBC Wales' new-found networked success is heavily dependent on the staffing axis of Davies–Gardner, and on Russell T. Davies' telefantasy output (as the creator of two *Doctor Who* spin-offs). Even publicity for the 2008 BBC Wales-commissioned networked show, *Merlin*, referred to Davies' creative vision for Saturday night BBC TV, despite the fact that he had no substantive involvement in the programme's production.[94] Rejecting BBC Wales' telefantasy, the chairman of the National Assembly's broadcasting committee, Alun Davies, recently argued that Wales still lacks shows such as BBC Scotland's *Monarch of the Glen*: 'What you don't have is the portrayal of life in Wales, and in that sense Wales really is the forgotten nation on the BBC.'[95] *Torchwood* is dismissed as non-representative, presumably on the basis that it is fantastical rather than naturalistic (though its predominantly urban, Cardiff setting may also be felt to preclude it from fully representing 'life in Wales').

Responding to the National Assembly's broadcasting committee, Controller of BBC Wales, Menna Richards, countered with a celebratory account of *Doctor Who*'s role:

> I think that it has had a very positive and beneficial effect not only on BBC Wales but on Wales ... I think the idea that Wales is producing the single most successful television series on British television for a generation says something not only about the talent that exists here, but also about the confidence Wales has about going out there and producing output that is as good as – indeed, better – than anything else.[96]

But if twenty-first century *Doctor Who* is arguably important to Welsh pride and national identity, the reverse is still not equally true: Welshness is not semiotically and symbolically important to the narratives of *Doctor Who*. After attempts to integrate discourses of tourism into series one, Cardiff has subsequently re-entered the series only briefly, allowing a TARDIS 'refuelling stop' in the pre-credits sequence of 'Utopia' (3.11), and appearing as Torchwood's base of operations at the conclusion of 'Last of the Time Lords' (3.13) and in 'The Stolen Earth'/'Journey's End' (4.12–4.13). Having passed the 'burden of Welsh representation' over to *Torchwood*, *Doctor Who* has continued in its metropolitan, London-centric routines. The climactic Dalek–Cyber–Torchwood battle of series two occurs in Canary Wharf; series three introduces Martha Jones who (just like Rose Tyler) works in London, whilst series four's companion, Donna Noble, hails from Chiswick.

If the programme can be viewed as a centralised London commission allocated to BBC Wales for both contingent, deal-brokering
and devolutionary BBC policy reasons, then in diegetic terms, BBC
Wales' *Doctor Who* nevertheless treats London as its narrative centre.
Recognisable London landmarks have formed part of spectacular special effects sequences regularly: the Doctor's implicit home, 2005–9,
is surely England's capital city. Cardiff remains a train journey or a refuelling stop away. As such, the show's networked success resonates
with Steve Blandford's observation that 'the BBC's faith in the need
for a broader, more flexible idea of Britishness does not yet extend to
its commissioning of programmes that they hope will have genuinely
broad appeal'.[97] *Torchwood*'s promotion to BBC1 as 'event TV' in 2009
challenges that notion to an extent, but such a move comes four whole
years after transmission of *Doctor Who*'s first BBC Wales series.[98]

In this chapter I have considered the (de)materialising authorship
of showrunner Russell T. Davies, arguing that egalitarian discourses
of multiple authorship – drawn from *Doctor Who*'s fan culture – have
been taken up industrially in this case. At the same time, however, Davies has provided a conventional 'author-function' for new *Who*, and
has used extra-textual statements both to self-interpret the series as
part of his established body of work, and to reinforce the 'non-agenda
agenda' of his approach to queer identity. Additionally, new *Who* has
been contextualised within debates over Welsh TV production and
the balance of power between BBC London and Wales, resulting in
the temporary adoption of 'discourses of tourism' in series one, pre-
*Torchwood*.

Continuing Part I's focus on the relationship between production
and fandom, in the following chapter I want to focus more directly
on how fan identities have affected the re-creation of *Doctor Who*. Fan
'poachers'[99] have now become official producers, or 'textual gamekeepers'. However, in what follows I want to analyse this development
critically rather than merely celebrating it as a shift in fan/producer
power relationships.

## NOTES

1   Kim Newman, (2005) *BFI TV Classics:* Doctor Who, BFI Publishing, Lon-
    don, p.113.
2   See, for example, David Richardson (2004) 'Russell T. Davies', *TV Zone
    Special* 56, Visual Imagination, London, pp.74–5 and 78–9.

3    More precisely, BBC Wales is based in Llandaff; *Doctor Who* at the Upper Boat studios near Pontypridd

4    James Chapman (2006) *Inside the TARDIS: The Worlds of* Doctor Who, I.B.Tauris, London and New York, p.185.

5    Rolinson, Dave (2007) '"*Who* done it": discourses of authorship during the John Nathan-Turner era', in David Butler (ed.) *Time and Relative Dissertations in Space: Critical Perspectives on* Doctor Who, Manchester University Press, Manchester and New York, p.188.

6    Russell T. Davies (2005) 'Bad Wolf/The Parting of the Ways', in *The Shooting Scripts*, BBC Books, London, p.431.

7    See Jason Mittell (2006) 'Narrative complexity in contemporary American television', *The Velvet Light Trap* 58 (Fall), pp.29–40, on 'narrative complexity' and US TV.

8    Dave Rolinson's book chapter on *Doctor Who* and authorship ('*Who* done it', 2007) does not endorse this discourse, but merely observes it at work.

9    See, for example, Matt Hills (2002) *Fan Cultures*, Routledge, London and New York, and Henry Jenkins (1995) '"Do you enjoy making the rest of us feel stupid?": alt.tv.twinpeaks, the trickster author and viewer mastery', in David Lavery (ed.) *Full of Secrets: Critical Approaches to* Twin Peaks, Wayne State University Press, Detroit, pp.51–69.

10   Jonathan Bignell and Andrew O'Day (2004) *Terry Nation*, Manchester University Press, Manchester and New York; Andy Murray (2007) 'The talons of Robert Holmes', in David Butler (ed.) *Time and Relative Dissertations in Space: Critical Perspectives on* Doctor Who, Manchester University Press, Manchester and New York, pp.217–32.

11   See Lynnette Porter and David Lavery (2007) *Unlocking the Meaning of* Lost, Sourcebooks, Illinois, pp.29–30, on *Lost* fans, and Maire Messenger Davies (2007) 'Quality and creativity in TV: the work of television storytellers', in Janet McCabe and Kim Akass (eds) *Quality TV: Contemporary American Television and Beyond*, I.B.Tauris, London and New York, pp.180–2, on *Star Trek* fandom. Though *Buffy* fans might argue that it 'is not at all difficult ... to locate the author' of the text (David Lavery (2002) 'Afterword: the genius of Joss Whedon', in Rhonda V. Wilcox and David Lavery (eds) *Fighting the Forces: What's at Stake in* Buffy the Vampire Slayer, Rowman and Littlefield, Maryland, p.252), they also read for the impact of the work of Jane Espenson or Marti Noxon.

12   Rolinson: '*Who* done it', p.183.

13   Russell T. Davies (2008) 'Introduction' in *Doctor Who Magazine Special Edition: The* Doctor Who *Companion — Series Four*, Panini Magazines, Tunbridge Wells, p.5. (See also Russell T. Davies (2006) 'Production notes: Phil's space', *Doctor Who Magazine* 366, Panini Comics, Tunbridge Wells, p.125.)

14   Ibid., p.5.

15   Scott, Suzanne (2008) 'Authorized resistance: is fan production frakked?', in Tiffany Potter and C.W. Marshall (eds) *Cylons in America: Critical Studies in* Battlestar Galactica, Continuum, New York and London, p.219.

16   Ibid., p.218.

17 See  http://www.bbc.co.uk/doctorwho/s4/misc/commentaries.shtml,  accessed 27 August 2008.

18 See Neil Perryman (2008) '*Doctor Who* and the convergence of media: a case study in "transmedia storytelling"', *Convergence: The International Journal of Research into New Media Technologies* xiv/1, pp.21–39.

19 Michel Foucault, Michel (1979) 'What is an author?', *Screen* xx/1, p.19.

20 John Tulloch and Henry Jenkins (1995) *Science Fiction Audiences: Watching Doctor Who and Star Trek*, Routledge, London and New York, p.188–90.

21 Ibid.

22 Russell T. Davies (2005) 'Have a Russell T. Davies TV festival', the *Guardian*, 1 January, available online at *http://www.guardian.co.uk/theguardian/2005/jan/01/weekend7.weekend4*, accessed 19 August 2008.

23 Murray: 'The talons of Robert Holmes', p.223.

24 Ibid.

25 Ibid.

26 Matt Bielby, (2008) 'The *Death Ray* interview: Steven Moffat', *Death Ray* 15, Blackfish, Bath, p.77.

27 See Steven Moffat in Bielby: '*Death Ray* interview', p.71 and Steven Moffat (2008) 'Production notes', *Doctor Who Magazine* 397, Panini Comics, Tunbridge Wells, pp.4–5 and (2008) 'A letter from the Doctor', in *Doctor Who Storybook* (2009) Panini Books, Tunbridge Wells, p.5, for further examples of his characteristic approach to non-linear narrative.

28 See Cornel Sandvoss (2005) *Fans: The Mirror of Consumption*, Polity Press, Cambridge, p.110; and on audiences' readings of the programme also shifting as they age across their own life-courses, see Brian Longhurst (2007) *Cultural Change and Ordinary Life*, Open University Press, Maidenhead and New York, p.113.

29 In Nick Setchfield and Steve O'Brien (2006) 'When Russell Met Verity', *SFX* 150, Future Network, Bath, p.54.

30 Charles Norton (2008) 'Evolution of a monster hit', *The Stage*, 15 May, pp.52–3.

31 See the arguments of Tulloch and Jenkins: *Science Fiction Audiences*.

32 In Norton: 'Evolution of a monster hit'.

33 See Jonathan Bignell and Andrew O'Day (2004) *Terry Nation*, Manchester University Press, Manchester and New York, p.89 on the play of author(ity) functions; see also Richard Berger (2008) 'GINO or dialogic: what does 're-imagined' really mean?', in Josef Steiff and Trista D. Tamplin (eds) *Battlestar Galactica and Philosophy: Mission Accomplished or Mission Frakked Up?* Open Court, Chicago and La Salle, IL, pp.317–28 on the 'dialogic' reimagining of *Battlestar Galactica*.

34 Umberto Eco (1995) *Faith in Fakes: Travels in Hyperreality*, Minerva, London, p.199.

35 Compare this situation with Sarah Cardwell (2002) *Adaptation Revisited: Television and the Classic Novel*, Manchester University Press, Manchester and New York, p.23 on the TV adaptation of classic literature.

36 Janet Staiger (2003) 'Authorship approaches', in David A. Gerstner and Janet Staiger (eds) *Authorship and Film*, Routledge, New York and London, pp.45–6.

37 Foucault: 'What is an author?'.
38 Staiger: 'Authorship approaches', p.51.
39 See Cardwell: *Adaptation Revisited*, p.25.
40 Steven Capsuto in Glen Creeber (2004) *Serial Television: Big Drama on the Small Screen*, BFI, London, p.130.
41 See Benshoff, Harry M. (1997) *Monsters in the Closet: Homosexuality and the Horror Film*, Manchester University Press, Manchester and Alan McKee (2002) 'Interview with Russell T. Davies', *Continuum: Journal of Media and Cultural Studies* xvi/2, p.239.
42 Glyn Davis (2007) *BFI TV Classics: Queer as Folk*, BFI, London, p.125.
43 Cited in ibid.
44 Sarah Nathan (2003) 'Duckie *Who*: Time Lord has gay show writer', the *Sun*, 27 September, p.33, available online at *http://www.cuttingsarchive. org.uk/news_mag/2000s/cuttings/ukls/duckie.htm*, accessed 28 August 2008.
45 Thom Hutchinson and Matt Bielby (2008) 'The gay agenda', *Death Ray* 15, September, Blackfish, Bath, p.59.
46 Ibid.
47 See Russell T. Davies in McKee: 'Interview with Russell T. Davies', p.238.
48 Quentin Letts (2008) 'Who's the greatest?', *Daily Mail*, 4 July, available online at *http://www.dailymail.co.uk/tvshowbiz/article-1031715/Whos-greatest.html*, accessed 28 August 2008.
49 In Ben Dowell (2008) 'Amy Winehouse would be a great Doctor', *Guardian*, 7 July, available online at *http://www.guardian.co.uk/media/2008/jul/07/television.bbc*, accessed 7 August 2008.
50 In Matthew Todd (2006) 'Any queries? Where you ask the questions – John Barrowman', *Attitude* 152 (December), pp.34–9.
51 Ibid.
52 Sara Gwenllian Jones (2002) 'The sex lives of cult television characters', *Screen* xliii/1, p.82.
53 Ibid., p.87.
54 Ibid., p.88.
55 Ibid., p.89.
56 See Robin Nelson (2007) *State of Play: Contemporary 'High-End' TV Drama*, Manchester University Press, Manchester and New York, p.196, and Sarah Cardwell (2005) 'The representation of youth in the twenty-something serial', in Michael Hammond and Lucy Mazdon (eds) *The Contemporary Television Series*, Edinburgh Press, Edinburgh, pp.131–2.
57 Russell T. Davies in Benjamin Cook (2007) 'There's no way we want to let her go', *Doctor Who Magazine* 385, Panini Comics, Tunbridge Wells, p.18.
58 Russell T. Davies in Ian Berriman (2007) 'Writing *Who*', *SFX Collection*, special edn 28, Future Network, Bath, pp.11–12.
59 See Neil Lambess (2006) 'Errant nonsense', *Time Space Visualiser* 73, pp.67–9.
60 See Tim Robins (2003) 'Sutekh's gift', *In-Vision* 109, Cybermark Services, Borehamwood, p.28.
61 Ibid.

62    Lambess: 'Errant nonsense', pp.67–8.
63    See Nick Setchfield (2007) 'When Russell met Verity: the outtakes', *SFX Collection*, special edn 28, Future Network, Bath, pp.123–4.
64    Lambess: 'Errant nonsense', p.69.
65    Russell T. Davies in McKee: 'Interview with Russell T. Davies', p.240; see also Davis: *BFI TV Classics – Queer as Folk*, p.101.
66    See Davis: *BFI TV Classics – Queer as Folk*, pp.32–3, and Robin Nelson: *State of Play*, p.82.
67    Russell T. Davies (1991) *Dark Season*, BBC Books, London, p.153.
68    Russell T. Davies (1996) *Damaged Goods*, Virgin, London, pp.242–3.
69    Davis: *BFI TV Classics – Queer as Folk*, p.96.
70    See Andrew Osmond (2005) 'Sexing up the Tardis', *Sight & Sound* (December), p.88.
71    Mark Aldridge and Andy Murray (2008) *T Is For Television: The Small Screen Adventures of Russell T. Davies*, Reynolds and Hearn, Surrey, pp.89–90, also compare these sequences of dialogue, yet somewhat paradoxically conclude that '*The Grand* does not comfortably fit into our analysis of Davies's ... recurring narrative devices and motifs'. *Contra* this, I would argue that the series acts as a significant precursor of Davies' *Who* work.
72    Russell T. Davies and Benjamin Cook (2008) *The Writer's Tale*, BBC Books, London, p.125.
73    For example, Davies and Cook demonstrate the extent of Davies' reworking of a section of script from James Moran. Much of the opening Doctor–Donna dialogue, as transmitted, was in fact Davies' work (Davies and Cook: *The Writer's Tale*, pp.194–6).
74    See Russell T. Davies (2005) 'Pitch perfect', in *The* Doctor Who *Companion: Series One*, Panini Comics, Tunbridge Wells, p.40.
75    This is detailed in Kevin Williams (2006) 'An uncertain era: Welsh television, broadcasting policy and the National Assembly in a multimedia world', *Contemporary Wales: An Annual Review of Economic, Political and Social Research*, vol. xviii, University of Wales Press, Cardiff, p.228.
76    BBC (2006) *Annual Report and Accounts 2005/2006*, Broadcasting House, London, p.56.
77    Mark Bould (2008) 'Science fiction television in the United Kingdom', in J.P. Telotte (ed.) *The Essential Science Fiction Television Reader*, University Press of Kentucky, Kentucky, p.224.
78    Steve Blandford (2005) 'BBC drama at the margins: the contrasting fortunes of Northern Irish, Scottish and Welsh television drama in the 1990s', in Jonathan Bignell and Stephen Lacey (eds) *Popular Television Drama: Critical Perspectives*, Manchester University Press, Manchester and New York, p.178.
79    Ibid., p.173.
80    Ibid., p.176.
81    See Chapman: *Inside the TARDIS*, p.187.
82    Julie Gardner in Benjamin Cook (2005) 'Gardner's world', *Doctor Who Magazine* 354, Panini Comics, Tunbridge Wells, p.15.
83    Julie Gardner in ibid., p.14.
84    John Geraint (2008) 'For Wales, see England": network television from "the Nations", 1996–2006', *Cyfrwng: Media Wales Journal* 5, p.47.

85   Ibid.
86   Kevin Williams (2008) 'Broadcasting and the National Assembly: the future of broadcasting policy in Wales', *Cyfrwng: Media Wales Journal 5*, p.95.
87   David Barlow, Philip Mitchell and Tom O'Malley (2005) *The Media in Wales: Voices of a Small Nation*, University of Wales Press, Cardiff, p.222.
88   Williams: 'An uncertain era', p.228.
89   BBC: *Annual Report 2005/2006*, p.56.
90   Russell T. Davies in Benjamin Cook (2005) 'New series preview: Boom Town', *Doctor Who Magazine 357*, Panini Comics, Tunbridge Wells, p.27.
91   See Bould: 'Science fiction television', p.224, and Sarah Herman (2008) 'Lleoliad, lleoliad, lleoliad!', *Torchwood: The Official Magazine 8*, Titan Magazines, London, p.16.
92   Julie Gardner in Simon Hugo (2008) 'Executive decisions', *Torchwood: The Official Magazine 8*, Titan Magazines, London, p.10.
93   Bould: 'Science fiction television', p.224.
94   See Julie Gardner in Mark Sweney (2008) 'Merlin: BBC cues up TV and cinema ads', 29 August, available online at *http://www.guardian.co.uk/media/2008/aug/29/bbc.television* accessed 27 September 2008.
95   In David Williamson (2008) 'BBC Wales won't depend on *Doctor Who*', *Western Mail*, 10 June, available online at *http://www.walesonline.co.uk/news/politics-news/2008/06/10/bbc-wales-won-t-depend-on-doctor-who-91466-21047606/*, accessed 18 September 2009.
96   Ibid.
97   Blandford: 'BBC drama at the margins', p.180.
98   And, it should be noted, *Torchwood: Children of Earth* combined its move to BBC1 with a new-found diegetic emphasis on London as a setting.
99   See Henry Jenkins (1992) *Textual Poachers*, Routledge, New York and London.

# 2

# 'THE *DOCTOR WHO* MAFIA':
# FANS AS TEXTUAL POACHERS
# TURNED GAMEKEEPERS

*D*octor Who's fan culture has undoubtedly been instrumental in its return to TV screens. As Clayton Hickman, then editor of *Doctor Who Magazine* told *Guardian* journalist Andy Bodle in 2004, 'The *Doctor Who* mafia ... That's why the show's coming back. If it wasn't for all the fans in high places, it would have just faded away.'[1] The programme's first producer, Verity Lambert, seemed amused by this turn of events, observing that '[m]ost of the writers seem to be members of the *Doctor Who* Appreciation Society (laughs) so they've kind of lived and immersed themselves in ... *Who*'.[2] And all of the participants in a *DWM* feature, 'We're gonna be bigger than *Star Wars*!',[3] have by now either worked directly on the BBC Wales' series or have written tie-in novels (Russell T. Davies, Mark Gatiss, Steven Moffat, Lance Parkin, Gareth Roberts).[4]

Davies would later remark in a 2003 *Doctor Who Magazine* special edition:

> I work in television and, as the years blunder past, I meet more and more *Doctor Who* addicts in this industry ... And I have come to tell

you now: *Doctor Who* made us clever ... I do meet Trekkers working in television. Making my coffee and driving me. Ha ha! *Making my coffee and driving me!* I liked that so much I said it again.[5]

Drawing on established *Who* fan lore that being a *Doctor Who* fan correlates with being an anti-fan of *Star Trek*, Davies further posits that fans' love of the show has inspired their desire to go into the media industry. In contributions to special editions of *DWM*, Davies developed his thesis that *Doctor Who* was always structured through absences and gaps, both textually and extra-textually (many early episodes having been junked by the BBC). As a result, he depicts *Who* fans as being forced to use their imaginations:

> I've always believed that the programme has survived and enriched itself because of the gaps in its production, the space between what was intended, what is, and what could be. Those gaps allow our imagination to slip inside. And there's a crucial gap, right there, right at the start: we don't know the central character's name. It's a clumsy device ... It's a slender premise ... Technically, it's a mess ... Genius doesn't make sense, it isn't nice and clean and shiny.[6]

And because stories such as 'Fury from the Deep' (1968) are no longer retained by the BBC (apart from a few short clips), their absence allegedly incites and invites fans to

> make these stories better in our imaginations ... We rewrite and censor and extrapolate ... This gorgeous, clumsy show gives us no choice but to exercise our brains ... We were brought up to fill in the gaps. We see foam and imagine the creature inside; we know that one pipe represents a vast array ... Consider the poor *Star Trek* fans. They were given so much, they were sorely deprived ... their imaginations never had to try.[7]

Flawed, permeated by gaps and (extra-)textual absences; Davies, writing as a fan for a fan readership, insistently romanticises *Doctor Who* as a lure to creativity and imagination. Despite his anti-*Trek* jokes, *Star Trek* has been analysed in cultural studies as a spur to the Space Programme in America, acknowledged as a childhood inspiration by NASA workers and astronauts.[8] *Doctor Who* fandom has seemingly had a closer link to professional media production, writing or performance, rather than inspiring careers in science. Indeed, following the 2005 success of *Who*, a 'literaturisation'[9] of *Doctor Who* fandom occurred, which was strongly akin to Nick Hornby's confessional account of his Arsenal fandom.[10] Journalist-fans published memoirs such as *Dalek, I Loved You*[11] and wry non-fiction *Wiffle Lever to Full*,[12] as well as comedy confessionals in the form of Toby Hadoke's one-man stage show *Moths Ate My Doctor Who Scarf*, adapted for BBC Radio 7 broadcast. Even the tenth Doctor, David Tennant, celebrated his childhood *Doctor Who* fandom in a piece for the *Telegraph Magazine*.[13] The cultural productivity of a generation of fans was, it seemed, fully integrated into the UK's creative industries, and into the programme itself. Executive producer Russell T. Davies and producer Phil Collinson were card-carrying fans; the actor playing the tenth Doctor was a fan; writers such as Paul Cornell, Mark Gatiss, Steven Moffat, Gareth Roberts and Rob Shearman were all fans; even *Radio Times* writer Nick Griffiths had grown up as a *Doctor Who* fan.

Such a scenario differs radically from the vision of media fandom ushered in by 1990s cultural studies, for instance in Henry Jenkins' seminal book *Textual Poachers*.[14] Jenkins used French theorist Michel de Certeau's work[15] to argue that:

> Like the poachers of old, fans operate from a position of cultural marginality and social weakness. Like other popular readers, fans lack access to the means of commercial cultural production and have only the most limited resources with which to influence entertainment industry's decisions.[16]

Fandom was thought of as essentially different from – and frequently opposed to – 'official' media production. And it was resistant 'poaching' that provided the key metaphor for this fan/producer difference. Fans were creative but relatively powerless; producers had power over 'official' media texts. Such a view was also carried through into John Tulloch and Henry Jenkins' study of *Star Trek* and *Doctor Who* fans, *Science Fiction Audiences*.[17] However, as Alan McKee has argued, by the time of this book's publication, binaries between *Doctor Who* fandom and professional media production were already eroding:

> by dint of the fact that Tulloch's research was completed several years before its publication in 1995, we are presented with a startling fact: by the time that [Gary] Russell is presented publicly proclaiming his powerlessness [as a fan], he has already been the editor of the official BBC-licensed *Doctor Who Magazine* ... the BBC has published several of his original *Doctor Who* novels; and he is only a year away from writing the official novelisation of the only new episode of *Doctor Who* produced ... in 1996.[18]

McKee goes on to pose these questions:

> at what point did [Gary] Russell [now working for BBC Wales] stop being powerless? When did he stop being a fan and start being a producer? Can he be a producer, in the media itself ... and still be a fan?[19]

In *Fan Cultures*, I explored similar issues, suggesting that 'the supposed "empowerment" of textual poachers who are able to turn "textual gamekeepers" ... occurs quite precisely within the economic and cultural parameters of niche marketing'.[20] My argument then was that fans able to 'go pro' could do so only as a result of, and indeed as part of, target-marketing aimed at their own fan culture. Similarly, Daniel O'Mahony suggests that *Who* fans became official producers due to the programme being off-air as a TV show and subsisting as a niche proposition: 'post-television forms of *Doctor Who* have seen ... fans-turned-gamekeepers with their own varying takes on fan discourse'.[21]

This argument simply no longer holds true, just as Jenkins' 'poachers' model and fan/producer binary has been qualified by the movement of *Who* fans into the TV industry. Now, 'official' producers are fans who combine communal knowledge with professional industry-insider status, making the programme for BBC Wales – and as a flagship BBC show, no less. Poachers have turned gamekeeper at the highest levels of official TV production aimed squarely at the mass market:

> petty producers [move] ... from the realm of production on the request of members of an enthusiasm, to production for the market itself. Here, production, rather than being located within patterns of network sociation [e.g. specifically by fans for fans], begins to be increasingly directed towards an anonymous market, where the consumers of the goods can only be *imagined*.[22]

Fan studies has moved away from fan/producer binaries, beginning to focus instead on fans' 'career paths'.[23] And Henry Jenkins' work has also moved beyond the fan/producer binary of the 'poaching' metaphor, arguing that under conditions of twenty-first century media convergence:

> Corporations imagine [fan] participation as something they can start and stop, channel and reroute, commodify and market. The prohibitionists are trying to shut down unauthorized participation; the collaborationists are trying to win grassroots creators over to their side

> ... Contradictions, confusions, and multiple perspectives should be anticipated at a moment of transition where one media paradigm is dying and another is being born ... Within companies ... there are sudden lurches between prohibitionist and collaborationist responses.[24]

Rather than being viewed simply as 'poachers', fans have become part-time collaborators with official producers seeking to incite and retain dedicated fan audiences, and part-time co-opted word-of-mouth marketers for beloved brands.[25] But these convergence-led shifts beyond the fan as 'poacher' do not quite address the generational experiences of *Doctor Who* fans who have now become official media producers, being called upon to 'keep faith' with established, 'old' fandom,[26] and professionally reach out to new audiences and new fans.

What discernable impact, if any, has official fan-production had on the series? Common-sense notions might suggest that 'if we're going to be honest with ourselves, the very fact that we're paid up *Doctor Who* fans ... puts us among the least appropriate candidates to ... dictate the future of the programme'[27] and that, in general, '[p]utting a fan in charge of producing a TV show is a really bad idea'.[28] But what is feared within such approaches? How might professionalised fandom pose problems for the very show that is loved? I shall turn to these questions in the following section, specifically examining the assumed perils of so-called 'fanwank'. I shall then conclude by considering how professionalised fandom has participated in the creation of a new *Doctor Who* 'brand' unlike anything that has come before in the show's history. And whilst aspects of this branding may seem to return us to a scenario of textual 'poaching', I will argue that BBC Wales' *Doctor Who* amounts to a 'fanbrand', at least in terms of its fetishised consistency. First, though, what is so threatening about this strange, devalued term, 'fanwank'?

## Fanwank and Continuity:
## 'The Gift of Fandom, and the Danger'

'Fanwank' has a specific meaning within *Doctor Who* fandom, being 'a continuity reference thrown into a story and having little relevance to the plot, but there purely as a device to please fans'.[29] This makes it a noun, whereas the term's variant use — frequently in US media fandom — treats it as a verb, with 'fanwanking' being the practice of correcting a continuity error in an official text by inventing some explanatory scenario, typically in fan-written fiction, or 'fanfic'. Each meaning nonetheless retains a shared sense that 'fanwank' and 'fanwanking' are concerned with specifically pleasing a given fan culture.[30] *DWM* reviewer and novelist Craig Hinton sometimes claimed to have invented the term, as used in *Who* fandom,[31] or at least to have 'popularised' it following 'references ... in fanzines from the early 80s'.[32]

It might be assumed that 'fanwank' is valued by fans, but as professional writer Paul Magrs has noted:

> I had never heard of the ... term ... until I started looking at the reviews and discussions of *Doctor Who* books and audios on the Internet ... [It] seemed, more often than not, to be levelled at the material produced for the marketplace by ... 'fan-professionals'. 'Fanwank' sounded naughty and silly but, as I read on, ... I started to gather that it was a phenomenon to be avoided – by both writer and discerning fan.[33]

The term began to circulate more widely within *Doctor Who* fandom in the 1990s and early noughties, when *Who* was no longer an ongoing TV series, existing through original novels (published by Virgin) and then audio adventures (produced by Big Finish). Fanwank was a product of *Doctor Who*'s target-marketed status, since Virgin's New Adventures and Big Finish's audios frequently were created by professionalised fans for fans. Unlike the fans as 'petty producers' of Abercrombie and Longhurst's definition, who are 'returned ... to general capitalist social relations, [being] ... as much at the mercy of structural forces as ... consumers',[34] these fans were producing professional content within 'patterns of network sociation'.[35] They were writing for an established fan culture that shared forms of knowledge and communal experience. As a result, pro fan-writers such as Gary Russell and Jim Mortimore would include detailed continuity references in their work, knowing that fan-consumers would 'get the reference'.

However, 'fanwank' began to take on a powerfully negative meaning for *Who* fandom. Magrs attempts to explain this negativity:

> I don't know why this 'fanwankery' is despised by the fans at large. Perhaps because it's infantile ... It seems to me that Fanwank is the worst thing that the fan-consumers can think to call these latterday *Doctor Who* novels and audios. Because what they mean by that is: 'Just like something I could have written. Something like I'd have written when I was ten. As crappy and as self-indulgent as that. Of course, I'd never

do that now. Oh, no. I'm much more grown-up and discerning than that now...' Such self-hatred.[36]

Fan culture was, in effect, internalising criticisms from without. Prior to the show's triumphant return, fans sought to distance themselves symbolically from pathologisations of fandom as 'sad', infantile, and living in the past. After all, in the wilderness years, *Doctor Who* was definitively an 'old', 'dead' show, popular in the 1970s. At that time, admitting to *Who* fandom seemed to imply that devotees had failed to grow up and move on, instead becoming trapped in regressive, infantile tastes. Fandom had even been represented visually by an anorak in the 1992 BBC2 documentary *Resistance is Useless*. In this cultural context, fans appropriated discursive attacks on their cultural identity, 'poaching' from negative stereotypes and reusing these through the term 'fanwank'. Tat Wood calls it an 'infantile state of mind',[37] and this captures the legacy of fanwank: it worked as a symbolic distancing, projecting infantilism onto other(ed) sections of fandom.

Fans' dislike of 'excessive' continuity was also related to the shared history of *Who* fandom, given that the TV programme's cancellation in 1989 had been explained within fandom precisely as a result of excess continuity referencing. As Chris Howarth and Steve Lyons put it:

> Only online *Doctor Who* fandom could invent a derogatory word for tie-in fiction that's, er, aimed at ... [*Doctor Who* fandom]. The argument goes that excessive references to the Doctor's past put off new viewers in the eighties, so any references to the show's rich history are now taboo.[38]

Fanwank is therefore something aimed at pleasing fans, but it has been used as a label to disavow negative fan stereotypes, as well as critiquing official texts allegedly targeting 'fans' rather than the 'general audience'. The perceived fan-cultural danger of having a fan in charge of the BBC Wales series was, then, that it would lead to a welter of fan-pleasing references rather than to stories with mass appeal. Rather than this scenario occurring, the fan-cultural term 'fanwank' has itself been destabilised by the work of official fan-producers as 'gamekeepers'. Howarth and Lyons bring home the absurdity of 'fanwank' debates:

> It would have been awful, after all, if the legions of non-fans who were surely reading the ... [BBC Eighth Doctor Adventures] and ... [Past Doctor BBC novels] had been confused and put off them – you know, like

they were by mentions of the Time Lords, K9, Eternals, the Nestene Consciousness, Cybermen, Daleks, two hearts, regeneration, mummies ... UNIT, Sarah Jane, International Electromatics ... etc in the new TV series.[39]

Here, 'fanwank' anxieties are shown to be wholly misplaced. Given that the term worked strongly as a discursive othering (other fans are 'infantile'), it is perhaps unsurprising that it may have failed as referential language, that is, supposedly labelling an existent phenomenon. When fans attacked original novels for their excessive continuity, these novels were really only being targeted at card-carrying fans. The point was that 'non-fans' simply *weren't reading them*, and so were hardly likely to be alienated by continuity. And now that millions of 'non-fans' are again watching *Doctor Who* on BBC1, they seem not to have been put off by the types of continuity referencing cited by Howarth and Lyons, all of which hail from episodes of new *Who*.

Fan-producers seem to have integrated 'fanwank' into the new series, but not in a way that reproduces the show's 1980s history, or alienates non-fans. In fact, rather than fans-as-producers simply adding fanwank to new *Who*'s ingredients, their work as media professionals reveals flawed fan-cultural assumptions underpinning the term. As *Tachyon TV*'s John Williams argues:

> The battle of the Daleks and Cybermen [in 'Doomsday' (2.13)] was characterised by some as pure fanwank ... But this fanwank episode was watched by over 8 million ecstatic viewers, only the merest fraction of whom could be described as fanboys. Surely something as niche a concept as fanwank loses all meaning if it's applied to something that appeals to a mainstream channel's popular audience?[40]

BBC Wales' *Doctor Who* effectively deconstructs the concept of 'fanwank'. It does so by critiquing the binary logic that sustained it – that of 'fans' versus the 'general audience', and 'continuity' versus 'new stories'. If academia in the 1990s got caught up in sometimes unhelpful binaries (powerless poachers against powerful producers) then *Doctor Who* fandom spent much of the decade embroiled in similar binary thinking. It became fan lore that 'what fans wanted' was diametrically opposed to 'what general audiences wanted'. As I argued after 'Doomsday' (2.13): 'Here's a mission-statement you'll probably never hear Russell T. Davies admit to in any promotional and publicity material: what he ... wants is to prove that 'fanwank' is the new black.'[41] What needs to be added to this is that if alleged 'fanwank' becomes fashionable then it ceases to be 'fanwank', at least as the term has been deployed within *Who* fandom:

> Once a fan got to make the series in Wales ... [there was] a trend towards fanwank, but it's only to do with things Joe Public might know about, like Daleks, Cybermen, or BBC Wales' own new monsters ... So far, they're reluctant to have too many overt acknowledgements of the 'old' past, unless you count the Macra in 'Gridlock' [3.3]... and the Isop Galaxy references.[42]

However, the new series appears to do all of these things – it references continuity assumed to have some nostalgic currency outside fandom, such as the Autons, the Daleks, Cybermen, the Master, Sontarans, Davros, as well as referencing its own continuity very heavily (consider the predominance of flashbacks in the finales of series three and four). And it references 'old' continuity that long-term fans might be expected to pick up on, for example, mentioning 1965's 'The Romans' in 'The Fires of Pompeii' (4.2), or 1975's 'Genesis of the Daleks' in episodes 4.12–4.13. The new series also self-consciously revisits its predecessors – this time we see glass break as Autons burst out of shop windows, as a textual gap from 'Spearhead from Space' (1970) is supplemented on-screen some 35 years later. For non-fans or new fans, this scene can be enjoyed narratively. For long-term fans, it represents additionally an extra-textual shattering of programme history, as well as being readable via Davies' own confessional fan narrative of imagining, as a child, such a moment in 'Spearhead'.[43]

New *Who* has embraced continuity as a multi-layered and polysemic tool that can be equally meaningful for old fans, new fans and more casual 'followers' of the series.[44] Though the many returning monsters and characters might look like 'fanwank', they consistently operate inclusively:

> most of the central planks of the old series are back at the hearts of new stories, and the whole of Britain got stupidly excited at seeing UNIT ... the Master, [and] Gallifrey ... all in one episode (... 'The Sound of Drums'[3.12]).[45]

Deconstructing 'fanwank' means collapsing this into its binary opposite, popular TV: 'current *Doctor Who* viewers are the fanwank obsessed fans. That's the point. They like fanwank. For fanwank and continuity, read "modern television storytelling".'[46]

Fan-cultural attacks on fanwank thus lose their semiotic coordinates in this altered context. Though the term continues to be used in online fandom, its 1990s meaning and function have been deconstructed decisively by fan-producers working on the BBC Wales' series. It no longer makes sense to accuse 'the Russell T. Davies era' of fanwankery, precisely because professionalised fans have challenged fan discourse on this count rather than simply accepting its binaries.

Fan 'gamekeepers' have, however, extended specific fan-cultural discourses (e.g. the notion of multiple authorship considered previously). And Russell T. Davies has elaborated on his thesis that *Doctor Who* uses textual gaps to incite fans' imaginative play, arguing that he has no final authority over the programme:

> once a script has been made and transmitted, I honestly believe it belongs equally to those who watch it ... I've got no more authority over the text than you! ... [I]f Gary [Russell] thinks [the Cruciform] ... was Gallifreyan, then he's got every right to think so. It's not mine any more! And yet, and yet ... I'm still glad we changed the [Cruciform] entry, 'cos ... the Encyclopedia's status as an official BBC book, sanctioned by the production office, would have given the Gallifrey theory more weight. It would have become that awful thing, a fact. And that's taking it away from you. It's taking away the choice.[47]

Likewise, although Davies could have taken the opportunity to 'retcon' (retroactively fix) continuity by explaining, say, the eighth Doctor's half-human identity, he has self-consciously refrained from doing so. As a fan, Davies may have 'funny little moments' where he wants to explain away the TV movie,[48] but its inconsistency has been left firmly in place thus far. And the dating of UNIT stories, another major fan controversy, is joked about in 'The Sontaran Stratagem'/ 'The Poison Sky' (4.4–4.5, scripted by Helen Raynor), with the Doctor recalling working for UNIT 'back in the 70s. Or was it the 80s?' Both textually and extra-textually, Davies acknowledges the continuity errors of previous production teams, and leaves them in place. As a fan-producer, he deliberately introduces new textual absences:

> The Golden Age, the Cruciform, the fall of Arcadia ... all of 'em. They're yours. Just as I've treasured my own versions of Ancient Silurian Civilisation, and the origin of the Great Intelligence, and whatever-happened-to-the-rest-of-the-Zygons, for years and years and years. I think that's *Doctor Who*'s greatest legacy – an imagination that goes way beyond the screen, and all the way into your head, where it's yours, forever.[49]

Refusing officially to close down fan debates over continuity, Davies has created a massive new textual gap in the form of the Time War.[50] As a result, unofficial publications can fill in these absences, but their in-filling remains purely speculative, with no greater status than fan fiction.[51]

However, Davies' disavowal of textual authority, and his fannish romanticisation of absence and imagination as *Doctor Who*'s key values, appear somewhat disingenuous. Though he represents his fan-producer identity as mirroring that of 'ordinary' fans on some occasions, Davies evidently realises that any 'fact' sanctioned by the production office has a distinct value for fandom. And the BBC Wales series cannot avoid creating new sets of textual 'facts', such as the show's first reference to the Doctor having a brother in 'Smith and Jones' (3.1), followed by refutation of fans' speculation that the Doctor and the Master are brothers ('Last of the Time Lords', 3.13). As such, the information that Davies chooses to provide and endorse does carry symbolic authority, however much he may resist this discursively in order to align himself as a 'collaborationist' with fandom.[52] Indeed, his relationship with socially organised and online fandom has not always been harmonious (see Chapter 7).

The creative input of fan 'gamekeepers' on *Doctor Who* has counter-intuitively deconstructed fanwank and resisted smoothing out prior textual discontinuities, against what might have been expected. But it has nonetheless sought to incite fans' speculation, disavowing production authority – even whilst enacting it – in favour of a romanticised view of *Doctor Who* and 'unfettered' audience imagination. Fan-producers have also incorporated other 'fan discourses' into the official text, such as celebratory affect.[53] The fact that fans love the Doctor has been imported into the text, most obviously via fan-like admirers shown in 'Love & Monsters' (2.10), which had the working title 'I love the Doctor',[54] but also through the affection displayed for the Doctor by his companions:

> This kind of hysterical in-show advertising is a fan's offering ... about selling the Doctor as the best thing going ... But 15 years of having him to ourselves, and then a sudden dazzling splash of the limelight means we get material like this, material that demands we apprehend the Doctor as God's first choice, if not God himself. We [in fandom] love him, therefore his assistants love him.[55]

Davies' recollections of his childhood daydreams about *Doctor Who* also seem to uncannily reiterate the end of 'Rose' (1.1), which represents the eponymous character running, in emotionally heightened slow motion, into the open TARDIS:

> for me, the reason why ... [*Doctor Who*] got into my heart, and, it's that connection thing that you can be part of it ... what I specifically mean is that I used to walk home from School when I was a little tiny kid, and you could walk around a corner and you could imagine the TARDIS would be there, and you would run through that door![56]

Rose Tyler can hardly be interpreted as Russell T. Davies' 'Mary Sue' (a fan fiction character standing in for the author, and representing their desire to enter the text). But the collision of extra-textual and textual discourses is nevertheless striking; Thom Hutchinson and Matt Bielby note that, in a sense, 'Rose is a big fan' of the Doctor.[57] Unlike all previous representations of the character – and hugely divergent from the show's beginnings in 1963 – this Doctor is an outright hero: a textually celebrated, mythicised figure. And this, journalist-fans have alleged, represents both 'the gift of fandom, and the danger',[58] even tending towards 'canonisation' of the character in 'The Doctor's Daughter' (4.6). Here, the Doctor effectively founds a new social order in his own image, taking on an almost quasi-religious role that the classic series had depicted as authoritarian and highly problematic (e.g. in 'The Face of Evil' from 1977). God-like status haunts the ninth and tenth Doctors, arguably as an over-determined result of the show's redesign for a new, non-fan audience (i.e. the Doctor is more conventionally heroic than ever before) as well as the incorporation of fan affect.

Thus far I have argued that fan 'gamekeepers' both oppose and incorporate specific fan discourses, undermining negative meanings of 'fanwank' whilst leaving the continuity contradictions of earlier production teams in place. And though fan gamekeepers disavow textual authority via the romanticisation of fannish 'imagination', they also textually incorporate – and thus authorise – prior fan affects in relation to *Doctor Who*'s 'genius'. But if textual continuity has been left open in favour of fan speculation and debate, textual *consistency* has formed a more transparent target for fan-producers' endeavours, and it is this topic that I will explore next. How have the *Doctor Who* brand and branding practices of corporate power been affected by fans taking charge? Fan creativity might be mirrored discursively and incited by gamekeepers, but bringing fandom and branding together symbolically seems a more difficult task. I will argue that although new *Who* positions spoiler-pursuing fans as 'pre-textual poachers' intent on challenging the timeline of brand-reinforcing PR 'strategy', it also draws on fan critiques of the classic series to shape a highly consistent 'fanbrand'.

## 'Fanbrand' and Consistency:
## From Pre-Textual Poachers to 'Semiotic Slimness'

One of the major industrial shifts accompanying *Doctor Who's* return has been its repositioning as a modern TV franchise. Although the classic series was merchandised heavily across its existence – and continues to function as a largely separate brand – *Doctor Who* has now been firmly re-conceptualised within the contemporary TV industry's 'will-to-brand'.[59] In the twenty-first century, media professionalism in the entertainment sector has been shaped and defined by discourses of branding: '[i]f the function of branding is to pattern [consumers'] activities across time and space, the process of selling entertainment has come to rely, increasingly, on the principle of deepening audience involvement in immersive brand worlds'.[60] The BBC terminology for this brand immersion is '360-degree commissioning', which aims to integrate a single commission's multi-platformed presence.[61] Indeed, *Doctor Who* has been applauded as a key success story within the BBC's pursuit of this multi-platforming ambition.[62]

Along with multi-platforming, merchandising today also acts as 'a kind of brand extension that needs to share and convey the brand values of the programme'.[63] Different types of consumer brand-immersion are possible, and as Catherine Johnson argues, merchandising strategies can be diegetic, pseudo-diegetic and extra-diegetic.[64] The first involves products that belong to the given programme's fictional world, such as replicas of the Doctor's sonic screwdriver. 'Pseudo-diegetic' merchandise stems from a programme's narrative universe, without necessarily appearing in it, such as remote -controlled, scale-model Daleks, or perhaps Dalek-shaped bubble bath. Finally, extra-diegetic merchandise deals with 'the series as a television programme', covering episode guides, posters, books, soundtracks, DVDs and so on.[65] Johnson argues that diegetic and pseudo-diegetic merchandise 'encourage the consumer to act out their involvement with the diegetic world',[66] being better suited to programmes that convey an 'authentic fantasy world' distant from viewers' everyday lives.[67]

BBC Wales' *Doctor Who* is policed carefully in terms of merchandising consistency so as to ensure that brand values are properly reflected:

> a new 'Style Guide' was produced to ensure that all items licensed under the 'New Series' banner had a consistent look and feel. [It included] ... two pages on the new logo and how to use it ... Then there was a pantone colour chart of all the allowable colours for the brand, samples of the 'Deviant Strain' commercial font that was being used on all merchandise ... BBC Worldwide had swung around to dictating in detail exactly what products should look like.[68]

Though the range of *Doctor Who* products covers all three kinds of merchandise identified by Johnson, it has been argued that '[t]oday, the action-figures and the voice-changer masks are like badges of honour, while the books ... well, they *sell*, but they seem somehow irrelevant'.[69] Extra-diegetic merchandise, especially of the type linked to cultural values of literacy, has allegedly been marginalised in favour of diegetic and pseudo-diegetic merchandise enabling immersive child's play. As such, educative or thought-provoking merchandise potentially has been displaced by purely brand-reinforcing product.[70] And though older fans may well consume products such as remote-controlled Daleks, it is notable that *Doctor Who*'s diegetically immersive merchandise is usually and ostensibly targeted at children. Diegetic merchandise aimed specifically at the fan or 'collector' market tends to consist of more expensive 'replica' content, such as Millennium FX's range.

Each of these market sectors has been served by new waves of product, series-on-series. For example, *DWM* reviewer Dave Owen remarks of 'The Stolen Earth'/'Journey's End' (4.12–4.13) that director 'Graeme Harper [offers] ... screen-filling eyestalk close-ups of the new red Dalek supreme (it's like the launch of a new iPod!)'.[71] The simile is telling; each fresh Dalek story in new *Who* has brought redesigned, minor variations on the iconic '2005 standard' model ('Dalek', 1.6); flame-thrower types and the Dalek Emperor ('The Parting of the Ways', 1.13); blacked-out Sec and the Cult of Skaro ('Army of Ghosts'/ 'Doomsday', 2.12–2.13); Hybrid Sec ('Daleks in Manhattan'/'Evolution of the Daleks', 3.4–3.5); and the Supreme Dalek model, Davros, opened-up Caan, and Crucible variants ('The Stolen Earth'/'Journey's End', 4.12–4.13). The same tendency toward design variation is also true of the Cybermen, who returned with an additional Cyberleader model in 'Doomsday' (2.13) and then Cybershades, the new-look Cyberleader and Cyberking all in 'The Next Doctor' (4.14). Piers Britton and Simon Barker argue that the original series redesigned its Cybermen due to 'changes in the sci-fi aesthetic', shifting from extreme stylisation in the 1960s to a 'more highly textured' 1980s design aesthetic influenced by *Star Wars*.[72] The constant redesigns in new *Who* are, however, not at all about changes in industry and cultural context. Precisely like 'a new iPod' they are, instead, updates to a brand, always visually recognisable as revisions, and consistently feeding into 'this year's must-have' diegetic or pseudo-diegetic merchandise.

The contemporary brand of *Doctor Who* means agreeing 'a coordinated approach – saying the same simple things (such as a tag line about "Adventures in Time and Space" for example), [and] referring to our style guide', notes the series' first Brand Manager, Ian Grutchfield.[73] As such, brand management also involves 'a lot of "enforcement"'[74] to keep product licences aligned with brand values, identified as:

> *Entertainment:* Please remember, however many awards the creatives behind *Doctor Who* win (and richly deserve) that this is only TV. I believe most people pay their licence fee for a fix of news and to make them smile. *Friendship:* Yes I would like to time travel with that crew! *Monsters:* The hardest things to create, so imaginative. *An eternal optimism.*[75]

You can't imagine Russell T. Davies, or other fan 'gamekeepers', stating that *Who* 'is only TV' as part of an on-message interview. Evidently, brand management follows a different set of corporate discourses from those of *Doctor Who*'s 'creatives', implying, as Henry Jenkins has argued, that corporations can oscillate between contradictory approaches to fan collaboration and prohibition.[76]

Indeed, whilst Davies may romanticise fan creativity, BBC Worldwide (the BBC's commercial/licensing arm) became news in its own right when it contacted one fan over third-party eBay sales of her knitted Adipose figures:

> A BBC Worldwide spokesman said ... that it had to act in the interest of licence-fee payers by protecting the *Doctor Who* trademark. 'If you don't protect your trademark, it's taken away from you. And *Doctor Who* is massive for the BBC. It's up to us to earn money from it so we can re-invest it in the BBC ... It's not that we don't admire creativity from fans – most of the time, we take the view that if it's small-scale

and not for profit, then we turn a blind eye ... This lady ... wanted to share with friends, family and fans ... But there were some unscrupulous people taking these patterns and using them on eBay to make profit for themselves. Unfortunately, we had to get to the source of the patterns.'[77]

Such a scenario returns us squarely to brand 'policing' and to the assumed protection of intellectual property rights against fans' poaching, which has been widely documented in fan studies.[78] Speaking on BBC News, Wayne Garvie, director of content for BBC Worldwide, further defended Worldwide's actions by arguing that it had a duty to 'protect the brand' and make sure that 'everything that is associated with *Doctor Who* is of the highest quality'.[79] Garvie then rather awkwardly stated that 'we love the creativity of *Doctor Who* fans, and we want to work with them ... we would like to talk to [this fan] ... about potentially licensing her knitting patterns'.[80] The BBC evidently is willing to enforce its brand ownership against unofficial fan-related activity that it perceives as profit-making, rendering its corporate practices indistinguishable from those of commercial entities. Here, it defined *Doctor Who* in legal terms, as a trademark, which it alleged was being infringed by fan and eBay activity.

This corporate 'prohibitionist' stance seeks to restrict fan productivity or 'poaching'. Though the fan concerned, known online as Mazzmatazz, had adapted and transformed the BBC's Adipose design, she was nevertheless treated as somebody who could only produce online patterns if she had a commercial licence. Garvie's notion that the BBC wished to discuss such a licence seemed unlikely – the 'ordinary fan' concerned was an individual rather than a company able to afford a BBC licence, or, indeed, be considered suitable to win such a licence. Negative publicity generated for the BBC (by the BBC) suggests that their prohibitionist strategy was at the very least problematic here, tending to reinforce a 'David versus Goliath' journalistic narrative of corporate power victimising one individual fan.

How, then, can such a situation involve what I am terming a 'fanbrand'? Quite to the contrary, *Doctor Who* seems mired in a classic struggle between TV art and TV commerce, between creatives and brand managers, between fan discourses of romanticised imagination and legal discourses of trademarking. Even where certain fans become 'gamekeepers' it appears that less privileged fans outside the TV industry continue to be addressed as problem 'poachers'. And furthermore, fans are left in the position of disempowered 'poachers' not only when it comes to trademark protection, as I will now consider briefly with reference to the phenomenon of 'set reports'.

Since new *Who* makes extensive use of location filming, fans based in or around Cardiff are able to witness the shooting of new material, sometimes many months before its eventual broadcast. Personally, I have been fortunate enough to watch Autons marauding in Cardiff's city centre, Daleks being filmed on the streets of Riverside, and sequences from the likes of 'Boom Town' (1.11), 'Rise of the Cybermen' (2.5) and 'The Sound of Drums' (3.12). And the repeated use of Howell's department store ('Rose', 1.1; 'The Christmas Invasion', 2.X; 'The Runaway Bride', 3.X) has also afforded many fans the opportunity to watch *Doctor Who* filming at close quarters.[81] This situation means that online fandom is able to share set reports and filming photos, piecing together and speculating over forthcoming storylines. In pursuit of narrative 'spoilers', sections of fandom are thus able to gain limited access to *Doctor Who*'s future episodes by tracking, witnessing and documenting public filming.[82]

At first glance, this doesn't much seem to resemble the 'poaching' described by Henry Jenkins. As Karen Hellekson has suggested in her analysis 'Poaching *Doctor Who*', fan poachers 'rewrite the [official] texts to their own liking', with the Mini-UNIT Minstrels (MUM) making their own fan videos that combine behind-the-scenes personnel with narrative incidents from the series.[83] Hellekson argues that: 'In MUM's world, [controller of BBC1] Michael Grade and producer John Nathan-Turner get what they deserve for "sabotaging" *Doctor Who*'.[84] 'Poaching' has usually meant the creation of fan material such as reworked storylines in fanfic,[85] or, indeed, the likes of Mazzmatazz's knitting patterns. Setting the 'poaching' metaphor to one side, Henry Jenkins describes spoiler-gathering instead as 'collective intelligence' at work, with online fan communities pooling their knowledge.[86]

However, *Doctor Who*'s public filming puts spoiler-gathering fans in opposition to official PR strategy. The production team (and PR specialists) seeks generally to control the release of narrative information as part of their media professionalism, by granting 'exclusives' to *Doctor Who Magazine* or the *Radio Times*, for example. Information is purposefully put into the public domain so that it is best timed to promote upcoming episodes – often emerging only a week or two in advance of broadcast.[87] For example, whilst series one was filming in

2004, the BBC did not make official photos available despite the online circulation of fan photos and paparazzi images in the press:

> the BBC told us [commercial fan magazine *Starburst*] that they 'do not want people getting bored of *Doctor Who* before next year', a comment which refers to the amount of unauthorised images already available to view from fan and Press sources ... When we then asked the BBC why they had not released even a single authorised image ... from the new series – a seemingly obvious notion which could probably do much to help stem the tide of unofficial images – *Starburst* was told that this was not the 'strategy' the BBC is employing.[88]

By powerful contrast, spoiler-seeking fans do not want to wait for narrative information or official press releases. They desire foreknowledge of *Doctor Who* as soon as possible, trading rumours along with 'set reports' and photos. Official producers have a vested interest in prohibiting the spread of these pre-transmission spoilers, especially because '[i]ncreasingly, spoiled information is finding its way into ... mainstream news outlets'.[89]

Rather than allow unofficial fan photos to make their way into the mass media, and speak 'for the brand', press releases have sometimes been timed to trump and overwrite fan-gathered spoilers, taking informational control back into the hands of producers and PR strategists. Billie Piper's return to series four, for instance, was documented by fans who witnessed filming on the streets of Cardiff on 26 November 2007. Posting blurred digital images of Piper online, the fan community scored a minor, tactical victory over the producers' PR control. However, an official press release had been timed for 27 November, meaning that rather than unofficial fan images being picked up in a news vacuum, producers were instead able to maintain brand 'quality' through the release of official information.[90]

Nevertheless, PR control over the 'public discourse'[91] surrounding *Who* is not held inevitably by *Doctor Who*'s production team, nor indeed by Taylor Herring, the specialist media PR firm tasked with handling *Doctor Who* from 2006.[92] To give one example: unlike Billie Piper's return, filming for 'The Stolen Earth' (4.12) was not followed by a press release; producers presumably didn't want to publicise how series four would be ending just a few weeks before it was due to be launched. And as a result of this lack of official information, fan photos were picked up by the *Sun* on 15 March 2008.[93] In this instance, fandom's pursuit of narrative information arguably damaged the BBC's preferred PR strategy.

On rare occasions, *Doctor Who* is filmed in public spaces without any spoilers making their way online. Russell T. Davies strikes an almost victorious note when he discusses this outcome during filming for 'Voyage of the Damned' (4.X):

> At the Tone Meeting, we had endless discussions about how to keep the cameras away. We'd seal off the area. Issue security wristbands ... Draft the police in. Put up fences to stop footage being ruined by camera flashes ... And no-one turns up! Not a soul. Not even a fan! ... So we film, in secret, in public, for just about the first time ever.[94]

This info-war between fans and producers — the skirmishing of fan set reports and professional press releases — represents an arena of conflict distinct from that of the broadcast text itself. Fans pursuing spoilers are not struggling against official fan-producers' control over textual content per se. Unlike 'poachers' of the early 1990s, they are instead contesting producers' control over pre-transmission information. These fans are 'pre-textual poachers'. Their struggles with fan-producers necessarily pre-date rather than follow the text's transmission.[95] From a position of relative weakness, since their access to spoiler information is dependent typically on public filming or unnamed industry contacts, fans seek to challenge more powerful strategies of brand publicity, finding chinks in the PR armour of *Doctor Who* where possible.

Publicity and marketing have become vital components of the programme's identity, as witnessed by the choice of title for 'The Next Doctor' (4.14), and successful attempts to preserve the secret of David Morrissey's identity in the Christmas 2008 episode. But the apotheosis of new *Who*'s PR info-war undoubtedly occurred on 3 January 2009, when a behind-the-scenes show, *Doctor Who Confidential*, revealed on-air on BBC1 the actor cast as the 11th Doctor. The subject of intense fan speculation and spoiler-chasing, this information was kept under wraps by the Beeb until only a day or so before broadcast. A media event treated as news by the BBC, and thus heavily cross-promoted, the episode of *Confidential* scored higher ratings than ITV's FA Cup football coverage and its launch of a new telefantasy series, *Demons*. For arguably the first time in *Doctor Who*'s history, the controlled release of production information had become (almost) equal in stature to the fiction itself.

In terms of trademark policing and public relations strategy, new *Who* might appear to resemble textbook industry practice. Also seemingly textbook, its branding strategies bear little relationship to the kind of merchandise and spin-offs linked to the classic series. These were frequently 'riddled with contradictions and surreal interpretations of the show's protagonist',[96] such as the Doctor wearing a Batman-style utility belt, displaying vengeful bloodlust against his enemies, or being depicted as a human inventor 'who had built a transdimensional time ship in his back yard'.[97] Scholar-fan Neil Perryman argues that the first emergence of a 'cohesive fictional world' in *Doctor Who*'s history, running across spin-off books, comics and audios, was not at all a matter of corporate branding but was, instead, due to fan collaboration within a community:

> The authors/fans [producing professional niche products] were already connected by a loose and informal grassroots network that would eventually be reinforced by the growing popularity (and usability) of the Internet, and they communicated with each other via email, online forums, and real-life locales, like the Fitzroy Tavern in London, where they would discuss story arcs and ensure that continuity and consistency existed throughout the [Virgin New Adventures] range. In short, they began to create a cohesive fictional world, something the producers of the television show had almost always failed to achieve.[98]

Perryman argues convincingly that before *Doctor Who*'s return in 2005, 'fans were already used to regarding [the show] as a transmedia franchise that could be linked together to form a coherent and satisfying whole'.[99] It is hence difficult to interpret *Who*'s newfound brand consistency simply as an imposition of the current TV industry's 'will to brand'. In part, its fetishisation of consistency can also be read as a result of fandom's movement into official production.

One of the perils of the classic series was the unevenness of its stories. For example, the much celebrated 'City of Death' (1979)[100] is followed by 'Creature from the Pit' (1979); 'Earthshock' (1982) by 'Time Flight' (1982); 'Timelash' (1985) by 'Revelation of the Daleks' (1985); and 'Silver Nemesis' (1988) by 'The Greatest Show in the Galaxy' (1988–9): it is not difficult to find hardy fan favourites immediately adjacent to consensually devalued episodes. To give another example, in the 1998 *DWM* vote covering all classic series' stories the title voted number three, 'Caves of Androzani' (1984), nestles in broadcast chronology between mid-table number 78, 'Planet of Fire' (1984), and the least-loved *Doctor Who* story of the survey, 'Twin Dilemma' (1984).[101] The classic series is marked frequently by startling variations in textual consistency and tone. New *Who*, run by fans, sets out to avoid this fate. The BBC Wales production team may have left diegetic continuity wrangles alone, but they were evidently keen to evade problems of episodic consistency. Russell T. Davies, as a fan, would have been keenly aware of the problems created by, say, just one risky visual effects decision in an otherwise startling story (as with, for example, the Skarasen in 'Terror of the Zygons', 1975).

In an implicit critique of the classic series – particularly its unevenness across and within stories – Davies thus instigated a production practice of 'tone meetings', bringing all key production staff together for a discussion of every story's intended identity. Seeking to even out tonal variation within stories, tone meetings ensured that all the different production departments were tasked with achieving similar meanings and textual effects. Asked to focus on a single, guiding word, the intent was that distinct areas of design and direction would then cohere stylistically, avoiding conflicts of interpretation between members of the production team.[102]

Some tone words make clear the generic 'feel' called for in an episode – for example, 'disaster movie' for 'Voyage of the Damned' (4.X).[103] Others draw on established, successful TV series to indicate a rule-of-thumb for production decisions, such as *'Cold Feet'* for 'Partners in Crime' (4.1)[104] and *'Rome'* as guidance on 'The Fires of Pompeii' (4.2).[105] Tone words have also been warnings rather than associative reminders, as with 'beware' for 'The Unicorn and the Wasp' (4.7),[106] cautioning staff not to exaggerate the episode's Agatha Christie pastiche too greatly. And in some cases, tone words cite the work of specific director-auteurs, such as 'Ridley Scott' for 'Planet of the Ood' (4.3).[107] Whether proper names, TV series, or generic cues like 'Haunted House' for 'Blink' (3.10), tone words and meetings seek to pre-emptively police the creative decisions made across each production. Though it may seem odd for a multi-generic show, marked by moments of comedy, drama, horror and romance, to be guided semiotically and delimited, this activity is as much one of fan critique (of the classic series) as it is a matter of conserving 'brand values' per se. Davies has justified tone meetings as being about protecting each script's integrity:

> Above all, tone comes from script ... You get 57 dozen people working on a drama, and they all wander off ... they're creative people, they're employed to use their imaginations, but everyone creates in a slightly different way ... The director, the producer, the design teams etc, should be interpreting the show in the *same* way.[108]

However, he also self-critiques this position, going on to suggest:

a lot of [what was just said] was crap – the tone stuff. It was based on the assumption that the script is good, and then gets ballsed up by various levels of creativity. It was written too much from the writer's point of view. Truth is, tone goes astray not because of interference, but because, simply, most scripts don't work. That doesn't mean it's anyone's fault.[109]

Despite this disavowal, the production processes overseen by Davies (such as tone meetings) indicate that key production areas and teams should, indeed, 'be interpreting the show in the same way', regardless of whether or not this is writer-centric. Shared production interpretation didn't always happen on the classic series, and massive tonal variations present in certain stories have been responsible for marking these out as 'least loved' within fandom, as with, for example, intratextual variations in acting style (Paul Darrow's turn in the disliked 'Timelash' from 1985), or difficulties in creature design (1982's 'Time Flight' and 1984's 'Twin Dilemma'). Such inconsistencies were captured by what became the most infamous theoretical statement in *Doctor Who*'s history, cited in the 1987 story 'Dragonfire': 'Tell me ... what do you think about the assertion that the semiotic thickness of a performed text varies according to the redundancy of auxiliary performance codes?'[110] This was paraphrased from Tulloch and Alvarado's Doctor Who: *The Unfolding Text*,[111] when *Who*'s then script editor Andrew Cartmel was asked for some 'technical-sounding gibberish'.[112] By virtue of its textual inclusion, the quote has become emblematic of *Doctor Who* scholarship.[113]

Drawing on the work of drama and theatre theorist Keir Elam,[114] Tulloch and Alvarado argued that:

What Elam calls the semiotic 'thickness' (multiple codes) of a performed text varies according to the 'redundancy' (high predictability) of 'auxiliary' performance codes. Thus, for instance, if the sets, music and so on were simply to reinforce the actors' performance without adding to it or inflecting it in the direction of new associations, but simply overlaid the acted 'pace' and 'drama' with their own, they would be relatively redundant.[115]

Tulloch and Alvarado are tackling the subject of how *Doctor Who*'s multiple codes (set design, costume design, music) work together, or against each other, to create meaning. Redundant codes don't add new meanings to the text, but simply underscore meanings communicated elsewhere, and hence don't add to the semiotic thickness of the programme. By contrast, where 'auxiliary' codes add new meanings to major codes – such as acting styles and performances – then the text is said to have been 'thickened': 'in the Williams/Adams story, "The City of Death" [1979], the use of music and sets ... was more entropic, drawing on motifs which some audience members recognised as "very forties" ... therefore potentially relocating the "stolen art" theme in terms of, say, *The Maltese Falcon*'.[116] As Lance Parkin has noted of the 'semiotic thickness of the text':

> [H]ow do you measure it? There's no SI unit of semiotic thickness ... After all, roughly the same number of people worked on all the *Doctor Who* stories of a given era – they all had a writer, actors, directors, costume people and so on ... So you'd think there would have to be a roughly consistent 'thickness'.[117]

Though fully quantified scores for semiotic thickness may indeed be impossible, the term still has some comparative merit, because it indicates that new *Who*, with its tone words and meetings, aims to reduce semiotic thickness. Rather than 'entropic' production decisions leading to clashes between different sign systems (or varied production choices leading to wild fluctuations in the tonal impact of special effects, practical design and acting styles), new *Who* aims to coordinate its multiple codes. Increased textual consistency means avoiding the embarrassments and disappointments familiar to *Doctor Who*'s established fan culture, though it also militates against the 'amateur aesthetic' and unruliness of stories such as 'City of Death' so loved by fans.

Variations in acting style within stories have been fairly uncommon in new *Who*. Roger Lloyd Pack's heightened performance in 'Rise of the Cybermen'/'The Age of Steel' (2.5–2.6) seems to fall outside the sphere of naturalism displayed by other performers, offering a more directly melodramatic coding, but this is a rare instance of increased semiotic thickness. In terms of 'auxiliary codes', the music in new *Who*, though playfully drawing on a range of intertextual references (see Chapter 6), also tends to work consistently as a reinforcement of the show's codes of 'action-adventure' and emotional impact, again maintaining and reinforcing tone rather than 'thickening' texts. And design work has consistently used 'short-hand' science fiction/a sub-*Blade Runner* aesthetic to reinforce brand familiarity rather than constructing widely varied alien environments. Perhaps the comparatively 'thickest' texts of new *Who* were those produced earliest in its run, especially 'Aliens of

London'/'World War Three' (1.4–1.5). Noel Clarke's performance offers a broader, more comedic take on Mickey Smith here, settling into a consistent naturalism only subsequently, and the representation of the Slitheen is also noticeably uneven in special effects terms (mismatching practical costumes and computer generated imagery, CGI). Arguably, semiotic thickness has, in general, reduced across the run of the series. I would propose 'Voyage of the Damned' (4.X) as the slimmest, most semiotically integrated text of those transmitted between 2005 and 2008, with its 'disaster movie' tone word thoroughly permeating the screenplay structure, use of effects, codes of acting and directorial style.

The 'fanbrand' of BBC Wales' *Who* is thus not just a matter of fan culture's collaborative emphasis on a 'cohesive fictional world' being brought into the multi-platformed sphere of official production. More than this, *Doctor Who*'s 'fanbrand' is also a fannish critique of classic *Who*'s unevenness, leading to the 'semiotic slimness' of newer texts. Characteristically it aims to iron out the old series' production inconsistencies rather than correct its diegetic continuity errors.

In Part I of this book I have argued that fandom's role within production has resulted in the extension of fan discourses such as multiple authorship and textual consistency. Fan 'gamekeepers' have also rejected 'fanwank' arguments from the 1990s, which were premised partly on assumed difference between fans and non-fans, and which had worked to infantilise other(ed) sections of fandom. By moving from the position of marginalised 'poachers' to industrially powerful official producers, it would appear that *Doctor Who* fandom has, generationally, broken down the fan/producer binary. Despite this, I have suggested that online fans seeking spoiler information have become 'pre-textual poachers'. Rather than reading the broadcast text of new *Who* against producers' interests, these fans operate against producers' desire to control pre-transmission, or pre-textual, release of information.

Though *Doctor Who*'s 'fanbrand' may share fan-cultural values of textual consistency, corporate investment in brand protection and promotion has nevertheless sought to prohibit fan audiences' creative use of *Doctor Who* design, along with access to spoilers. Sections of fandom and fan-producers have followed profoundly opposed attitudes to pre-textual information, engaging in constant skirmishes within an ongoing info-war. Theories of fan 'poaching' therefore remain of some value to thinking through specific power relationships between professionalised fans and the wider fan culture. In a sense,

fan-producers such as Russell T. Davies and Phil Collinson oscillate between fan discourses and media professional production discourses.
As Michel Foucault reminds us:

> Thus conceived, discourse is not the majestically unfolding manifesta-
> tion of a thinking, knowing, speaking subject, but on the contrary, a
> totality, in which the dispersion of the subject and his discontinuity
> with himself may be determined. It is a space of exteriority in which a
> network of distinct sites is deployed.[118]

Following Foucault, we cannot accuse fan-producers of being
somehow self-contradictory, or displaying hypocrisy. Exhibiting self-
discontinuity, dispersions of the subject represent shifts between different discourses; in specific contexts fan-producers draw strongly on
fan discourse (such as when writing for *Doctor Who Magazine*), and
at other moments they draw centrally on production discourse (for
example, when berating a blanket vision of online fandom). Davies
and Cook illustrate this tension:

> Helen Raynor went on Outpost Gallifrey last month and read the re-
> views of her two Dalek episodes. She said that she was, literally, shak-
> ing afterwards. Like she'd been physically assaulted ... That bastard
> internet voice gets into writers' heads and destabilises them massively
> ... that endlessly critical voice. It's completely, *completely* destructive. I
> cannot see one iota of it that's helpful.[119]

Here, Davies writes purely as a media professional, with any sense of fan
discourse being wholly purged from his totalising attack on a 'bastard
internet voice'. These moments return us squarely to a scenario of producers versus fans, but they are not the whole story of new *Who* – they
represent just one set of discourses mobilised amongst others, making
it impossible to isolate a singular set of power relationships between
fans and producers. Rather, *different discourses appear to inhabit and
constitute differential power structures: fandom is sometimes shared by
official producers, sometimes targeted, and sometimes opposed.*
    In Part II, I turn my attention to the genre identities, and the precise
format, of new *Who*. The next chapter examines how time travel has
been used distinctively in the new series, before Chapter 4 then moves
on to consider, and theorise, the importance of monsters to this incarnation of *Doctor Who*. Though it might be assumed that time travel is
a singularly science-fictional, fantastical trope, I will argue that it has
been used multi-generically in BBC Wales' *Doctor Who*. Perhaps more

so than ever before in its cultural career, this *Doctor Who* has been all about time.

## NOTES

1    Clayton Hickman in Andy Bodle (2004) 'Who dares, wins', *Guardian: G2*, 23 March, p.4.
2    Quoted in Nick Setchfield and Steve O'Brien (2006) 'When Russell met Verity', *SFX* 150, Future Network, Bath, p.54.
3    Gary Gillatt (1999) 'We're gonna be bigger than *Star Wars*!'', *Doctor Who Magazine* 279, Marvel Comics, London, pp.8–12.
4    Indeed, this prescient feature was revisited in Gary Gillatt (2008) 'The sheer brilliance of *Doctor Who*', *Doctor Who Magazine* 400, Panini Comics, Tunbridge Wells, pp.16–26.
5    Russell T. Davies (2003) 'Fury from the deep: classical gas', in *The Complete Second Doctor: Doctor Who Magazine* special edn 4, Panini Comics, Tunbridge Wells, p.48.
6    Russell T. Davies (2004) '100,000 BC: how do you do it?', in *The Complete First Doctor: Doctor Who Magazine* special edn 7, Panini Comics, Tunbridge Wells, p.22; see also Russell T. Davies (2004) 'The stones of blood: super nature', in *The Complete Fourth Doctor, Volume Two: Doctor Who Magazine* special edn 9, Panini Comics, Tunbridge Wells, p.21.
7    Davies: 'Fury from the deep', p.48.
8    See, for example, Constance Penley (1997) *Nasa/Trek*, Verso, London, p.18, and John Tulloch and Henry Jenkins (1995) *Science Fiction Audiences: Watching Doctor Who and Star Trek*, Routledge, London and New York, p.213.
9    Steve Redhead (1997) *Post-Fandom and the Millennial Blues*, Routledge, London and New York, p.88.
10   Nick Hornby (1992) *Fever Pitch: A Fan's Life*, Gollancz, London.
11   Nick Griffiths (2007) *Dalek I Loved You: A Memoir*, Orion Publishing, London.
12   Bob Fischer (2008) *Wiffle Lever to Full: Daleks, Death Stars and Dreamy-Eyed Nostalgia at the Strangest Sci-Fi Conventions*, Hodder and Stoughton, London.
13   David Tennant (2006) 'My Time Lord is now', *Telegraph Magazine*, 8 April, pp.36–9.
14   Henry Jenkins (1992) *Textual Poachers*, Routledge, New York and London.
15   See Michel de Certeau (1988) *The Practice of Everyday Life*, University of California Press, Berkeley and London.
16   Jenkins: *Textual Poachers*, p.26.
17   Tulloch and Jenkins: *Science Fiction Audiences*.
18   Alan McKee (2004) 'How to tell the difference between production and consumption: a case study in *Doctor Who* fandom', in Sara Gwenllian Jones and Roberta E. Pearson (eds) *Cult Television*, University of Minnesota Press, Minneapolis and London, pp.171–2.
19   McKee: 'How to tell the difference', p.172.
20   Matt Hills (2002) *Fan Cultures*, Routledge, London and New York, p.40.

21    Daniel O'Mahony (2007) '"Now how is that wolf able to impersonate a grandmother?" History, pseudo-history and genre in *Doctor Who*', in David Butler (ed.) *Time and Relative Dissertations in Space: Critical Perspectives on* Doctor Who, Manchester University Press, Manchester and New York, p.65.

22    Nicholas Abercrombie and Brian Longhurst (1998) *Audiences*, Sage, London, p.150.

23    See ibid., p.140; Gary Crawford (2004) *Consuming Sport: Fans, Sport and Culture*, Routledge, London and New York, pp.42–9; Brian Longhurst (2007) *Cultural Change and Ordinary Life*, Open University Press, Maidenhead and New York.

24    Henry Jenkins (2006) *Convergence Culture*, New York University Press, New York and London, pp.169–70.

25    See, for example, Suzanne Scott (2008) 'Authorized resistance: is fan production frakked?', in Tiffany Potter and C.W. Marshall (eds) *Cylons in America: Critical Studies in* Battlestar Galactica, Continuum, New York and London, pp.210–23, on *Battlestar Galactica's* fanbase; Cochran, Tanya R. (2008) 'The browncoats are coming! *Firefly, Serenity* and fan activism', in Rhonda V. Wilcox and Tanya R. Cochran (eds) *Investigating* Firefly *and* Serenity: *Science Fiction on the Frontier*, I.B.Tauris, London and New York, pp.239–49, on co-opted fans of *Firefly* (Fox, 2002); and Derek Johnson (2007) 'Inviting audiences in: the spatial reorganization of production and consumption in "TVIII"', *New Review of Film and Television Studies* v/1, pp.61–80.

26    James Chapman (2006) *Inside the TARDIS: The Worlds of* Doctor Who, I.B.Tauris, London and New York, p.187.

27    Vic Camford (1999) 'If you tolerate this, your children will be next', in *Doctor Who Magazine* 284, Marvel Comics, London, p.9.

28    Alan McKee cited in Jesse Walker (2004) '*Doctor Who* and the fandom of fear: what happens when fans take over a franchise?', in *Reason Online*, available at *http://www.reason.com/news/show/33494.html*, accessed 21 September 2008.

29    Craig Hinton cited in Keith Topping (2006) 'Craig Hinton', available online at *http://keithtopping.blogspot.com/2006/12/craig-hinton.html*, 6 December, accessed 3 September 2008.

30    Nevertheless see also the online resource 'Fandom wank', described by Karen Hellekson as 'a blog-based online community that exists solely to describe – and mock – fandom blowups', thus providing evidence of fan debates and disagreements (see Karen Hellekson (2008) 'Fandom wank and history', available online at *http://khellekson.wordpress.com/2008/03/30/fandom-wank-and-history/*, accessed 2 October 2008).

31    Craig Hinton (2003) 'Live chat with Craig Hinton, *Doctor Who* Online, 14 May, 8pm–9pm', available online at *www.drwho-online.co.uk/chat-craighinton.doc*, accessed 26 August 2008.

32    Craig Hinton (2002) 'Dripping with camp menace', available online at *http://www.shockeye.org.uk/Freezer/Griller/Hinton/Hinton.html*, accessed 9 July 2007.

33    Paul Magrs (2007) 'Afterword: my adventures', in David Butler (ed.) *Time and Relative Dissertations in Space*, Manchester University Press, Manchester and New York, p.306.

34  Abercrombie and Longhurst: *Audiences*, p.140.

35  Ibid., p.150.

36  Magrs: 'Afterword', pp.307–8.

37  Tat Wood (2007) *About Time 6: The Unauthorized Guide to* Doctor Who *1985–1989*, Mad Norwegian Press, Des Moines, IA, p.13.

38  Chris Howarth and Steve Lyons (2006) Doctor Who: *The Completely Unofficial Encyclopedia*, Mad Norwegian Press, Des Moines, IA, p.49.

39  Ibid.

40  John Williams (2008) 'Whose fanwank is it anyway?', available online at *http://www.behindthesofa.org.uk/2008/07/whose-fanwank-i.html*, 4 July, accessed 3 September 2008; see also Thom Hutchinson and Matt Bielby (2008) 'Love & Monsters', *Death Ray* 15, Blackfish, Bath, p.58.

41  Matt Hills (2006) 'Triumph of a Time Lord (Part One): an interview with Matt Hills', available online at 'Confessions of an aca-fan: the official we-blog of Henry Jenkins', *http://www.henryjenkins.org/2006/09/triumph_of_a_time_lord_part_on.html*, 28 September, accessed 3 September 2008.

42  Wood: *About Time 6*, p.217.

43  Russell T. Davies (2002) 'Spearhead from space: back home', in *The Complete Third Doctor: Doctor Who Magazine* special edn 2, Panini Comics, Tunbridge Wells, p.15.

44  Tulloch and Jenkins: *Science Fiction Audiences*, p.23.

45  Wood: *About Time 6*, p.17.

46  Williams: 'Whose fanwank is it anyway?'

47  Russell T. Davies (2007) 'Production notes: between the lines', *Doctor Who Magazine* 388, Panini Comics, Tunbridge Wells, p.66.

48  Russell T. Davies in Ian Berriman (2007) 'Writing *Who*', *SFX Collection*, special edn 28, Future Network, Bath, pp.12.

49  Davies, 'Production notes', p.66.

50  At the time of writing it seems likely that the Time War will feature prominently in David Tennant's final episodes as the tenth Doctor. However, Davies is unlikely to give away all the details and secrets of the War. Adding information to this back-story simply leaves scope for further fan speculation.

51  See, for example, John Peel (2007) *I Am the Doctor: The Unauthorised Diaries of a Time Lord*, Zone, London, p.99.

52  Jenkins: *Convergence Culture*, p.169.

53  See Alan McKee (2001) 'Which is the best *Doctor Who* story? A case study in value judgements outside the academy', *Intensities: The Journal of Cult Media*, available at *http://intensities.org/Essays/McKee.pdf*, accessed 26 August 2008.

54  Russell T. Davies (2006) 'Second Sight', *The* Doctor Who *Companion: Series Two*, Panini Comics, Tunbridge Wells, p.9.

55  Hutchinson and Bielby: 'Love & Monsters', pp.58–9; for a related argument, see also Gillatt: 'The sheer brilliance', p.23.

56  Russell T. Davies in *Doctor Who Confidential* (2008) 'Do you remember the first time?', David Tennant (dir.), broadcast 9 June 2007, BBC3.

57  Hutchinson and Bielby: 'Love & Monsters', p.59.

58  Ibid.

59   Paul Grainge (2008) *Brand Hollywood: Selling Entertainment in a Global Media Age*, Routledge, London and New York, p.43.

60   Ibid., p.175.

61   BBC (2006) 'BBC reorganises for an on-demand creative future', press release, 19 July, available online at *http://www.bbc.co.uk/pressoffice/pressreleases/stories/2006/07_july/19/future.shtml*, accessed 3 September 2008.

62   See Martin Belam (2007) '"The Tardis and multiplatform" – Julie Gardner talks about *Doctor Who*'s multi-media incarnations', 28 September, available online at *http://www.currybet.net/cbet_blog/2007/09/the_tardis _and_multiplatform.php*, accessed 3 September 2008. This means attempting to strategically 'hold' fans and audiences, channelling them through a range of different platforms as well as spin-off texts; see also Matt Hills and Amy Luther (2007) 'Investigating "CSI television fandom": fans' textual paths through the franchise', in Michael Allen (ed.) *Reading CSI: Crime TV Under the Microscope*, I.B.Tauris, London and New York, pp.208–21.

63   Catherine Johnson (2007) 'Tele-branding in TVIII: the network as brand and the programme as brand', *New Review of Film and Television Studies* v/1, p.17.

64   Ibid., p.15.

65   Ibid., p.16.

66   Ibid.

67   Ibid., p.19.

68   David J. Howe and Arnold T. Blumberg (2006) *Howe's Transcendental Toybox Update No. 2: The Complete Guide to 2004–2005 Doctor Who Merchandise*, Telos, Tolworth, pp.16–17).

69   Lawrence Miles (2007) 'Secs sell', available online at *http://Beasthouse. LM2.blogspot.com*, 29 November, accessed 29 November 2007; see also Tat Wood and Lawrence Miles (2006) *About Time 1: 1963–66*, Mad Norwegian Press, Des Moines, IA, p.143.

70   See Whotopia (2006) '*Doctor Who* adventures number 3 review', available online at *http://newdoctorwhostuff.blogspot.com/2006/05/doctor-who-adventures-3-review.html*, accessed 6 June 2006.

71   Dave Owen (2008) 'Turn Left/The Stolen Earth/Journey's End', *Doctor Who Magazine* 399, Panini Comics, Tunbridge Wells, p.61.

72   Piers D. Britton and Simon J. Barker (2003) *Reading Between Designs: Visual Imagery and the Generation of Meaning in* The Avengers, The Prisoner, *and* Doctor Who, University of Texas Press, Austin, pp.171–2.

73   Ian Grutchfield (2005) 'Brand Aid!', *Doctor Who Magazine* 364, Panini Comics, Tunbridge Wells, p.39.

74   Ibid.

75   Ibid.

76   Jenkins: *Convergence Culture*, p.170.

77   See BBC News (2008) '*Dr Who* fan in knitted puppet row', available online at *http://news.bbc.co.uk/1/hi/entertainment/7400268.stm*, 14 May, accessed 25 August 2008.

78   See, for example, Rosemary J. Coombe (1998) *The Cultural Life of Intellectual Properties: Authorship, Appropriation, and the Law*, Duke Univer-

sity Press, Durham and London, and Rebecca Tushnet (2007) 'Copyright law, fan practices, and the rights of the author', in Jonathan Gray, Cornel Sandvoss and C. Lee Harrington (eds) *Fandom: Identities and Communities in a Mediated World*, New York University Press, New York and London, pp.60–71.

79  BBC News: '*Dr Who* fan in knitted puppet row'.

80  Ibid.

81  Indeed, Nick Griffiths goes on a fan pilgrimage to Howells department store as part of his quest to visit infamous *Doctor Who* locations in (2008) *Who Goes There: Travels Through Strangest Britain In Search of the Doctor*, Legend Press, London, pp.235–55.

82  See Tim Robins and Paul Mount (2004) 'Lights, camera, legal action!', *Starburst* 317, Visual Imagination, London, p.12, and, for example, photos contained in J. Shaun Lyon (2005) *Back to the Vortex*, Telos Press, Tolworth, and his (2006) *Second Flight*, Telos Press, Tolworth, as well as Stephen James Walker (2007) *Third Dimension*, Telos Press, Tolworth.

83  Karen Hellekson (1996) 'Poaching *Doctor Who*', available online at *http://www.frontiernet.net/~mumvideo/analysis.htm*, accessed 27 September 2008.

84  Ibid.

85  See, for example, Anon. (2008) 'Dreamers in the night', in Josef Steiff and Tristan D. Tamplin (eds) Battlestar Galactica *and Philosophy: Mission Accomplished or Mission Frakked Up?* Open Court, Chicago and La Salle, IL, pp.359–67, where the book *Textual Poachers* itself appears in a piece of *BSG* fanfic.

86  Jenkins: *Convergence Culture*, pp.26–8, drawing on Pierre Levy (1997) *Collective Intelligence*, Perseus Books, Cambridge, MA.

87  Although PR-related information management cock-ups can and do occur. For several spectacular instances see Russell T. Davies and Benjamin Cook (2008) *The Writer's Tale*, BBC Books, London, pp.158, 249. PR strategy is very far from being all-powerful and determining, even without fan intervention.

88  Simon Gerard (2004) '"Assault" at Temple at Peace?', *Starburst* 317, Visual Imagination, London, p.6.

89  Jenkins: *Convergence Culture*, p.55.

90  See BBC News (2007) 'Billie Piper to return to *Dr Who*', available online at *http://news.bbc.co.uk/1/hi/entertainment/7114699.stm*, 27 November, accessed 27 September 2008.

91  Paul Rixon (2008) '*Star Trek*: popular discourses – the role of broadcasters and critics', in Lincoln Geraghty (ed.) *The Influence of* Star Trek *on Television, Film and Culture*, McFarland, Jefferson and London, p.153.

92  See *http://www.taylorherring.com/doctorwho_case.html*, which details the firm's key objectives for the programme as follows: 'maintain and continue to build profile of the show, consolidate relationships with children's market and mainstream media alongside targeted press initiatives' (accessed 2 October 2008). Taylor Herring is *Doctor Who*'s first external PR agency, further indicating the importance of marketing and information management to this incarnation of the show.

93   See the *Sun* (2008) 'Billie is gunning for the Daleks', available online at *http://www.thesun.co.uk/sol/homepage/showbiz/tv/article920788.ece*, 15 March, accessed 27 September 2008.

94   Russell T. Davies (2007) 'Production notes: the Doctor calls', *Doctor Who Magazine* 387, Panini Comics, Tunbridge Wells, p.66.

95   A variant version of 'pre-textual poaching' concerns non-UK fans downloading new *Doctor Who* episodes before they are broadcast locally – sometimes even before a specific national broadcasting deal has been struck (see Jonathan Gray (2008) *Television Entertainment*, Routledge, New York and London, p.90).

96   Neil Perryman (2008) '*Doctor Who* and the convergence of media: a case study in "transmedia storytelling"', *Convergence: The International Journal of Research into New Media Technologies* xiv/1, p.23.

97   Ibid.

98   Ibid., p.24.

99   Ibid., pp.25–6.

100  See, for example, Alan McKee (2007) 'Why is "City of Death" the best *Doctor Who* story?', in David Butler (ed. *Time and Relative Dissertations in Space: Critical Perspectives on* Doctor Who, Manchester University Press, Manchester and New York, pp.233–45.

101  See Gary Gillatt (1998) 'The *DWM* Awards', *Doctor Who Magazine* 265, Marvel Comics, London, pp.4–7; Stephen Cole (1998) 'The Caves of Androzani: hatred and heroism', *Doctor Who Magazine* 265, Marvel Comics, London, pp.22–3; McKee: 'Which is the best *Doctor Who* story?'.

102  See, for example, Benjamin Cook (2007) 'Favourite worst nightmares!', *Doctor Who Magazine* 384, Panini Comics, Tunbridge Wells, p.45.

103  Andrew Pixley (2008) *Doctor Who Magazine Special Edition: The* Doctor Who *Companion – Series Four*, Panini Comics, Tunbridge Wells, p.14.

104  Ibid., pp.28–9.

105  Ibid., p.42.

106  Ibid., p.84.

107  Ibid., p.51.

108  Davies and Cook: *The Writer's Tale*, p.182.

109  Davies and Cook: *The Writer's Tale*, p.183.

110  In Wood: *About Time 6*, p.217.

111  John Tulloch and Manuel Alvarado (1983) Doctor Who*: The Unfolding Text*, Macmillan, London.

112  Andrew Cartmel (2005) *Script Doctor: The Inside Story of* Doctor Who *1986–89*, Reynolds and Hearn, London, p.78.

113  See Wood: *About Time 6*, p.209.

114  See Keir Elam (1980) *The Semiotics of Theatre and Drama*, Methuen, London, p.45.

115  Tulloch and Alvarado: *The Unfolding Text*, p.249.

116  Ibid.

117  Lance Parkin (2007) 'Re: *Time and Relative Dissertations in Space*', 18 December, 7:29pm, available online at *http://www.doctorwhoforum.com*.

118  Michel Foucault (2002) *The Archaeology of Knowledge*, Routledge, London and New York, p.60.

119  Davies and Cook: *The Writer's Tale*, pp.76–7.

# PART II

## GENRE AND FORMAT

How might [a] 'generic function' operate like Foucault's author-function? ... Genres obviously primarily work to classify texts together, much like authorship ... Genres also serve as sites of interpretive consistency, as generic interpretations posit core meanings for any given genre ... Finally, genres are activated in systems of cultural value, with nearly every genre located on the highbrow/lowbrow axis ... [G]enres do not emerge from their assumed central site of origin, the text, but rather are formed by the cultural practices of generic discourses.

Jason Mittell (2004) *Genre and Television*, Routledge,
New York and London, p.15.

# 3

# TIME TRAVEL IN NEW *WHO* AS COMEDY, SOAP OPERA, ADVENTURE ... AND SCIENCE FICTION

Cultural theorist Alec Charles notes that '*Doctor Who* is primarily, as Rose Tyler ... immediately recognises, about time.'[1] Indeed, the very phrase 'About Time' has been used for an entire series of unofficial guides to the classic series.[2] The equation '*Doctor Who* = time travel' is an obvious one, given that the show 'may provide the best-known time traveller in the world',[3] yet Charles' observation continues: '*Doctor Who* is primarily ... about time *and timelessness*.'[4] By this, he means that time travel can be interpreted as a metaphor for the way we live in the twenty-first century: 'in the era of relativity and relativism, it is not continuity but discontinuity which defines us. In a postmodern time ... it is a sense of ahistoricality or anachronism which makes us who we are'.[5] In the here-and-now in which the show is made, we are all everyday time-travellers; we borrow styles from the past (nostalgia for the 1980s has been popular recently), watch digitised 'archive' TV shows and recombine these tastes into a new pattern of now-ness. Set against such a view of contemporary culture, *Doctor Who*'s post-2005 success can be attributed to how it represents 'anachronism ... [its] ahistoricism recalls the junking of history which

Terry Eagleton (1987) identifies as a defining characteristic of postmodernity'.[6] Here, time travel is not viewed as a marker of genre but rather as a reflection of the real society in which new *Who* is produced:

> temporal paradoxes ... lie at the heart of ... the entirety of the programme's 2005 season: it is the philosophical opposite of the grandfather paradox. Existence is at once self-generating and therefore self-contradictory; nothing is any longer equal to itself. This dissolution of our defining absolutes takes place ... also in the realm of social history. This may perhaps to some extent explain why Russell T. Davies's 'Bad Wolf' mystery and paradox so gripped the public and media imagination.[7]

Rose discovers signs of 'Bad Wolf' throughout series one, only to send these messages back in time as a signal to herself in 'The Parting of the Ways' (1.13), and as a warning to the Doctor in 'Turn Left' (4.11). The 'grandfather paradox' appears where a time traveller goes back in time and kills their own grandfather. They then can't have been born, and so can't go back in time in the first place. It is a paradox of self-destruction; if the self cancels itself, then how can it have existed? The opposite referred to by Charles is a paradox of self-creation: Rose Tyler becomes the super-powered entity 'Bad Wolf', capable of manipulating the energies of the Time Vortex, because of the messages sent back through time by SuperRose. Yet Rose can only go on to become a god-like being in the future because she has already become god-like in that already-realised future.

Alec Charles reads this paradox of self-creation as another reflection of postmodern society, in which we can potentially make and remake our self-identities through consumer choices. But these interpretations of BBC Wales' *Doctor Who* are rather limited. They tell one theoretical story about society, find a version of that same story in the programme, and speculatively conclude that the success of the 2005 series was a result of the alleged similarity. A major problem for 'reflectionist' readings like this is that there may be a host of different representations of time travel in BBC Wales' *Doctor Who*. Rather than merely 'postmodern' anachronisms or paradoxes, we might be able to analyse a wide range of approaches to temporality in the series.[8]

In this chapter, then, I will resist the temptation to offer one master narrative of diegetic time travel, rather exploring differing time travels, plural, in the series. Investigating types of time travel traversed by the ninth and tenth Doctors calls for a taxonomy, and I will hence argue that time travel works in the show as a multi-layered device linked to genres of SF, comedy, adventure and soap opera. Though Jason Mittell's concept of a Foucauldian 'generic function' shifts its focus usefully from 'the text' to circulating discourses of genre, I am interested here in how genre discourses are themselves also embedded in production decisions and textual structures.[9] In the final section, I will consider one element of production discourse, the 'celebrity historical', and whether this has given rise to a view of time travel as 'tourism'.[10] Have historical scenarios increasingly provided branded familiarity, reducing history to a version of 'the present in costume'?[11] First, though, what are the many meanings of time travel in *Doctor Who*? And how can these multiple meanings contribute to an emphasis on the programme's '*proprietary* characteristics ... over *sharable* determinants like genre'?[12]

## About Time Taxonomies:
## Setting Parameters Versus Series Finale Paradoxes

A number of writers have sought to classify 'chronomotion' stories, amongst them the celebrated SF writer Stanislaw Lem.[13] George Slusser and Danielle Chatelain argue that despite the apparent variety of material, such stories can be reduced to one over-arching family, that of the 'temporal paradox' narrative,[14] and William Burling seeks to refine this argument further.[15] By contrast, writers such as Gordon and Penley have studied Hollywood representations of time travel via a psychoanalytic framework.[16] Television is under-represented within such debates, though *Doctor Who*'s and *Star Trek*'s depictions of 'chronomotion' have been repeatedly contrasted.[17]

Rather than mapping academic discussions per se, my focus is on time travel and discourses of TV genre.[18] It is sometimes assumed that the presence of a time machine, the Doctor's TARDIS, automatically prescribes *Doctor Who* as science fiction:

> The character of the Doctor has at his disposal the TARDIS, a machine capable of travelling to any moment in time and any point in space. It is, in effect, a metaphor for an imagination unfettered by the constraints of realism and empiricism; *the TARDIS is a physical manifestation of the potential of science fiction.*[19]

Writing about the classic series, Tulloch and Alvarado use Darko Suvin's influential definition of SF.[20] This argues that science fiction is distinguished by the

> introduction of a *novum* – a cognitive innovation 'super added to or infused into the author's empirically "known" – i.e. culturally defined – world'. In *Doctor Who* of course ... the novum is the possibility of time travel and the experimental and estranging 'wisdom' this allows the time traveller ... Hence time travel ... is a novum allowing for a variety of social interactions.[21]

SF is said to rely on a thought experiment, a cognitive addition to the narrative world. The TARDIS and its journeys have been central to the format of *Doctor Who*, that is, its original, copyrighted 'production category with relatively rigid boundaries'.[22] This tends to mean that, for long-term fans of the series, 'when "science fiction" is discussed, it is as a default or invisible value'.[23] And yet, the TARDIS can visit Earth's history as well as the far future, potentially weakening the assumed linkage of *Who* with SF. As Daniel O'Mahony notes, 'if science fiction is the thesis of *Doctor Who* then historicals are its antithesis'.[24]

Indeed, the 'straight' historical story (in which the TARDIS is the only SF novum) has not been pursued at all in the first four series of BBC Wales' *Who*, which has resolutely stuck to the SF 'thesis' of the show's presumed identity. Where history has featured, it has always been coupled with an SF monster: Charles Dickens and the Gelth (1.3); the 1980s meets the Reapers (1.8); the Second World War and nanogenes (1.9–1.10); Queen Victoria and a werewolf (2.2); Madame de Pompadour and clockwork droids (2.4); Queen Elizabeth II's coronation and The Wire (2.7); Shakespeare and Carrionites (3.2); post-First World War Daleks (3.4–3.5); pre-First World War and the Family of Blood (3.8–3.9); and Agatha Christie and a Vespiform (4.7). Given that alien forces are recurrently represented as attacking Earth's history, this alters 'the Doctor from being an observer into an active defender of history ... the genre expectations of the "future" stories leak through to the "past"'.[25] Whether time-travelling to the historical past or a wholly imagined, projected future, new *Who* would thus appear to be consistently coded as science-fictional. Historical stories offer similar narrative pleasures to iconic SF tales: the Doctor is still battling against some spectacular, alien creature, just within a different milieu. This was something that developed across the run of the classic series, taking hold relatively early in the 1960s,[26] and which fans developed a language to describe: 'The phrase "pseudo-historical" is an invention of fan discourse, though one that fed back to the perception of *Doctor Who*'s producers.'[27]

However, new *Who* has added 'pseudo-futurological' stories to its 'pseudo-historicals'; one recurrent fan complaint has been that depictions of the future in the series have not been 'proper' science-fictional extrapolations from contemporary society. Instead, the far-futures represented have frequently been satirical, metaphorical versions of the present-day. Rather than history being critiqued academically as 'the present in costume', this style of argument seems to have been carried over into fan responses to some future-set *Who* stories, such as this from *Back to the Vortex*:

> Where I'm not comfortable with 'The Long Game' [1.7] is in its dreadful realisation of the future. Styrofoam cups? Burger joints? If this had been the year 2100, maybe … [b]ut 200,000? … 197,900 years and we're still drinking flavoured ice and eating out of styrofoam tins? If that's not stagnation, I don't know what is.[28]

Rather than present-day identities being defamiliarised, they seem to be projected, as-is, into far-future narrative settings. In theorist Fredric Jameson's terms this mode of 'science fiction … corresponds to the waning or blockage of … historicity',[29] by failing to imagine a plausible, extrapolated future which differs from the here-and-now:

> Perhaps, however, what is implied is simply an ultimate historicist breakdown in which we can no longer imagine the future at all, under any form – Utopian or catastrophic. Under those circumstances, where a formerly futurological science fiction … turns into … an outright representation of the present, the possibility … [of] an experience of our present as past and as history … is slowly excluded.[30]

In Lyon's terms, 'The Long Game' is seemingly just bad SF. However, this neglects to consider production discourses circulating around the pseudo-futures of new *Who*. In his pitch for series one, Russell T. Davies originally set this story in the year 8922:

> 8922 … then became 200,000 instead … I was really getting into this History of Humanity stuff – I wanted a fairly ordinary sci-fi future, and yet set in a far-flung date, to suggest that culture and technology have risen and fallen countless times. It's the Fourth Human Empire, we've been through some peaks and troughs to get this far.[31]

Though arguably it is not dwelt on in the transmitted episode, there is a sense within this justification that history is being conceptualised as cyclical. However, this production discourse is somewhat out of alignment with dominant cultural views of 'history'. As Barney Warf has noted: 'Western conceptions of history ... rely upon a linear, rather than cyclical, conception of time ... Causation and determination in history have frequently been attributed to teleological forces.'[32] And whilst faith in a 'teleological' view of history – a series of progressions towards some positive end-point – may have subsided, the concept of history as linear undoubtedly remains powerful. By responding to 'The Long Game' (1.7) only as an 'ordinary sci-fi future' and not as embedded in a cyclical conception of history, fans such as J. Shaun Lyon treat the show as 'linear' SF, assuming that things haven't changed enough for a narrative gap of 198,000 years between now and then. The same is true of critiques of 'Bad Wolf' (1.12), where use 'of the trappings of three familiar television shows – nearly two hundred thousand years in the future... – caused some consternation among viewers'.[33] There is a tension between fan and production discourses here, with fans tending to read some of *Who*'s future representations as 'failed' SF extrapolations across linear history, and fan-producers defending those same SF futures via cyclical concepts of history.

What such analyses demonstrate is that cultural constructions of history inevitably are drawn upon within discussions of *Doctor Who*, genre and time travel. But what are the rules of the time-travel narrative game? How does the branded format of the regenerated series engage with philosophies of time travel? Answering these questions means thinking about alternative, hybridised genre identities beyond SF that are mobilised by the production, including comedy, adventure and soap opera. Fixing time travel as a science-fictional novum misses the point that *Doctor Who*'s visions of time travel use the device multi-generically to define the series' exact format. As Rick Altman has argued, genre can be thought of as a 'by-product of discursive activity',[34] because media producers are primarily interested in creating individualised, copyrighted formats that can be owned – quite unlike genre, which is a shared set of conventions spanning across texts. Altman suggests that genre, in the form of an imitative cycle of products, emerges through copies of a highly successful branded format – for example, *Primeval* (ITV, 2007–9), *Robin Hood* (BBC, 2006–9) and *Merlin* (BBC, 2008) – forming a renewed sense of 'British telefantasy' or

'Saturday night family drama' following *Doctor Who's* success. But this narrative, where genre emerges from format, plays down the fact that, in turn, branded formats are themselves generated by specific re-combinations of existent genre discourses. The dynamic between format and genre can be thought of as:

Multiple genre discourses → combined specifically into the branded proprietary format of *Doctor Who* → altered genre (and TV schedule) discourses via imitating shows.

Therefore, it remains important to identify the range of genre discourses that are drawn upon to generate a format – here BBC Wales' *Doctor Who* and its kinds of 'chronomotion'. Stanislaw Lem, in his taxonomy of time travel, argues that there are two kinds of time loop story: 'minimal' and 'maximal'.[35] The minimal loop concerns the time-travelling of an individual within coincident generations, for example, someone going back to encounter their parents or grandparents before their own conception. 'Father's Day' (1.8) is a version of the minimal loop story, and it is these sorts of narrative which have typically been subjected to psychoanalytic readings.[36] On the other hand, the 'maximal' time loop deals with events at a cosmological scale, for example, with the creation of the universe occurring as a result of particles being sent back in time to the Big Bang. Lem also differentiates between cases where the time loop is 'the backbone of a work's causal structure' and those which involve the 'far looser motif of journeys in time per se',[37] the latter usually being a more accurate reflection of *Who's* storylining. Lem goes on:

There are actually two possible authorial attitudes, which are mutually exclusive: either one deliberately demonstrates causal paradoxes resulting from 'chronomotion' with the greatest possible consistency, or else one cleverly avoids them. In the first instance, the careful development of logical consequences leads to situations as absurd as the one cited [e.g. an individual becoming his own father], and usually has a comic effect.[38]

In fact, within its multi-generic use of time travel, *Doctor Who* displays both of these supposedly 'mutually exclusive' approaches. On the whole, it appears keen to avoid the paradoxes that can be generated by time travel. The classic series introduced the 'Blinovitch Limitation Effect' under producer Barry Letts, to try to rule out time paradoxes.

This stated that time travellers couldn't return to a point earlier in their own timestream, altering their own personal history.[39]

'Father's Day' (1.8) deals with the same problem by suggesting that the fabric of time is weakened by time travellers looping round, as well as introducing the Reapers, monsters which repair time in a catastrophic manner for anyone caught up in a self-encountering paradox. This may be a less minimalist solution than the 'Blinovitch' label, but it achieves the same result in formatting terms: paradoxes such as 'the "two-body" problem [or] consciousness of a dual existence in time'[40] are ruled out.

A further narrative problem that the new series' format has to deal with, in terms of setting its own parameters, is the issue of when the Doctor can and can't intervene in history. Anthony Thacker observes that 'Father's Day' (1.8) again tackles this:

> it establishes ... for viewers the limits to the Doctor's powers. He can't go into the past and prevent the holocaust, it appears. (However, he will still go into the future and stop Dalek holocausts!) It is this inconsistency Rose challenges:
>
> 'So it's OK when you go to other times and you save people's lives, but not when it's me saving my Dad?'
>
> The Doctor: 'I know what I'm doing; you don't! ... My entire planet died, my whole family; do you think it never occurred to me to go back and save them?'[41]

Some events are presented as 'naturally' unchangeable. As a result, though aspects of Earth's history can be amended, there are also fixed points. As Thacker notes in *Behind the Sofa*, 'the reason why script editors [and latterly, executive producers] invented such laws of time is clear enough'.[42] It is partly to provide solid reference points for character and narrative development; otherwise the Doctor could go back in time and alter events in order to change character psychologies.[43] And he might seek to alter the tragedies of his own past, such as the Time War, which he believes is 'timelocked' in 'Journey's End' (4.13). This language of 'timelocking' does suggest, unlike the notion of specific events being naturally unchangeable, that the Time War has been frozen through some decision or agency (akin to a design being 'locked' prior to *Doctor Who*'s production; production discourses of management and consistency seem almost to invade the diegesis here).

As well as fixing character and back-story, generally applicable 'rules of time' also work to introduce a sense of danger into tales set in the Earth's past. For, if history were always fixed then there would be nothing at stake: alien forces could never triumph by changing established history; threats to destroy the Earth in the time of Dickens or Shakespeare would be utterly pointless. It took a surprisingly long time for the classic series to address this, until 'The Pyramids of Mars' (1975) finally demonstrated that history *could* hang in the balance:

> the Doctor uses the TARDIS to do something he's never done before: he takes the Ship to a version of Sarah [Jane Smith]'s own time [1980] in which they didn't bother to stop [the villainous] Sutekh, and it's a blasted, lifeless, storm-wracked planet circling a dead sun ... This ... suggests that the Doctor can hop forward to check the results of his work, then hop back if they're not satisfactory, an incredibly useful tool which he never, ever uses at any other point.[44]

This very scene – showing that established history can be derailed with disastrous consequences – was almost a part of the first 'pseudo-historical' of series one, 'The Unquiet Dead' (1.3). In his initial outline, Russell T. Davies planned for the ninth Doctor to 'hop forward' in an analogous manner:

> Rose is from 2005, so obviously, the world can't end in 1860, there can't be any *real* danger ... Not so. Halfway through this episode ... the Doctor takes Rose into the Tardis, and sets the controls for 2005. The doors open on a new 2005, a barren wilderness, the human race extinct. History can change, it's always changing. Only the Doctor can see the patterns binding our lives together. They have to go back to 1860, because the world *needs* saving. (All credit to the original series, which once did this exact scene; it needs repeating)[45]

The scene, poached from 'Pyramids of Mars', was drafted by writer Mark Gatiss but ultimately not used. Though its purpose was to establish a sense of historical threat, it was deemed to take 'away the danger, the ticking clock' of the story by letting the Doctor and Rose get back to the safety of the TARDIS.[46] Though the possibility of history taking a dangerous new path is set up in the story, this parameter is most strongly revisited in 'The Fires of Pompeii' (4.2). Here, the Doctor insists, against Donna's entreaties, that he cannot interfere:

> Pompeii is a fixed point in history. What happens, happens ... It's still part of history ... Some things are fixed, some things are in flux ... that's

> how I see the universe. Every waking second, I can see, what is, what
> was, what could be, what must not. It's the burden of the Time Lord,
> Donna. I'm the only one left.

The 'implication is that Time Lords are in some way time-proof, set
apart from normal causality or ... immune to the course of history. Time
doesn't affect them the way it affects ordinary mortals, even ordinary
mortal time-travellers.'[47] Due to his unique sense of time seemingly
only the Doctor has genuine free will; only he knows when time can be
changed,[48] even if time-travelling Daleks appear capable of achieving
the diegetically 'impossible' by intervening in time-locked events.

New *Who*'s approach to time-travel parameters is thus highly flexible. Showrunner Russell T. Davies reconciles two seemingly irrecon-
cilable philosophies of history: that it can branch into different possibilities, or that it is fundamentally fixed. However, as Stanislaw Lem
notes:

> In a way ... the two [philosophies] are reconcilable: history can as a
> whole be ... not very responsive to local disturbances, and at the same
> time such exceptional hypersensitive points in the causal chains can
> exist, the disturbance of which produces more intensive results.[49]

What is especially useful for Davies' attempt to police and avoid temporal paradoxes – one of the two major authorial attitudes identified
by Lem – is that his solution does not set out any narrative rules for
determining when history is fixed and when it is in flux at 'fateful moments'.[50] The only arbiter of this is the character of the Doctor. Whatever philosophy of history a given story calls for, overall textual consistency can thus be maintained along with narrative flexibility.

Despite this clever catch-all, it is not only in the case of Dalek Caan
and the Time War that Davies dispenses with parameters aimed at
avoiding temporal paradox. He also over-rides his own apparent strictures in the series one 'Bad Wolf' story arc, and via the Doctor–Donna
hybrid of 'Journey's End' (4.13), where the single heartbeat of the
Time Lord–human 'metacrisis' occurs before its cause, rippling back
in time. These Davies-scripted transgressions are focused on the resolution of story arcs, typically occurring in series finales – Captain Jack
and the Face of Boe being an example from series three, where the an-
cient being knows that the Doctor is 'not alone' as a Time Lord (3.3),
presumably having been involved in these very events millennia earlier as Captain Jack (3.11–3.13). The Face of Boe/Jack knows what will

happen in the Doctor's future ('You Are Not Alone' dialogue) because this has already happened far in his own past (meeting the hidden Time Lord, Professor Yana, in 'Utopia', 3.11).

The regular appearance of time paradoxes at the end of series' runs suggests that the confusion of ordinary cause and effect is linked to the need to produce moments of massive narrative shock or revelation (who or what is 'Bad Wolf'?; what is the significance of Professor Yana's name?; how can an ordinary woman be the most important person in the universe?). The motif and structure of the temporal paradox enables the disruption of character identities, allowing unexpected and unpredictable narrative twists by suspending norms of diegetic logic. Series three even formalises this through its creation of a 'Paradox Machine', representing a 'maximal' loop in Lem's terms, whereby the remnants of humanity from the very end of time seek to travel back and supplant the human race of the twenty-first century (3.11–3.13). And this narrative deployment of temporal paradox is again articulated with a revelatory moment: the Toclafane are not marauding aliens, they are desperate, deranged humankind. Paradoxes may produce seeming absurdities, as Stanislaw Lem says, but introduced as narrative shocks – as they repeatedly have been by Russell T. Davies – their function is far from comedic.

Temporal paradox is one narrative strategy, then, for climactically surprising the audience and for generating the unexpected (even if this has become a routinised strategy). *Doctor Who's* formatting of time travel is, here, sharply integrated with TV industry requirements for story-arc escalation at the end of each run of episodes. It underpins the 'event TV' status of each series finale (series two working slightly differently as a result of being linked to the *Torchwood* spin-off). Whereas an increase in narrative stake is structured into reality TV and talent shows that progress towards a final – forms of light entertainment *Doctor Who* has had to compete against since 2005 – Davies' use of temporal-paradox-as-revelation proffers an equivalent for SF TV. And though the use of the 'looping' form is science-fictional, its last-minute reversals and unmaskings of true identity bind it strongly to genres such as melodrama/adventure. I will return to the question of time travel as adventure, but for now I want to consider other instances of time-looping in new *Who*.

Whilst Russell T. Davies permits himself to break apparent parameters of format logic, there is another contributor who has repeatedly been given the freedom to play with temporal paradoxes – Steven Moffat. An accomplished comedy writer, Moffat's use of paradox is not framed by story-arc resolution, but instead occurs within stand-alone stories. 'Blink' (3.10) is one example, as here the Doctor learns his part in a DVD-recorded dialogue by reading a transcribed version of what he has yet to say, but simultaneously has already said. Rather than offering a detailed explanation of this, Moffat gives the Doctor the following exposition: 'People assume that time is a strict progression of cause to effect, but actually, from a non-linear, non-subjective viewpoint it's more like a big ball of wibbly wobbly ... timey wimey ... stuff.' 'Blink' is probably the most intricately structured of all *Doctor Who* episodes, almost a horological mechanism in its own right. The same pieces of David Tennant's dialogue interact with different narrative contexts, whilst the Doctor effectively knows everything that is going to happen in advance; as he says, 'things don't always happen to me in quite the right order. It gets a bit confusing at times.'

This intricacy is given a comedic edge, however, just as Lem argues: 'a circular causal structure may signalize a frivolous type of content, [though] this does not mean that it is necessarily reduced to the construction of comic antinomies for the sake of pure entertainment'.[51] This comedy is partly down to Moffat's dialogue and Tennant's performance, as well as the absurdities of the situation, but it is not without serious meaning. The use of 'wibbly wobbly timey wimey' in place of logical explanation is a marker of the episode's reflexive, comedic construction. Time paradox is recognised as such, but via child-like language rather than scientific-seeming technobabble. Invented technical jargon would give the impression of a science-fictional generic frame, whereas 'wibbly wobbly timey wimey' momentarily breaks the frame: paradox is self-reflexively acknowledged as an absurdity rather than rationalised. Moffat repeats this device in 'Time Crash' (Children in Need special, 2007), in which the TARDIS crashes into an earlier version of itself, piloted by the fifth Doctor (Peter Davison). The solution, a feat of TARDIS control beyond even the Doctor's usual abilities, is explained as follows:

> Fifth Doctor: You remembered being me, watching you, doing that. You only knew what to do because *I* saw you do it.
>
> Tenth Doctor: Wibbly wobbly –
>
> Both: timey wimey!

Moffat cites his own catchphrase for inexplicable paradox, again covering over logical problems with a reflexive awareness that what has occurred is impossible. Drawing on the work of theorist Theresa Ebert, Jan Johnson-Smith argues, of American SF TV, that it has become increasingly 'meta' in terms of calling attention to its own fictional construction.[52] Moffat's 'wibbly wobbly' slogan seems closer to this scenario than anything else in BBC Wales' *Who*, perhaps bar elements of Davies' 'Love & Monsters' (2.10). Moffat also deploys time-shifting in a 'meta' way in 'The Girl in the Fireplace' (2.4). Here, Arthur the horse, apparently from the eighteenth century, trots around a fifty-first century spaceship, a fiercely incongruous detail which, though setting up part of the Doctor's eventual rescue mission, again has a comedic, 'meta' feel by virtue of its deliberate visual and narrative collision of elements of pre-industrial 'costume drama' and iconic SF (complete with spacecraft and droids).

Additionally, 'The Girl in the Fireplace' is a 'time-travel-fuelled romantic' tale.[53] The Doctor's time-travelling is used to posit a romance experienced out of sequence by its participants: a reunion awaited for years by Madame de Pompadour (Sophia Myles) happens moments later for the Doctor. Moffat returns to this conceit, a relationship where time is out of joint, in 'Silence in the Library' and 'Forest of the Dead' (4.8–4.9). This time around, the Doctor's significant other, River Song (Alex Kingston), has known the Time Lord for a long while, whereas on his timeline the Library incident is their first encounter. Whilst calling attention to the 'fictivity' of time travel, Moffat's scripts multi-generically articulate time-travelling with the conventions of comedy and soap opera. It is not the case that time travel is monovalently 'science-fictional', with other textual elements bolting-on the melodramatic, emotionally focused aspects of soap. Instead, temporal disorientation becomes part of *Doctor Who*'s 'soap drama':

> in many ways this new type of television drama employs many of the characteristics of soap opera, in particular, its use of close-up (of people's faces) in order to convey intimate conversation and emotion, its concentration on dialogue rather than visual image to impart meaning, and its tendency towards quickly-edited scenes as a way of mixing and bringing together a number of varied and multiple storylines.[54]

Soap drama shares traditional soap opera's 'interest in close-knit communities and friends echoing ... preoccupation with private existence ... and its use of time tends to parallel actual or contemporary time'.[55] New *Who*'s 'soap drama' status is thus partly indicated via its repeated use of contemporary London settings, but also via its stress on the Doctor's elective 'family' of helpers, and his private life ('dancing', in Moffat's euphemism). The novum of time travel is itself integrated with these representations of 'private existence' and emotional belonging: 'the very hybridity of "soap drama" ... while utilising soap conventions ... can also break the genre boundaries upon which traditional 'soap opera' is ... made and understood'.[56]

In the re-imagining of *Who*, time travel is thereby given a new-found 'emotional realism'.[57] In Ien Ang's terminology, 'the same things, people, relations and situations which are regarded at the denotative level as unrealistic, and unreal [adventures in the past or future, involving monstrous entities – MH] are at [the] connotative level ... seen ... as "recognizable"' emotionally and psychologically.[58] Rose travels to the future to witness the end of the world (1.2), but wants to stay in touch with her Mum, and so phones home – across time – to indicate awkwardly the love she feels for her. All the while, Rose's mother, Jackie (Camille Coduri), is caught up in her everyday life of work and laundry. The scene emphasises how far Rose has travelled, and the fantastical nature of what she is witnessing, by contrasting present-day 'now' with a distant, SF future. But it also emotionally connects these two time periods, the contemporaneous ordinary and the extrapolated extraordinary:

> Magnificent sfx of the atmosphere boiling away and the continents crumbling into dust – *but the most important thing is the close-up on the Doctor and Rose*, as they watch the end of the world, together. CUT TO Piccadilly Circus, 2005. Cars, noise, people. Rose stands with the Doctor and the Tardis behind her, as she looks around at everyday life. We think this world will last forever. It will not. But it's not a sad ending – it's wonderful. To Rose, now, every second matters, she feels more alive than ever.[59]

Precisely as TV scholar Glen Creeber argues of soap drama, the close-up is stressed here rather than SFX as visual spectacle. This approach 'places an emphasis on the *reactions* of characters to the unknown over the representation of the fantastic itself', as Catherine Johnson has suggested.[60] However, this 'intimacy is balanced by action sequences',[61] meaning that dialogue and characters' looks or glances are not focused upon purely in opposition to visual spectacle, but *in addition to this*, albeit with production prioritisation still going to the 'close-up'.

Private, emotional relationships – the typical terrain of soap – are represented as having psychological depth, with this being brought out via time-travel scenarios. Amongst other examples, Paul Cornell's 'Father's Day' (1.8) works in this way, combining its time-paradox plotline with constructions of 'emotional realism' – with Rose's father, Pete Tyler (Shaun Dingwall), realising that her description of him as a good Dad is unlikely to be true and with Jackie mistaking Rose for someone carrying on with her husband. Whether concerning the Doctor's romances, or his companion's family ties, it can be suggested following theorists Creeber and Johnson that time-travelling intimacy is central to BBC Wales' *Doctor Who* as soap drama/telefantasy. The show's format frequently trades on melodramatic 'contagion of emotion passed from screen response to audience affect',[62] as in the melancholy of the Doctor and Rose's parting in 'Doomsday' (2.13), or indeed when they first part company in series one:

> The most evocative ... moment at the end of this new *Doctor Who* did not come from the title character but his companion ... Rose. On returning to her home – and our time – she was horrified at the banality of life, work, tasteless food and a quiet night in front of the telly. In remembering the adventure, the challenge and the good fights in the Tardis, Rose remarks that 'The Doctor showed me a better way of living your life. You just don't give up. You make a stand. You say no.' ('The Parting of the Ways', 1.13)[63]

Again, this works by contrasting yet emotionally connecting different imagined time zones. William S. Burling's taxonomy of time travel stories offers a way of thinking about this device; rather than the temporal paradox, or the 'dislocation form' of narrative,[64] Burling identifies an alternative, which he calls the *temporal contrast form*:

> The principles and results of *temporal contrast* time travel differ considerably from those of temporal dislocation. The narrative structure ... emphasizes historical specificity ... This 'blasting' contrast of ... the present with the alternative era which the time traveller visits *emphasizes not an abstractly scientific mediation on the 'how' of time travel, but rather a dynamic historical critique.*[65]

The 'temporal contrast' of new *Who* is one where the contemporary world is both celebrated (as in the life-affirming conclusion of 'The

End of the World', 1.2) and critiqued, as in representations of Rose's sense that her life on Earth lacks the agency and purpose of travelling with the Doctor. Via the emotional articulation of different times, Fredric Jameson's call for 'historicity' is met – that is, a sense is created of *the present as history*, as open to change for the better, or as connected (through similarity and difference) to past and future times. For Rose in 'The Parting of the Ways' (1.13), the future is 'happening now' and she wants desperately to make a difference in that 200,100 world. One implication is that time travel has been a consciousness-raising activity.

Yet the 'adventure' Rose desires is present simultaneously on an epic scale (the Dalek invasions of 1.13 and 4.12; 2.8–2.9's 'Beast' from before time; 2.13's Daleks vs Cybermen; 4.13's end of all parallel universes) and in intimate 'close-up' (Rose's affection for, separation from, and eventual reunion with the Doctor). As soap drama, the show's multi-generic time-travelling format might best be characterised as that of *intimate epic* given that the 'temporal contrast' between differing times and worlds is balanced recurrently with characters' emotional connections and choices. Nowhere is this more evident than the conclusion to 'Last of the Time Lords' (3.13), where an SF invasion storyline – itself a time paradox – is followed by Martha Jones' decision to stop travelling with the Doctor in order to get over her unrequited love. Likewise, 'Journey's End' (4.13) connotatively represents the Doctor's 'family' of helpers, with this emotional belonging being set against a Dalek plot to destroy 'reality itself'.[66]

However, this 'intimate epic' formatting marginalises the possibility of the Doctor and his companions making a political difference in the present day. Instead, the 'emotional realism' of recognisable feeling is grafted into epic, alien invasion narratives such as 'The Sontaran Stratagem'/'The Poison Sky' (4.4–4.5). Here, the Doctor, Donna and Martha defeat a Sontaran plan to choke the Earth's atmosphere with toxic gases rather than tackling, say, issues of actual climate change. Emotional realism plus science-fictional narrative results, at best, in a metaphorical cloaking of directly political content, and, at worst, in a displacement of political critique. The time-travelling consciousness-raising of Rose Tyler, Martha Jones and Donna Noble is predominantly affective rather than being cognitively focused on specific political issues. It is about *feeling empowered to make a difference* rather than actually contesting political issues such as, say, environmentalism. Even where the Doctor brings down a government in 'The Christmas Invasion' (2.X), he does not do so through any specific political objection. And 'Planet of the Ood' (4.3) refuses to connect its slavery narrative with present-day exploitations of third-world labour.

*Doctor Who*'s 'intimate epic' format demonstrates a further generic mobilisation of time travel, this time as 'action-adventure'. In *The Dialogic Imagination*, Mikhail Bakhtin studies what he calls the 'chronotope'. Bakhtin argues that 'it is precisely the chronotope that defines genre and generic distinction',[67] defining the concept as follows:

> We will give the name *chronotope* [literally, 'time space'] to the intrinsic connectedness of temporal and spatial relationships that are artistically expressed in literature ... In the literary artistic chronotope, spatial and temporal indicators are fused into one carefully thought-out, concrete whole. Time, as it were, thickens, takes on flesh, becomes artistically visible; likewise, space becomes charged and responsive to the movements of time, plot and history.[68]

This suggests that the representation of time is always closely linked to different genre discourses, whether or not one is specifically tackling the issue of time travel. Distinct chronotopes can be analytically identified as characteristic of particular genres. A number of these are studied by Bakhtin, including 'the unique chronotope of [the chivalric romance:] ... *a miraculous world in adventure-time*'.[69] Though I am not arguing that *Doctor Who* is an example of 'chivalric romance', Bakhtin's work remains helpful in this radically different context. He argues that the chronotope of 'adventure-time' involves a fantastical world, and that:

> In this world the hero is 'at home' (although he is not in his homeland); he is every bit as miraculous as his world. His lineage is miraculous ... He is flesh of the flesh and bone of the bone of this miraculous world.[70]

As a Time Lord, the Doctor very neatly resonates with this account. And in new *Who*, he is both 'at home' with alien worlds or future-historical timeframes, and permanently cut off from his 'homeland' of Gallifrey, destroyed in the Time War. Writing of adventure films, as opposed to the thriller genre, Martin Rubin similarly suggests that the 'primary operation in adventure tales is a movement away from the ordinary world into an adventurous environment, rather than the bringing of those adventurous elements into the ordinary world'.[71] However, *Doctor Who* explores both of these narrative-generic possibilities: whilst the Doctor's ability to travel in time marks him down as part of a 'miraculous' or 'adventurous' world, the TARDIS also visits contemporary Earth repeatedly (as a part of its 'soap drama'). In these episodes, the 'miraculous world' of the adventure genre crosses, temporarily, into thriller-like representations of our ordinary world – Slitheen penetrate to the heart of government (1.4–1.5); Krillitanes impersonate school teachers (2.3); the Master seeks election as Prime Minister (3.12); ATMOS car-emission devices go rogue (4.4–4.5), and so on. This sense of dramatic transformation (ordinary-to-extraordinary) also resonates with Bakhtin's generic analysis of adventure-time, which further argues that

> Moments of adventuristic time occur at those points when the normal course of events, the normal, intended or purposeful sequence of life's events is interrupted. These points provide an opening for the intrusion of nonhuman forces – fate, gods, villains – and it is precisely those forces, and not the heroes, who in adventure-time take all the initiative.[72]

*Doctor Who*'s 'adventure-time', as a TV format, deals consistently with the intrusion of villainous forces, against which the Doctor must battle heroically. He never takes a Time Lordly initiative in this regard; episodes do not begin with him deciding to take the battle to the Daleks, to hunt them down and do away with their schemes. There is no 'War on Terror' in the *Doctor Who* universe: no narrative legitimation of pre-emptive action, no *a priori* surveillance or monitoring of the enemy. And whilst it could perhaps be argued that the events of 'Boom Town' (1.11), 'Bad Wolf' (1.12), 'Love & Monsters' (2.10) and 'Army of Ghosts' (2.12) can be traced back to actions taken by the Doctor, these stories still involve 'the intrusion of non-human forces' other than the last Time Lord. Likewise, his decision to become the human John Smith in 'Human Nature'/'The Family of Blood' (3.8–3.9) is a reactive one. And where we, as the audience, encounter the Doctor in medias res (he is mid-adventure in 'Rose' (1.1), 'School Reunion' (2.3) and 'Smith and Jones' (3.1)) then he is again responding to prior narrative disruptions. As such, the Doctor's time-travelling journeys are consistently either unmotivated or reactive; he has no narrative agenda of his own. Planned time travel seems to occur largely where the Doctor wants to visit celebrated historical events, persons, or alien worlds; his impulsive wandering represents the 'normal course of events' rather than an intrusion of disruptive forces.

For Bakhtin, adventure-time carries another major quality, that of being 'momentary'. He identifies the many 'moments of adventure-time, all these "suddenlys" and "at just that moments"'.[73] Of course, this generic use of time need not involve time travel at all, being even more fundamental to the series' narrative construction. In a sense, rather than *Doctor Who*'s generic identity being reliant on a science-fictional novum, as has been assumed, it could be argued that its dominant chronotope is, instead, derived from action-adventure TV. Rather than 'action' simply meaning 'fast-paced narratives ... and (increasingly) sensational special effects',[74] with SF being linked to virtues of 'imagination' or social critique,[75] Bakhtin's work demonstrates that elements of 'adventure-time' can themselves involve the realisation of fantastical worlds and non-human powers. And, in line with my overall argument here, although 'adventure-time' may exceed representations of time travel, it also impacts on these in new *Who*, again rendering 'chronomotion' multi-generic rather than simply science-fictional. For example, SuperRose's arrival at the Game Station, provoking the denouement to 'The Parting of the Ways' (1.13), is time travel as an adventure-time 'at just that moment'. And the TARDIS' return to the Crucible in 'Journey's End' (4.13) is a knowing riff on this plot device, appearing to offer an at-just-that-moment resolution of the Dalek threat, but promptly failing to do so. 'The Runaway Bride' (3.X) visualises TARDIS 'adventure-time' highly unusually for the series, since rather than materialising at the exact moment that it is called for, the Police Box is instead shown flying along a motorway, only then hovering ready to rescue Donna Noble. The TARDIS' generic colouration by, and contextualisation within, 'adventure-time' is marked frequently by a shift in its representation: in these cases, its arrival tends to be intercut with wind-swept character reaction shots, and its doorway temporarily back-lit – along with 'The Parting of the Ways' (1.13) and 'Journey's End' (4.13), a further example of this occurs in the family rescue sequence of 'The Fires of Pompeii' (4.2).

Thus far, I have argued that *Doctor Who*'s time travelling is linked to a range of hybridised genres including SF, comedy, soap drama, and adventure. The show's format involves articulating these different genre discourses via a 'generic function' that sets discursive parameters (and consistencies) to *Who*'s identity. I want to focus, finally, on the production discourse of the 'celebrity historical', something that has been a major component of the new series' portrayal of time travel.[76] 'The Unquiet Dead' (1.3) ushered in this part of the format of new *Who* and it has been iterated successfully in each series. What are the consequences of this style of pseudo-historical, time travelling representation? And to what extent does it position the Doctor and his companions problematically, not just as time travellers but, more specifically, as time *tourists*?

## About Time Tourism: History as Quasi-Brand Familiarity and Residual Public Service

The classic series of *Doctor Who* began with a very specific view of how history should be represented in its time travel stories. As Matthew Kilburn has argued, it set off

> with the intention that its predominantly youthful audience should be shown that ... the past events which had shaped their world were the province of ordinary people as well as members of the pantheon of great men and women celebrated by, for example, the Ladybird history books of L. Du Garde Peach.[77]

Kilburn suggests that the initial production team was wary of over-emphasising a view of history as the province of 'Great Men', though that implication did creep back in.[78] Within this perspective, *Doctor Who* was conceptualised as an educational primer for children. From the very first discussion of a precise 'format ... at the BBC Script Department on Tuesday 26 March 1963' the classic series was distinguished via its time machine's proposed ability to go backwards, forwards and sideways into 'all kinds of matter',[79] though historical stories carried a hefty ideological weight insofar as they were freighted with the BBC's public service ideals. For example, James Chapman's cultural history of *Who* notes the 'moral seriousness' of John Lucarotti's scripts such as 'Marco Polo' (1964) and 'The Aztecs' (1964).[80] And Daniel O'Mahony argues that long-term *Doctor Who* fandom has constructed a prelapsarian narrative concerning these early, 'pure' historicals, adjudging them to be 'an example of what *Doctor Who* was like ... before it fell away from the initial instincts of its creators (which only appear uniform in hindsight)'.[81] Pure historicals hence represent 'a set of virtues invested in that genre ... high-minded storytelling, educational content and historical fidelity'.[82]

Set against these fan discourses, the new series has been far less wary of featuring infamous historical personages. Quite the reverse, in fact, as the production discourse of the 'celebrity historical' links iconic familiarity, the 'fame' of historical renown, to this newly formatted sub-genre. The term 'celebrity' in this context thus offers a shorthand for history (or history-as-shorthand); the crucial format element is *familiarity*. Time travelling into history should not alienate or distance the imagined audience; it should be 'pre-sold' in terms akin to brand recognition, hence being intertextually pre-digested. This is not so different to the positioning of history-as-genre-pastiche embedded in 1970s *Doctor Who*,[83] but it does mark out one key formatting difference. Whereas classic *Who* from the 'Hinchliffe–Holmes era' often premised its familiarity on other popular texts (*Frankenstein*; *Jekyll and Hyde*; *Fu Manchu*, etc.), the new series is less keen to annex its textuality to an array of predecessors. Instead, its familiarity is premised not on imitating pop-cultural predecessors or competitors, but on the recognition of specifically brand-like non-brands: historical figures. This is a 'safe' region of intertextuality for BBC Wales since it achieves the effect of brand citation, or 'product placement' if you like, without actually transgressing BBC guidelines on the matter. Historical 'celebrities' hence take on the role of quasi-brands in the new series. This absolves the show of direct commercialism, whilst also meaning that new *Who* can conserve a sense of its own original, copyrighted identity, since its format is not too obviously intertextually derived from other fantasy-adventure brands. The 'celebrity historical' is a textual solution to an implicit question: how can history be pre-sold to audiences without relying on other branded pop-cultural texts or seeming to surrender public service ideals? The irony is that this pursuit of familiar, pre-sold 'history' is entirely part and parcel of commercial logics. One staunch defender of the BBC's public service remit, Lawrence Miles, has acerbically argued:

> the modern [i.e. new series] *Doctor Who* historical can be seen as a kind of time-tourism. History plays up all its regional clichés in order to attract the casual traveller, without doing anything that might scare the crowds away or – God forbid – tell them anything they didn't already know ... [T]he more things change, the more we re-write the past in order to make it look as if they don't. Shakespeare is like a rock star ... while the teenagers of ancient Pompeii act just like teenagers from a BT commercial.[84]

The tourism discourse is important here because it captures Miles' objection to 'celebrity historicals', namely that they 'rewrite the past' as a version of the present day, giving the audience *faux* history.[85] Figured as a tourist attraction, history is reduced to the 'present in costume ... without ... historical particularity'.[86] Representations of the past in new *Who* seem to take on the role of 'heritage' icons, exportable in a global marketplace, and 'British with an eye to international marketability. National icons, including people (Charles Dickens), places (the London eye and Big Ben) and events (the London Blitz) [have] figured prominently.'[87] These examples from Nicholas Cull are all from the 2005 series, but later runs share the same tendency, with time travel into the past again being familiarised as 'in effect a tourist trip'.[88] Indeed, Russell T. Davies has indicated that well-known historical figures and events were used deliberately in series two to smooth over the disruption of replacing Christopher Eccleston:

> I was still aware of the Tenth Doctor being 'new'. By playing stories with both Queen Victoria and Madame de Pompadour (and with Mark [Gatiss] adding Queen Elizabeth II), I was making an effort to write the Doctor into history, to make him part of established events, to create the impression for new, young viewers that this Doctor had always been there.[89]

Tara Brabazon argues that at transitional points in the new show's development, Davies has 'wielded the safe and comfortable Christmas format' as a 'frame (and shield)'[90] against threats to the programme's identity (a change of Doctor, and new companions). Her argument is persuasive, but Davies has evidently not just used Christmas specials in this way. History, specifically the 'celebrity historical', has been similarly deployed.

This being so, Lawrence Miles' description of new *Who*'s time travel as 'time-tourism' does more than extend a simile used by the ninth Doctor.[91] It identifies a problem of interpretation: how can the historical Other – people and cultures from different times – be depicted, 'without reducing it [all] to the terms' of present-day understanding?[92] History treated as 'heritage', according to Robert Hewison in *The Heritage Industry*, becomes 'costume drama and re-enactment'[93] offering contemporary entertainment rather than education.

However, does this non-educational characterisation really exhaust the functions of the 'celebrity historical'? Across series one to four, *Doctor Who* has featured Charles Dickens (Simon Callow), Queen Victoria (Pauline Collins), Madame de Pompadour (Sophia Myles), William Shakespeare (Dean Lennox Kelly) and Agatha Christie (Fenella Woolgar). And it has featured historical settings without 'celebrity' involvement, presumably where the events depicted were assumed to be sufficiently well known in their own right (the Blitz, the coronation of Queen Elizabeth II, the eve of the First World War, Pompeii). To dismiss these episodes on the basis that they do not match up to the 'moral seriousness' of specific 1960s stories seems rather hasty. Academic John Frow has contested the Hewison/Miles style of argument, pointing out that this

> forgets not only that 'costume drama and re-enactment' have always been important vehicles of historical understanding, but that 'history' is always a textual construct; the question cannot at all be about the gap between representations of history and history 'itself', but only about the relative effectiveness, the relative political force, of different representations.[94]

The fact that new *Who* has sometimes deployed history as 'scenery for monsters',[95] and as a vehicle to articulate historically inaccurate sentiments, should not lead us to conclude that such representations are entirely without merit. It is, rather, a matter of 'relative effectiveness'. Tommy's relationship with his father in 'The Idiot's Lantern' (2.7) might say more about contemporary social norms than those of the 1950s, and the family interactions in 'The Fires of Pompeii' (4.2) may be, in part, stereotyped versions of 2008 identities. Similarly, both Charles Dickens and William Shakespeare are depicted as celebrities who tolerate their 'fans', selective representations which resonate with contemporary cultures of 'stardom'.[96] But these cases of time-tourism still convey researched details about their respective time periods, as well as capturing specific elements of social milieux and the lives of historical 'celebs'. Furthermore, the type of history drawn upon is often literary (though Agatha Christie's appearance is diegetically represented via her status as a 'bestseller' rather than as a literary figure).

However much history becomes a quasi-brand within new *Who*'s format, then, it is also linked to residual value-systems of education and the 'literary canon'. Unlike classic *Doctor Who*, the BBC Wales series has refrained from visiting celebrities linked to science fiction (such as H.G. Wells, for example), or 1960s Britain whilst a series called *Doctor Who* is on TV.[97] There is an established tradition of literary time travel stories in which SF celebrities are visited,[98] and TV SF such as *Star Trek: Deep Space Nine* (Paramount, 1993–9) has revisited its own earlier incarnation, *Star Trek: The Original Series*.[99] In contrast, new *Who*'s time-tourism is outward-looking – albeit skewed in terms of Britishness – rather than being generically inward-facing and rampantly 'meta'. The closest the show comes to this is 'The Idiot's Lantern' (2.7), given that it is a television episode about a well-known episode in the medium's history. Generally, pseudo-historicals in new *Who* have remained focused on 'intertextual cultural capital' rather than 'intertextual subcultural capital'.[100] The former are references to other texts and representations that have official cultural status, that is, they would be widely recognised as having educational value: the life of Charles Dickens, or Queen Victoria, or Shakespeare. And the latter are references to texts or representations that have value as a kind of currency ('capital') for subcultures of fans and audiences, but are far less likely to be part of formal education. Indeed, Dickens, Queen Victoria and Shakespeare would seem to represent almost hysterical, exaggerated versions of 'intertextual cultural capital', as if the producers were keen to avoid any accusation that they were 'dumbing down' by converting history into quasi-branded time-tourism. When new *Who* does, finally, start to move tentatively in the direction of a 'celebrity historical' with an overtly popular-cultural bent, then it dignifies Agatha Christie as an authorial icon, treating the character with reverence, and proclaiming her 'genius'. Here, popular culture is handled as if it is high culture, and as if Christie is paradigmatically interchangeable with Dickens and Shakespeare, given that she occupies the same discursive space in the format. Indeed, the episode's coda stresses the (fictional, intergalactic) timelessness and endurance of Christie's work.

In this chapter, I have considered how new *Who*'s time-travelling format operates. Genres cannot be owned, copyrighted or franchised by media producers, but by drawing multiple generic discourses into a precise format, BBC Wales' *Doctor Who* takes on its distinct, copyrighted and 'generative' character.[101] Just as Foucault's 'author-function' works to bring consistency and value to a set of texts, then so too does the broadly Foucauldian 'generic function', whereby genre discourses in cultural circulation can be drawn on, recombined, and threaded together in textually individualising ways (with this formatting process subsequently leading to recontextualised, extra-textual genre discourses). As 'intimate epic', new *Who* has sought to combine a 'close-up' focus on emotion and characters' private lives with large-scale, spectacular SF conceits such as alien invasions. Far from just being a science-fictional device, the TARDIS has become a genre machine as much as a time machine, a formatting vehicle for entwining multiple generic discourses and deploying historical 'celebrities' as quasi-brands. Whilst the classic series was also highly marked by generic hybridity, new *Who* displays a far clearer use of time travel both as 'emotional realism',[102] and as a distinct source of revelatory series-finale paradoxes. These types of time travel bring *Doctor Who's* format firmly into line with the TV industry norms of the twenty-first century, linking it to the increased presence of 'personal/emotional concerns' in 'soap drama'[103] and the 'TV event' of the light-entertainment final.

One important genre I have deliberately excluded from my analysis thus far is horror. I will focus on this generic component of new *Who* in the next chapter, considering how the programme functions as 'TV horror' suitable for a prime-time, family audience, and how monstrosity is portrayed. Kim Newman has argued, in *The BFI Companion to Horror*, that the classic series 'was often more horror than s-f'.[104] Chapter 4 asks whether this is equally true of the BBC Wales' regeneration, using academic theories of monstrosity to address the characteristic structures of new *Who's* scare stories.

## NOTES

1    Alec Charles (2007) 'The ideology of anachronism: television, history and the nature of time', in David Butler (ed.) *Time and Relative Dissertations in Space: Critical Perspectives on* Doctor Who, Manchester University Press, Manchester, p.113.

2    See, for example, Tat Wood and Lawrence Miles (2006) *About Time 1: 1963–66*, Mad Norwegian Press, Des Moines, IA.

3    Jan Johnson-Smith (2005) *American Science Fiction TV:* Star Trek, Stargate *and Beyond*, I.B.Tauris, London and New York, p.166.

4    Charles: 'The ideology of anachronism', p.113.

5    Ibid., p.111.

6    Ibid., p.121; see also Julian McDougall (2008) *OCR Media Studies for AS*, 3rd edn, Hodder Education, London, p.109, on 'Tooth and Claw' (2.2).

7    Charles: 'The ideology of anachronism', p.112.

8    See, for example, James Chapman (2006) *Inside the TARDIS: The Worlds of Doctor Who*, I.B.Tauris, London and New York, p.199, on 'Father's Day' (1.8).

9    Jason Mittell (2004) *Genre and Television*, Routledge, New York and London, p.15.

10   Lawrence Miles (2008) *'Doctor Who* 2008, week two: the past is another country ... it's full of bloody tourists', cited in *Doctor Who* Forum posting 5, 'At Last The Lawrence Miles Show', 13 April, available at *http://lawrencemiles.blogspot.com/2008/04/fires-of-pompeii.html*.

11   John Caughie (2000) *Television Drama: Realism, Modernism, and British Culture*, Oxford University Press, Oxford and New York, p.211.

12   Rick Altman (1999) *Film/Genre*, BFI Publishing, London, p.117.

13   See Stanislaw Lem (1991) 'The time-travel story and related matters of science-fiction structuring', in *Microworlds*, Mandarin, London, pp.136–60.

14   George Slusser and Danielle Chatelain (1995) 'Spacetime geometries: time travel and the modern geometrical narrative', *Science Fiction Studies* xxii/2, pp.161–86.

15   William J. Burling (2006) 'Reading time: the ideology of time travel in science fiction', *KronoScope* vi/1, pp.5–30.

16   Andrew Gordon (2004) *'Back to the Future*: Oedipus as time traveller', in Sean Redmond (ed.) *Liquid Metal: The Science Fiction Film Reader*, Wallflower Press, London, pp.116–25; Constance Penley (1990) 'Time travel, primal scene and the critical dystopia', in Annette Kuhn (ed.) *Alien Zone*, Verso, London, pp.116–27.

17   See, for example, Nicholas J. Cull (2006) 'Tardis at the OK Corral: *Doctor Who* and the USA', in John R. Cook and Peter Wright (eds) *British Science Fiction Television*, I.B.Tauris, London and New York, p.58; Johnson-Smith: *American Science Fiction TV*, p.173; and Daniel O'Brien (2000) *SF:UK, How British Science Fiction Changed the World*, Reynolds and Hearn, London, p.77.

18   See Mittell: *Genre and Television*.

19   Peter Wright (1999) 'The shared world of *Doctor Who*', *Foundation: The International Review of Science Fiction* xxviii/75, pp.95–6 (my italics).

20   Darko Suvin (1979) *Metamorphoses of Science Fiction*, Yale University Press, London.

21   John Tulloch and Manuel Alvarado (1983) Doctor Who: *The Unfolding Text*, Macmillan, London, pp.114–15.

22   Graeme Turner (2001) 'Genre, format and "live" television', in Glen Creeber (ed.) *The Television Genre Book*, BFI Publishing, London, p.6; see also Albert Moran (1998) *Copycat TV: Globalisation, Program Formats and Cultural Identity*, University of Luton Press, Luton.

23   Daniel O'Mahony (2007) '"Now how is that wolf able to impersonate a grandmother?" History, pseudo-history and genre in *Doctor Who*', in David Butler (ed.) *Time and Relative Dissertations in Space: Critical Perspectives on* Doctor Who, Manchester University Press, Manchester and New York, p.56.

24   Ibid.

25   Ibid., p.59.

26   Wood and Miles: *About Time 1*, p.69.
27   O'Mahony: 'Now how is that wolf...?', p.57.
28   J. Shaun Lyon (2005) *Back to the Vortex*, Telos Press, Tolworth, p.307.
29   See Fredric Jameson (1991) *Postmodernism, or, The Cultural Logic of Late Capitalism*, Verso, London and New York, p.284.
30   Ibid., p.286.
31   Russell T. Davies (2005) 'Pitch perfect', in *The* Doctor Who *Companion: Series One*, Panini Comics, Tunbridge Wells, p.47.
32   Barney Warf (2002) 'The way it wasn't: alternative histories, contingent geographies', in Rob Kitchin and James Kneale (eds) *Lost in Space: Geographies of Science Fiction*, Continuum, London and New York, p.18.
33   Lyon: *Back to the Vortex*, pp.363–4.
34   Altman: *Film/Genre*, p.120.
35   Lem: 'The time travel story', pp.141, 151.
36   Penley: 'Time travel, primal scene'; Slavoj Zizek (1989) *The Sublime Object of Ideology*, Verso, London.
37   Lem: 'The time travel story', p.144.
38   Ibid., pp.144–5.
39   See Lawrence Miles and Tat Wood (2005) *About Time 5: 1980–84*, Mad Norwegian Press, Des Moines, IA, p.199.
40   D.N. Rodowick (1997) *Gilles Deleuze's Time Machine*, Duke University Press, Durham and London, p.116.
41   Anthony Thacker (2006) *Behind the Sofa: A Closer Look at Doctor Who*, Kingsway Publications, Eastbourne, p.107.
42   Ibid., p.104.
43   See Steven Moffat (1996) 'Continuity errors' and 'Afterword', in Andy Lane and Justin Richards (eds) *Doctor Who: Decalog 3*, Virgin Publishing, London, pp.214–39, 304.
44   Lawrence Miles and Tat Wood (2004) *About Time 4: 1975–79*, Mad Norwegian Press, Des Moines, IA, p.66.
45   Russell T. Davies (2005) 'Pitch Perfect', in *The* Doctor Who *Companion: Series One*, Panini Comics, Tunbridge Wells, p.45.
46   Ibid.
47   Lawrence Miles and Tat Wood (2004) *About Time 3: 1970–74*, Mad Norwegian Press, Des Moines, IA, p.69.
48   Ibid., p.71. This places the character in a position of diegetic knowledge; what defines the Doctor, as much as his ability to time travel, is thus *his Time Lordly epistemological privilege* – i.e he *knows* when timelines are sacrosanct or otherwise.
49   Lem: 'The time travel story', p.146.
50   See Anthony Giddens (1991) *Modernity and Self-Identity: Self and Society in the Late Modern Age*, Polity, Cambridge, p.113.
51   Lem: 'The time travel story', p.145.
52   Johnson-Smith: *American Science Fiction TV*, p.183.
53   J. Shaun Lyon (2006) *Second Flight*, Telos Press, Tolworth, p.203.
54   Glen Creeber (2004) *Serial Television: Big Drama on the Small Screen*, BFI Publishing, London, p.115.
55   Ibid.

56    Ibid., p.116.
57    Ien Ang (1985) *Watching Dallas*, Routledge, London and New York, p.41.
58    Ibid., p.42.
59    Davies: 'Pitch perfect', p.45 (my italics).
60    Catherine Johnson (2005) *Telefantasy*, BFI Publishing, London, p.80.
61    Ibid.
62    Linda Ruth Williams (2005) '*Twin Peaks*: David Lynch and the serial-thriller soap', in Michael Hammond and Lucy Mazdon (eds) *The Contemporary Television Series*, Edinburgh University Press, Edinburgh, p.46.
63    Tara Brabazon (2008) 'Christmas and the media', in Sheila Whiteley (ed.) *Christmas, Ideology and Popular Culture*, Edinburgh University Press, Edinburgh, pp.160–1.
64    William J. Burling (2006) 'Reading time: the ideology of time travel in science fiction', *KronoScope* vi/1, p.7.
65    Ibid., p.12 (italics in original).
66    For familial readings of time-travel narrative see Gordon: *Back to the Future* and Wyn Wachhorst (1984) 'Time-travel romance on film', in *Extrapolation* 25, pp.340–59.
67    M.M. Bakhtin (1981) *The Dialogic Imagination: Four Essays*, University of Texas Press, Austin, p.85.
68    Ibid., p.84.
69    Ibid., p.154.
70    Ibid.
71    Martin Rubin (1999) *Thrillers*, Cambridge University Press, Cambridge, p.16.
72    Bakhtin: *The Dialogic Imagination*, p.95.
73    Ibid.
74    Bill Osgerby, Anna Gough-Yates and Marianne Wells (2001) 'The business of action: television history and the development of the action TV series', in Bill Osgerby and Anna Gough-Yates (eds) *Action TV*, Routledge, London and New York, p.28.
75    Wright: 'The shared world of *Doctor Who*', pp.78–96; Burling: 'Reading time'.
76    Russell T. Davies (2007) 'Three-volution', in *The* Doctor Who *Companion: Series Three*, Panini Comics, Tunbridge Wells, p.6.
77    Matthew Kilburn (2007) 'Bargains of necessity? *Doctor Who*, Culloden and fictionalising history at the BBC in the 1960s', in David Butler (ed.) *Time and Relative Dissertations in Space: Critical Perspectives on* Doctor Who, Manchester University Press, Manchester, p.68.
78    Ibid., p.79.
79    O'Mahony: 'Now how is that wolf...?', p.58.
80    Chapman: *Inside the TARDIS*, p.36.
81    O'Mahony: 'Now how is that wolf...?', p.60.
82    Ibid.
83    See O'Mahony: 'Now how is that wolf...?', p.63.
84    Miles: '*Doctor Who* 2008, week two'.
85    See also Charlie Brooker (2007) who instead uses the discourse of tourism to criticise the tenth Doctor's characterisation, which he argues is

'scripted as a seen-it-all-before smartarse' in series two (*Charlie Brooker's Dawn of the Dumb*, Faber and Faber, London, p.199).

86   Caughie: *Television Drama*, p.211.

87   Cull: 'Tardis at the OK Corral', p.67.

88   See the arguments of Jonathan Bignell (2004) 'Another time, another space: modernity, subjectivity and *The Time Machine*', in Sean Redmond (ed.) *Liquid Metal: The Science Fiction Film Reader*, Wallflower Press, London, p.136, with regard to H.G. Wells' *The Time Machine*.

89   Russell T. Davies (2006) 'Second Sight', *The* Doctor Who *Companion: Series Two*, Panini Comics, Tunbridge Wells, p.7.

90   Brabazon: 'Christmas and the media', pp.161–2.

91   In 'The Long Game' (1.7); see Steve Couch, Tony Watkins and Peter S. Williams (2005) *Back in Time: A Thinking Fan's Guide to* Doctor Who, Damaris Books, Milton Keynes, p.32.

92   John Frow (1997) *Time and Commodity Culture: Essays in Cultural Theory and Postmodernity*, Clarendon Press, Oxford, p.73.

93   Robert Hewison (1987) *The Heritage Industry*, Methuen, London, p.135.

94   Frow: *Time and Commodity Culture*, p.78.

95   Miles: '*Doctor Who* 2008, week two'.

96   See Joe Moran (1999) *Star Authors*, Pluto Press, London.

97   In 'Timelash' (1985) and 'Remembrance of the Daleks' (1988), respectively.

98   See Brooks Landon (2002) *Science Fiction After 1900: From the Steam Man to the Stars*, Routledge, London and New York, and Steve Lyons (2004) 'All our Christmases', in Paul Cornell (ed.) *Short Trips: A Christmas Treasury*, Big Finish, Maidenhead, pp.185–94.

99   See Chris Gregory (2000) Star Trek: *Parallel Narratives*, Macmillan, Basingstoke.

100  Matt Hills (2005) *The Pleasures of Horror*, Continuum, London and New York, p.179.

101  Moran: *Copycat TV*, p.13.

102  Ang: *Watching Dallas*.

103  Creeber: *Serial Television*, p.117.

104  Kim Newman (1996) 'Doctor Who', in Kim Newman (ed.) *The BFI Companion to Horror*, Cassell, London, p.96.

# 4

# TV HORROR:

# THE IMPORTANCE OF MONSTERS

Contemporary audiences and critics can, perhaps, be forgiven for assuming that scary monsters have always been the *sine qua non* of *Doctor Who*'s format. On the contrary, early classic *Who* was not always reliant on the representation of monstrous forces.[1] Wood and Miles argue that the conceptual shorthand of 'Yeti-in-a-loo' — that is, that *Doctor Who* is essentially about alien threats invading the familiarity of present-day Earth — has led to 'a monolithic, uniform conception of how to do *Doctor Who*'.[2] They point out:

> [The programme] lasted for the whole of William Hartnell's tenure ... without a single space-travelling menace landing on twentieth-century Earth. Beyond the three years of the Doctor's exile in the 1970s, only around 13 per cent of 'old' stories involve extra-terrestrials trying to take over, blow up, or otherwise consume the world, whereas — astonishingly — more than 45 per cent of the episodes made in 2005 and 2006 do.[3]

In this chapter I want to consider why the re-invention of *Doctor Who*'s format for twenty-first-century audiences has focused so intently on the representation of monsters. BBC Wales' reimagining of the programme draws significantly on horror genre discourses, hybridising

these with science fiction, comedy, soap drama and adventure codings (as argued in Chapter 3).

However, the horror genre typically has been linked with film and
literature, and its specific content has to be made culturally 'safe' for
prime-time, family television audiences. When the classic series drew
on conventions of gothic horror in the 1970s, it became subject to the
cultural policings of the National Viewers and Listeners Association,
spearheaded by Mary Whitehouse.[4] And the inclusion of relatively
graphic violence in 1980s *Doctor Who* led to the series' then-producer
substituting comedy for horrifying, violent elements after critical comments from the Controller of BBC1, Michael Grade.[5] In short, the horror genre and its affects have posed problems for *Who*, calling for an
exceptionally careful management of tonality.

The new series was conceptualised and planned for a 7pm slot in
the Saturday night schedule. Russell T. Davies has explained: 'Knowing
right from the word go that we were up against Ant and Dec on ITV1
... enabled us to make sure people didn't channel hop over to them.
Our *Doctor Who* is very, very, very Saturday night.'[6] As such, there
are obvious limits to the type of violence and gore the programme
can feature: 'Russell has rules he won't break ... no blood and no human doing violence to another human.'[7] These 'self-imposed basic
rules'[8] ensure that *Doctor Who* is never too closely linked to the horror
genre. Even if it does spark audience complaints (as did 'The Unquiet
Dead' (1.3) in 2005), its content can be defended as fantasy violence
visited upon non-human entities, without human bloodshed. There
is a modality defence in place: the violence cannot be read 'as real'.
Thus, certain expectations of the horror genre are displaced in order
for *Doctor Who* to function as 'TV horror'. For instance, in her study of
special effects Michele Pierson argues that the

> association that some genres have had with particular types of special
> effects can still be discerned ... Audiences have come to expect ... the
> makeup and prosthetics that give the gore effects in horror films their
> special visceralness and viscosity.[9]

This type of visceral horror is structurally absent from *Doctor Who*'s
format; where related genre discourses of horror are drawn on, they
are transcoded so that 'viscosity' appears on screen not as leaking body
fluids or gore, but instead as the bright green gloop of a Sontaran clon-
ing tank, for example (as in 4.4–4.5).[10] As Jason Mittell points out:

> Although genres are constantly in flux and under definitional negotia-
> tion, generic terms are still sufficiently salient that most people would
> agree on a similar working definition ... Discourse theory offers a mod-
> el for such stability in flux – genres work as *discursive clusters*, with
> certain definitions, interpretations, and evaluations coming together at
> any given time to suggest a clear and coherent genre.[11]

To function as discursively and culturally safe 'TV horror', *Doctor Who*
can only draw on certain elements from the 'discursive cluster' char-
acterising contemporary horror (film), whilst excluding others – its
formatted 'generic function' does not permit visceral horror, but does
allow for specific representations of monstrosity. In *Gothic Television*,
Helen Wheatley cites Matthew Sweet's discussion of horror in *Doctor
Who*, originally broadcast as part of BBC2's *The Culture Show*. Wheatley, following Sweet, suggests that new *Who* has 'embraced [the] ...
gothic ancestry' of the mid-1970s Philip Hinchcliffe–Robert Holmes
era.[12] And in the official tie-in book, *Monsters and Villains*, Justin Richards goes further back in time than the 1970s in pursuit of a 'template'
for the BBC Wales version: 'from the second-ever story ['The Daleks'
in 1963–4] it was clear what the Doctor did – he fought the monsters
... With the new series, the monsters and villains have started off right
where they belong – as the very essence of the stories.'[13]

This narrative views the horror-genre borrowings of the new series as a direct return to its former incarnations, whether of 1963–4 or
1975 vintage; a kind of 'Greatest Hits' approach to the show's format,
dialogically made up out of previously successful genre hybridities
and debts. However, such an intratextual view – classically fannish in
its mode of reading[14] – fails to examine the distinctions of new *Who*'s
horror-related format. I want to take alternative routes into thinking
about the prevalence of monsters in new *Who* rather than approach-
ing this as a textual 'essence'.

In the following section, I consider the 'double-coding' of monsters – where they supposedly appeal differently to child and adult
viewers, being interpretable as horror/satire, or horror/comedy elements – and the monster as 'visual spectacle'. Reviewing 'The Lazarus
Experiment' (3.6) in *DWM* 384, Dave Owen noted that it was 'textbook *Doctor Who* – showing the monster's point of view first, then its
killing extremity, before giving us the full monty'.[15] This links monsters
with the titillating visual spectacle of a metaphorical strip tease; the
gradual reveal of 'the full monty'. But to what extent does the new

series adopt this 'textbook' horror technique of offering viewers the monster as spectacular object?[16]

Finally, I link scholarship on horror monsters to new *Who*. Such work has sought to analyse the narrative construction of monstrosity, arguing that there are patterns of meaning linked to the genre.[17] I will consider how *Doctor Who* adopts textual strategies for articulating and disarticulating its monsters to horror genre discourses, questioning what it means to be 'monstrous'.[18] Throughout, my focus in this chapter will be on the generic debts of *Doctor Who* as a family-friendly formatting of 'TV horror'.

## Textbook Monsters:
## Double-Coding and Visual Spectacle

Before the return of the series, Clayton Hickman espoused the following philosophy of *Who*'s monsters: 'something Tom Baker once, rather astutely, observed [is] ... that [the programme] ... can be watched on many levels – from the youngest child hiding from the monsters, right up to the adults being catered for with, perhaps, social satire'.[19] In this account, monsters are part of the show's multiple coding, being aimed primarily at scaring the child audience. Writer Steven Moffat also links monsters to the emotional experience of being a child:

> You know, I've never come face to face with a monster in real life ... The moment that the monster appears, I relax. I *know* that it's just a story, cos you never meet monsters in real life. But while the monster still lurks in the shadows, *Doctor Who* looks exactly like my bedroom at night ... Look, as an adult, I'm not really scared of the dark anymore. I'm scared of getting ill, or global warming ... but traditional horror scares belong to childhood ... This is what *Doctor Who* does so brilliantly: it returns you to childhood.[20]

This argument is slightly distinct: adults can become childlike by appreciating the scares, and the suspenseful build-up, of the programme. Nevertheless, there is still a child/adult binary here, with 'real-life' adult worries and concerns not really being about monsters at all. As soon as monsters appear, then child-focused 'traditional horror scares' supposedly take centre stage. These scares are still, however, based on imagination rather than on showing viscera or gore of any sort: as Moffat has stated, 'We can't really show anything.'[21]

Of course, monsters can carry multiple codings: they can be scary, comedic *and* satirical, hence evading identification simply as horror-genre creations. The Slitheen most directly exemplify this approach, combining aspects of horror characterisation (shedding human outer skins to reveal their inner alien-ness) with broad 'gross-out' comedy (the exaggerated actorly performance of farting and burping jokes). And they carry political satire in the form of a '45 seconds' claim, echoing political rhetoric of the UK's New Labour government.

What these visions of monstrosity share is a belief in the 'double-coding' of the series' monsters. Rebecca Farley has usefully interrogated this production discourse:

> The theory of double-coding argues that ... texts have one 'layer' of meaning ... which appeals to children, and a second 'layer' ... which appeals to adults. Though 'double-coding' is an academic term, the actual explanation is salient for industry professionals. Double-coding is, however, a deeply problematic theory.[22]

Farley argues that double-coding 'relies on ... false binary oppositions' by dividing 'an audience into "adults" and "children", two (apparently) mutually exclusive groups with (seemingly) opposed tastes'.[23] She notes that neither category is, in reality, internally homogeneous, and that there is no clear, identifiable line between imagined 'child' and 'adult' viewers: a '40-year-old is just as capable of appreciating ... farce or slapstick as a 7-year-old'.[24] Steven Moffat's production discourses come closest to direct recognition of this, via the notion that adults can watch *as-if* they have returned to a symbolically childlike state. But this is one-way emotional time travel: children cannot watch *as-if* they have become adults, which leaves in place a child/adult binary that grants 'childlike' viewing to all on the basis of alleged regression.

This double-coding perspective is also apparent through the monster-as-metaphor approach of the new series, with Cybermen representing a vision of digital technology, Daleks coded as religious zealots, and the Ood representing enslavement as well as consumer goods. Even the Master is represented as an insane Prime Minister, giving the character real-world resonances with debates surrounding democracy and dictatorship. To an extent, the monster-as-metaphor was present in the classic series, but new *Who* has far more consistently represented its monstrous creatures in this manner. By providing almost every villainous race or being with a programmed subtext, they have become one element of the show that can supposedly target child and adult audiences.

The format of the new series thus relies on monsters conceptualised as a double-coded device for reaching 'family' audiences. Not a single story has been devoid of monsters; when such an episode was proposed in the 2005 series, 'Father's Day' (1.8), 'Jane Tranter's response ... was "We haven't got enough monsters. More monsters!" So we fed that back to Paul [Cornell] ... and the Reapers sprang into existence.'[25] The 'half-born idea' of the Jagrafess was also developed in 'The Long Game' (1.7) to increase the monster count for series one.[26] With monsters thought of as a condensation of child/adult codings, their centrality to the show's format becomes understandable. They represent one solution to the question of how to reach a trans-generational audience. However, as Rebecca Farley's argument makes clear, this is an approach based on *imagined audiences* – according to production lore, very little focus-grouping was done for the series.[27]

In 'The child as addressee, viewer and consumer in mid-1960s *Doctor Who*', Jonathan Bignell argues against the idea that 'monster stories are too scary for children', following work in media studies by pointing out that such tales can develop children's media literacy.[28] There is still a sense of the 'child' versus 'adult' viewer here, though it is based on developmental understandings of childhood. Bignell suggests that monsters enable children to 'test their own maturity at coping with disturbing emotions ... by gaining the understanding of modality (the conventions of genre and narrative...) which will allow them to ... manage these emotions'.[29] Monsters can thus form an important part of developing media literacy and emotional management, offering children figures that partly represent their own desire for power/mastery, and partly indicate a desire for adult rationality and control.[30] Bignell also suggests that the monstrous threats of *Doctor Who* are made safe through the programme's viewing context, including domestic watching and

> the peripheral culture of toys, play and consumption related to the programme and selected features of its imagery ... In the case of *Doctor Who*, it was possible in the mid-1960s (and also today) to watch the programme while playing with toy Daleks, gazing at images of Daleks, and talking about them with fellow viewers.[31]

This 'peripheral culture' has included *Doctor Who* spin-offs aimed directly at the child audience, for example the kids' magazine show *Totally* Doctor Who (BBC 2006–7), which included behind-the-scenes content regarding monsters.[32] For instance, actor Paul Kasey appeared in Cyber costume after the transmission of episodes 2.5–2.6, both representing the Cybermen as scary and simultaneously defusing this via his own humorous unmasking ('Why does everyone run away from me when they see me?').[33] For theorist Jonathan Bignell, *Who*'s monsters have always been about containing threat, about restoring a sense of control and safety to child audiences as well as giving rise to 'testing' emotions such as scares. Monstrosity is rendered usable for children, developmentally, through imaginative play.[34] Indeed, Russell T. Davies has used the notion of childhood imagination as an explanation for specific production decisions. In the contemporary context, this play is heavily linked to the show's branding given that children are likely to be playing with a range of official, 'Character Options' toys. It is also worth noting that 'children' and 'fans' are relatively interchangeable within this romanticist production discourse of *Doctor Who* as 'inciting imaginative play' (see Chapter 2).

The combination of Cybermen and Daleks in series two was partly justified through Davies' notion that 'young viewers would love this idea', having already imagined such a meeting, or played out the Cyber–Dalek battle.[35] Likewise, the finale to series four was discussed by Davies as follows:

> We like to make things bigger and better each year ... because I think that's the way a child's imagination works. Imagine if the last Harry Potter book had been low-key, with Harry battling only to pass his exams! Kids would have been up in arms. And me too![36]

Rather than children's imaginative play contextualising the text, here there is a sense of play feeding back – albeit again in relation to an imagined child audience – into the text's very construction. The series four finale also featured different blue-suited and brown-suited Doctor characters, meaning that children could combine these variant action figures within their play. 'Journey's End' (4.13) created an official, narrative context for the combination of discrete toy figures, just as 'Doomsday' (2.13) had created a textual frame for bringing together Daleks and Cybermen in play. The discourse of playing child-consumers is further reinforced by details in 'Journey's End' (4.13); though the Doctor and his companions are described as becoming 'the play-things of Davros', it is the DoctorDonna who diegetically plays with the Daleks, controlling them as if they were remote control toys spinning around under her direct power. At the level of connoted meaning, *the fourth series' narrative is effectively resolved by the Daleks becoming remote control toys*, thus textually reinforcing the brand-specific play activities in which child-consumers are imagined to engage.

If double-coding has been one production rationale for the new series' reliance on monsters, then another 'textbook' production dis-course of monstrosity has involved the monster-as-spectacle. It is this that I will now consider briefly, before moving on to examine how *Doctor Who*'s monsters can be understood via academic work on the horror genre. Speaking of the classic series, Miles and Wood suggest that:

> the sight of the monster was a 'tease', usually left until the first cliff-hanger. In an odd sort of way the monster took the place of the decora-tive girl, something there primarily as a spectacle and with characteri-sation a poor second.[37]

This gender commentary appears to refer to an influential line of thought in film studies stemming from work by feminist Laura Mulvey on classic Hollywood cinema. Mulvey argued famously that female characters were taken as objects of a male gaze. As a result, women in film have played a

> traditional exhibitionist role ... simultaneously looked at and displayed, with their appearance coded for strong visual and erotic impact so that they can be said to connote to-be-looked-at-ness ... The presence of woman is an indispensable element of spectacle in normal narrative film, yet her visual presence tends to work against the development of a story-line, to freeze the flow of action in moments of erotic con-templation.[38]

Given the cultural development and presence of feminism, new *Who* does not subscribe so obviously to the positioning of female characters as 'objects of the gaze', and hence as 'spectacle' to be looked at (though the pre-credits appearance of Georgia Moffett in 'The Doctor's Daughter' (4.6) arguably comes close to this, albeit un-der the narrative alibi given by the episode title). As Miles and Wood suggest, the monster can instead be seen as functioning in this role of spectacular object. There is also a tradition of this substitution in classic horror cinema, as Linda Williams has argued:

> A key moment in many horror films occurs when the monster displaces the woman as site of the spectacle. In *King Kong*, Kong is literally placed on stage to 'perform' before awed and fearful audiences. In *The Phantom of the Opera*, the Phantom makes a dramatic, show-stopping entrance at the Masked Ball as the Masque of the Red Death...[39]

And Catherine Johnson has noted the tendency for telefantasy narratives to progress toward a related moment of unveiling where the 'event or object which confounds socio-cultural verisimilitude is *displayed* through a visual set-piece'.[40] The place of the monster-as-spectacle is certainly acknowledged by new *Who*. The appearance of a host of alien creatures in 'The End of the World' (1.2) is treated almost as a fashion show, with different models being paraded before both the characters and audience. And the literal unmasking of the monster is visually built up to as a climactic moment, as, for example, with the Sontarans in 'The Sontaran Stratagem' (4.4).

Though the new series follows the template set by the original, it also shows a differentiated use of spectacle. For, given the rise in industry use of CGI, new *Who* does not only represent its monsters as FX spectacle. Repeatedly, CGI shots are used to reveal alien vistas and planetary environments. As well as spectacular monsters, new *Who* deploys these effects sequences in ways that augment, or compensate for, the visual object of the monster. To take one example, in 'Midnight' (4.10) there is – very unusually – no visual FX monster, this narrative function instead being represented entirely through Lesley Sharp's performance. But, as if to make up for this lack of monstrous spectacle, the story is set on a diamond planet realised through CG matte paintings, and treated diegetically as a fabulous vision that can only be unveiled and gazed upon by characters for a short time. Here, it is the alien landscape that functions as the show-stopping spectacle rather than the monster, established relatively inexpensively through just four mattes.[41] Similarly, 'Planet of the Ood' (4.3), relying upon the return of an already-seen creature, offers CGI effects of a snowy, ice planet as visual compensation for the fact that the narrative cannot offer a new monster as spectacle (though the final Ood brain acts partly in this way). And 'The Fires of Pompeii' (4.2) culminates in a CGI volcanic eruption, again augmenting its monsters with environmental visualisation.[42] This augmentation of the monstrous with world-building spectacle occurs in the new series format as early as 'The End of the World' (1.2), where the audience is granted the visual privilege of witnessing the Earth's (SFX) destruction.

World-building special effects are also crucial to 'Gridlock' (3.3). Though this story does feature a conventional monster – giant CGI crabs known as the Macra – it is instead the visualised world of the motorway that performs the major show-stopping role as sublime, objectified spectacle. And 'New Earth' (2.1) also represents the Doctor and Rose observing a panoramic vista, placing themselves, and the audience, in the position of the 'tourist gaze'[43] rather than Mulvey's 'male gaze'. Whether looking through protective screens, at TV screens, or out of the TARDIS doors, the new series recurrently positions its characters and audiences as tourists gazing upon environmental spectacle, as much as – and sometimes in place of – deploying the monster-as-spectacle. The 'textbook' monster, withheld and revealed eventually as a moment of narrative-freezing spectacle, is therefore only one visual 'show-stopping' strategy used in the programme's contemporary format.

In the next section I want to consider in more detail how *Doctor Who*'s monsters are related to, and disarticulated from, horror genre discourses. I will draw on renowned work on horror and the 'fantastic'[44] to argue that new *Who* demonstrates similarities and differences from horror's 'discursive cluster' of generic meanings. Specifically, the monstrous is not always a given category in the new series, instead frequently occupying the role of a narrative or ethical problem.

## Horror *Who*: Defusing Genre and Refusing Evil

A considerable body of academic work exists on monstrosity, but two of the more influential horror genre accounts are in Noel Carroll's *The Philosophy of Horror*,[45] and Robin Wood's *Hollywood from Vietnam to Reagan*.[46] I will start by summarising Carroll's account before considering how it might illuminate *Doctor Who*'s monsters. I will then examine Robin Wood's work in relation to *Who*, arguing that Wood's theoretical approach is, in fact, strongly reminiscent of production discourses articulated by the likes of Russell T. Davies and Steven Moffat.

Noel Carroll's work distinguishes between different kinds of monsters, helping us to remember that the equation of 'monsters' with 'horror' need not always follow: 'In examples of horror, it would appear that the monster is an extraordinary character in our ordinary world, whereas in fairy tales and the like the monster is an ordinary creature in an extraordinary world.'[47] Horror monsters violate the norms of the given narrative world, and so characters standing in for the audience – figures of identification – react to these entities as transgressive and threatening. By contrast, what Carroll terms 'fairy tale' monsters may be fantastical, but their status is very much part of the accepted narrative world, with characters reacting to them matter-of-factly. Horror monsters are 'impure'[48] in the sense that they violate cultural categories, but simultaneously they are also threatening.[49] For a monster to be impure but non-threatening makes it a limit case; in Carroll's terms it superficially resembles a horror-genre monster, but is ultimately fantastical without being horrifying, hence being fairy tale-like.

Since this is a fairly technical argument, some *Doctor Who* examples might help. One instance of horror monster 'impurity', or of the transgression of cultural categories, is a creature that is both dead and alive, such as the ghost, vampire, or zombie. The Gelth-animated cadavers in 'The Unquiet Dead' (1.3) are impure, as are the skeletal victims of the Vashta Nerada in 4.8–4.9. A variation on this would be the monster that violates cultural categories of animate/inanimate, with sentience being granted to inanimate objects, as with, for example, The Wire existing inside television sets (2.7), or The Weeping Angel statues of 'Blink' (3.10) moving when unseen. Another infamous type of horror monster impurity is the human/beast hybrid, such as the werewolf, as in 'Tooth and Claw' (2.2). This impurity is also present in the pig-slaves of 3.4–3.5 and the Slitheen, since they transform from human-seeming to alien by shedding 'skin-suits'. The Krillitanes (2.3) can also be categorised as this type of shape-shifting monster, and one might additionally analyse human/machine impurity, as with the Cybermen.

To focus on the opening episodes of series one: the Autons in 'Rose' (1.1) are horror monsters because they are 'extraordinary' or 'impure', that is, they violate the norms of the narrative world, being living plastic, and they are also armed threateningly with 'hand-guns'. In contrast, the entities encountered by Rose Tyler at the beginning of 'The End of the World' (1.2) are not all horror monsters. The Face of Boe might seem to be impure or categorically incomplete (a giant, disembodied head in a tank), but his existence is treated matter-of-factly by others, and he is revealed to be non-threatening. Though the Face may be monstrous in visual terms, the reactions of characters providing audience identification are peaceable and unconcerned, cueing viewer responses.[50] In Carroll's terminology, creatures like the Face of Boe are therefore 'fairy-tale monsters' rather than belonging to the horror genre.

Where Carroll's limit case is concerned – the monster that is impure yet non-threatening – he offers the example of 'Brundlefly' in *The Fly* (dir. David Cronenberg, 1986). Here, a human scientist, Seth Brundle (Jeff Goldblum), is genetically spliced with a house-fly, creating a man–insect hybrid that violates cultural categories. However, 'Brundlefly' is not always threatening; the character's girlfriend reacts with 'disgust tinged with sympathy and care',[51] cueing the audience to react similarly. Series one of *Doctor Who* also proffers this type of monster, in the form of the last Dalek (1.6). Before resolving to put an end to its own life, the final Dalek wants only to feel sunlight on its exposed flesh. Rose's reaction is not one of fear, but is instead a compound of revulsion at the Dalek's organic form revealed inside its casing and sympathy at the entity's distress. Christopher Eccleston appeared to refer to this script when he observed in 2004 that:

> [T]his great, cold, steel instrument of destruction, all that [Dalek] casing, all that armour, is actually to protect this very vulnerable, strange, frightened creature. So yeah, you can think about that on different levels, and think about what it is that actually frightens us. It's good to be aware of that stuff, but the kids can also just take it as read that the Daleks are scary![52]

And yet, at the end of 'Dalek' (1.6), the eponymous alien is *not* represented as scary, temporarily becoming a not-quite-horror monster. This, indeed, is also the narrative position that it is first accorded, being depicted as a victim of torture at the hands of villainous technologist Henry van Statten. We begin and end 'Dalek' (1.6) being cued, as an audience, to feel sympathy for the alien. As Nicholas J. Cull has noted, '[i]n a direct comparison between an American [van Statten], and a Dalek, the American seemed much worse and the Doctor said as much'.[53]

This process of articulating and disarticulating the Daleks from horror genre discourses continues across later series. 'Doomsday' (2.13) introduces named, individuated Daleks – the Cult of Skaro –

who are said to have the capacity for imagination and, presumably, empathy of a sort since they exist outside any Dalek hierarchy and are tasked with thinking like the Daleks' enemies. And episodes 3.4–3.5 introduce a further Dalek–human hybrid that can exist independently of the usual machine casing, and which begins to desire a peaceful co-existence with other life forms. Episodes 4.12–4.13, meanwhile, feature Dalek Caan as a mad visionary ultimately intent on manipulating the Doctor's timeline so as to destroy the Daleks forever. Though it can be argued that the Daleks have been updated for a modern audience in terms of their visual FX plausibility and connoted meanings,[54] they have also been updated in a further sense: they are no longer always and only horror monsters. The classic series explored the 'human factor' as opposed to 'Dalek-ness',[55] but in comparison the new series has repeatedly made the cultural classification of the Daleks – are they wholly monstrous? – one of its key, ongoing narrative problems. Even 'The Parting of the Ways' (1.13), which seems to use the creatures simply as a marauding horde of aliens, partly undermines this categorisation by revealing that these Daleks have been made from human cells taken from the homeless and the dispossessed. They are a version of us; a lumpenproletariat deserted by humanity.

The Doctor's most infamous adversaries – the monsters taken frequently to define the 'essence' of the programme[56] – themselves have no essential position as a horror monster within the show's new format. Instead, they are sometimes articulated with the horror genre (as threatening and impure), and sometimes narratively disarticulated from the position of horror monster, sympathetically humanised and personalised. The same is true of the Cybermen who also fluctuate, narratively, between the role of horror monster (man–machine hybrids) and sympathetic not-quite-horror monster (human minds and memories tragically trapped inside metal shells). And though the classic series explored this territory in many 'possession' narratives, the new series has linked it firmly to headlining creations such as Daleks and Cybermen.

The Daleks' iconic design may have been left largely untouched by the new series,[57] but they have nevertheless been coded visually in a different way to their classic series' predecessors. Post-2005, the organic, tentacled, crenellated brain matter of the Dalek becomes more visible: a vulnerable softness within polycarbide armour.[58] The original series represented this, to be sure, as a narrative threat in its own right in 'Resurrection of the Daleks' (1984), and with the sign of a destroyed Dalek shell in various stories. But the new series takes this concept of the Dalek creature *and gives it a face*. Now, the Dalek casing becomes a kind of connotative mask, a pretence to hide behind, whilst the creature within is represented anthropomorphically and more sympathetically as a distorted human visage. Indeed, it is a design strategy that the Toclafane (3.12–3.13) literalise, since diegetically they *are* mutated human faces inside machine-like, spherical cases.

Noel Carroll's approach to monsters is useful, as I've suggested, in allowing us to distinguish between those typical of the horror genre and those that do not fit its characteristic discourses. However, there are many problems with Carroll's account, and I will address two here that are especially relevant to *Doctor Who*. First, Carroll assumes that audience-identification characters will all react in the same way to a monster, but what if this is not the case? And second, Carroll defines impure monstrosity statically, as a violation of cultural categories. But what of monsters that dynamically 'evolve', like the Daleks, beyond their initial diegetic identities?

Developing my first argument, series one stresses repeatedly the differences between the character reactions of the Doctor and Rose, questioning whose reactions to the 'alien' Other are most reasonable. Noel Carroll's definition of the horror monster hence fails to capture these complexities of new *Who*. Rather than positive protagonists reacting in shared ways – a major part of Carroll's definition of 'horror' versus 'fairytale' monsters – here they react in contrastive, opposed fashions. 'Rose' (1.1) contrasts the Doctor's intergalactic knowledge with the hesitancy of Rose herself. Are shop window dummies really coming to life? David Butler notes the importance of this hesitation[59] in constructing what literary theorist Tzvetan Todorov terms the 'fantastic'.[60] Perhaps it is coincidental that this same word forms the ninth Doctor's catchphrase, but in its literary–theoretical usage, the 'fantastic' is a textual moment in which audiences are unsure of the status of strange narrative events. Weird happenings could be explicable in realist terms (it was all a trick, a dream, a hallucination) or they may be based in 'supernatural' explanations (that is, paranormal creatures are real in this narrative universe; there are monsters). For the duration of the textual effect of the 'fantastic', audiences are not sure, and do not have enough evidence to decide:

the text must oblige the reader to consider the world of the characters as a world of living persons and to hesitate between a natural and supernatural explanation of the events described. Second, this hesitation may also be experienced by a character ... [this] second [condition] may not be fulfilled.[61]

The different reactions displayed by Rose ('Wilson, is that you?') and the Doctor ('Run!') mean that the Autons, at least in their very first appearance, do not correspond with Carroll's definition of the horror monster. It is only later in the episode that these aliens are established as impure and threatening, and their narrative function as traditional genre monsters is fixed. Indeed, David Butler has argued that the construction of 'fantastic' mystery enables *Doctor Who* to work most effectively as a drama, suggesting that where it foregoes this device in favour of matter-of-factly introducing alien races or planets, then it sacrifices a sense of wonder, explaining strangeness rather than drawing audiences into its enigmatic worlds.[62] Ascribing to a similar view, Russell T. Davies has stated that the creation of an experience akin to 'fantastic' hesitation was crucial to his plans for 'Rose' (1.1):

I decided to bring back the Autons ... because it was important that Rose, in her first adventure, could consider the whole thing to be one big trick. If, in the first five minutes of the episode, she saw a great big tentacled thing ... she'd know they were aliens! But plastic, even if it's living plastic, can keep her doubting for a long time, while she gets to know the Doctor.[63]

This strategy for inflecting horror genre discourses is rarely sustainable for long. Once a monster has been identified as a real, narrative threat then hesitation is resolved. Partly as a result of Rose Tyler's newfound diegetic knowledge of monsters, the following episode, 'The End of the World' (1.2), took a slightly different tack. However, the Doctor and novice time traveller Rose continued to react very differently to the creatures they encountered, again confusing applications of Carroll's philosophy of horror. This time, the parade of aliens introduced to Rose (and the viewer) is not disbelieved by her, but the question mark that ultimately hangs over this motley, spectacular collection is rather one of motive – who is responsible for the deaths on Platform One? It is the Doctor who establishes the truth eventually, but whilst this mystery persists then the 'monstrous' status of the creatures is suspended, that is, they are not obviously threatening. Rose's inability to detect which creature is or is not a monstrous entity extends into a comedic sequence where she talks to a plant cutting as if it is sentient: 'I'm talking to a twig.' Discourses of horror, hinging on clearly identifiable monstrous threats, are defused into mystery and comedy. Unlike the Doctor, Rose is shown as not yet having developed the ability to identify forms of alien life, let alone which creatures are monstrous threats.

'The End of the World' also plays a knowing game with clichéd representations of 'the monster', since the 'Adherents of the Repeated Meme' are falsely revealed as the villainous party. Yet these entities look like generic monsters, being described in the script as 'cowled ... figures, faces hooded in darkness, like the Ghost of Christmas Future crossed with a Dementor'.[64] The term 'meme' is drawn from the work of evolutionary biologist Richard Dawkins (who later appeared in 'The Stolen Earth', 4.12). It means an idea that is culturally successful in replicating itself, thereby becoming dominant and widespread. In this context, the particular meme is actually an idea of monstrosity – the Adherents are standard ideas of 'the monster' extra-diegetically, as well as being 'just an idea' within the storyline. By making monstrous identity a question, or a mystery, rather than a given, this episode continues to deflect generic discourses of horror.

'The Unquiet Dead' (1.3) continues in the same vein. Like 'Dalek' (1.6), this adventure dramatises strongly different character reactions to the assumed 'monster of the week', the Gelth in this case. Rose believes that the Gelth, gaseous beings, should not be allowed to possess dead human bodies, whilst the Doctor views their scheme as interspecies recycling. What appears as a monstrous threat to Rose Tyler nevertheless strikes the Doctor as perfectly acceptable, especially if the Gelth are otherwise going to perish: 'It's a different morality. Get used to it. Or go home.' The identification and classification of monstrosity thus again appears as a key narrative question, quite unlike the horror genre's direct use of monstrosity as threat. And unlike Noel Carroll's theorisation, there is no one character reaction that can cue audience sentiment, at least until the episode's closing scenes.[65]

Resembling 'The End of the World' (1.2), then, 'The Unquiet Dead' (1.3) is somewhat schizoid to the extent that it problematises standard horror monstrosity, this time disarticulating the Gelth from clear identification as 'monsters', only to finally reproduce highly standardised, generic 'impure and threatening monsters' (Cassandra/the demonic Gelth). Yet the latter adventure places considerable emphasis on *debate between audience identification figures*, suggesting that the issues it raises cannot be foreclosed so easily.[66] It dramatises a progressive discussion and working-through of monstrosity,[67] before resorting to a reactionary template of alien invasion.

New *Who* dances repeatedly around horror genre discourses. It calls into doubt the singular character reactions to monstrosity posited by Carroll, and challenges static versions of impurity. *The Philosophy of Horror* (1990) views monstrous impurity merely as a matter of cultural categories being violated. But more dynamically than this, *Doctor Who* violates its own established diegetic categories. Though many of its monsters correspond with Carroll's definitions, there is also an entire class of new *Who* monsters which violate classifications inherent to the 'Whoniverse' rather than culture-at-large. These represent a type of monster not theorised by Noel Carroll, being wholly proprietary to the brand of *Doctor Who*.

Such entities do 'not merely represent the collapse of cultural classifications such as dead/alive ... but ... instead challenge ... established ... narrative classifications'.[68] These brand-specific monstrous hybrids have included Dalek–human category transgressions (the Dalek army in 1.13; see *I Am a Dalek* by Gareth Roberts;[69] Dalek Sec in 3.4–3.5), human–Time Lord category combinations (the DoctorDonna and the genocidal blue-suited Doctor in 4.13) and Dalek–human–Time Lord hybrids (3.5). From the major sequence of recurring, hybridised identities involved in the programme – human, Time Lord, Dalek – the only boundary-crossing not to have been represented thus far is that of a Dalek–Time Lord monster.

*Doctor Who* hence works as TV horror because 'despite being visually restricted in terms of gore ... [it] puts forward doubled or extended notions of ... [impurity]'.[70] *Who* does not simply remain at the level of impurity whereby Daleks represent biological/machine hybrids (violating these cultural categories), but goes on to further hybridise these established creatures with other diegetic categories such as human and Time Lord. Brand-specific monstrosity was even represented promotionally on the cover of the *Radio Times* during the initial UK transmission of series three.[71] This featured an image of the Dalek Sec hybrid above the question: 'Half-Dalek, half-human, total monster?' As Bignell and O'Day point out, the Daleks have become:

a sign used to advertise *Doctor Who*, as revealed, for example, by their appearance on the cover of the BBC's listings magazine *Radio Times* ... These texts took on an author(ity) function that aimed to supervise and direct the programmes' meanings and the ways that audiences would engage with them.[72]

And here, it is the meaning of a brand-specific monster – violating the Whoniverse categories of Dalek/human – that is used to focus 'public discourse'[73] on monstrosity as a narrative puzzle rather than a fixed category.

Robin Wood's important work on the horror genre has, unlike Noel Carroll's, pondered whether monsters can be portrayed sympathetically. For Carroll, a sympathetic monster ceases to be a 'horror monster'. *Contra* this assumption, Wood argues that 'progressive' and 'reactionary' horror can be distinguished, in social/political terms, through 'the way the monster is presented and defined'.[74] Progressive horror challenges metaphysical concepts of 'evil' and pure monstrosity that can prop up all sorts of cultural Otherings and repressions. Reactionary horror, by contrast, subscribes to metaphysical evil as a given, suggesting that innate, pure evil requires unquestioning exorcism or destruction. Progressive horror seeks to understand monstrosity, whilst reactionary horror uses stock ideas of good and evil:

> characteristics that have contributed to the genre's reactionary wing [include:] ... [t]he designation of the monster as simply evil ... Horror films, it might be said, are progressive precisely to the degree that they refuse to be satisfied with this simple designation ... The progressiveness of the horror film depends partly on the monster's capacity to arouse sympathy; one can feel little for a mass of viscous black slime ... monsters are by definition destructive, but their destructiveness is capable of being variously explained, excused, and justified. To identify what is repressed with evil incarnate (a metaphysical ... definition) is automatically to suggest that the only recourse is to strive to keep it repressed.[75]

Wood's work thus stresses the 'ambivalence'[76] that progressive horror can generate, as monsters are both horrifying and yet simultaneously draw sympathy. The cultural politics pursued by Wood are, in fact, uncannily close to statements of intent made by Russell T. Davies in promotional interviews. Discussing 'The Satan Pit' (2.9), Davies argued that:

we have never used the word evil. Never. Every script that lands on my desk, with the Doctor using the word evil, I send back and write, 'Come up with a better word'. Words like good and evil stop all interesting debate. There's no such thing. People do terrible things and people do great things. None of it's a disembodied malevolent force.[77]

One project of new *Who*, unlike the classic series, thus appears to be a consistent opposition to reactionary, metaphysical evil. However, Wood cautions against adopting the expressed intentions of producers: 'I certainly don't wish to attribute any absolute authority to an artist's view of her/his own work ... it is the work that confers status on the artist's statement, not vice versa.'[78] How, then, does *Doctor Who* (2005–9) stand up to Davies' expressed intentions?

It certainly emphasises the fact that 'monsters' should be given a chance to reform or reconsider their plans. Indeed, this dimension of cross-species (or cross-cultural) understanding is central to the series' vision of the Doctor. He repeatedly rejects the possibility of carrying out an act of genocide against the Daleks, refusing this in 'The Parting of the Ways' (1.13), 'Evolution of the Daleks' (3.5) and 'Journey's End' (4.13). Where he expresses such a view, as in 'Dalek' (1.6), this results in a mirroring of Dalek and Doctor, the Time Lord being represented, highly unusually, as filled with rage and hatred.

The Doctor seeks dialogue with the Nestene Consciousness in 'Rose' (1.1), with this act seemingly defining the format's approach to monsters. Such a textual philosophy is pursued across all four series. Even the Doctor's hiding from 'The Family of Blood' (3.8–3.9) is represented as an act of charity – leaving them be, rather than punishing them. Amongst others, the Doctor also gives the Slitheen (1.5), Krillitanes (2.3) and Sontarans a chance to abandon their schemes peacefully; as he observes in 'The Poison Sky' (4.5): 'I have to give them a choice.'

Rather than metaphysical 'evil', the new series recurrently offers narrative understandings for the actions of its 'monsters'. As the authors of *Back in Time* have noted:

> Our first sighting of Christopher Eccleston's Doctor is in the bowels of a London department store, and after that commercially-tinged entrance, the issue of money is never far from the surface for the rest of ... series [one] ... in the 2005 version the vast cosmic schemes that he pits himself against often seem to be grounded in the mundane motivation of financial gain.[79]

This is true for Cassandra, the Slitheen, the Editor and even Captain Jack when we first encounter him. Insurance scamming, amoral entrepreneurialism, big business and confidence trickery: all manner of fiscal motivations underpin the villains of series one. *Doctor Who* has rarely been so economically aware; one of the markers of Davies' vision of the show has undoubtedly been a greater focus on understandable motivations for 'evil' actions. From the very first day of filming, 18 July 2004,[80] there has been an emphasis on visual monstrosity as something that can belie sympathetic, peaceable and non-monstrous actions. This filming featured actor Jimmy Vee as a pig-like creature, eventually shown to be fearful rather than a narrative threat. Only the Doctor discerned this fact; military characters opened fire on the entity. Such was the fan-audience appeal of this poor, sad creature – dubbed only 'Alien' in the end-credits of 'Aliens of London' (1.4) and unnamed in tie-ins such as the official *Doctor Who* books *The Shooting Scripts*[81] and *Monsters and Villains*[82] – that his likeness was eventually released as an action figure called 'Space Pig', echoing online fan discussions. Space Pig is not, however, just an example of fan power; his appeal articulates the values of the new series – that monstrous appearances can be deceptive, and that 'monsters', whether Space Pig or the Adipose, can be understood rather than narratively repressed or destroyed.

This shift towards sympathetic monsters has also been present recurrently in Steven Moffat's scripts. 'The Empty Child'/'The Doctor Dances' (1.9–1.10) feature alien technology that is simply trying to repair people in line with its programming, mistakenly producing distortions of humanity. Likewise, in 'The Girl in the Fireplace' (2.4), futuristic technology goes awry by seeking the actual Madame de Pompadour. And in 4.8–4.9, people are 'saved' (archived to data storage) as an act of mercy rather than an attack, with the shadowy Vashta Nerada simply going about their instinctual business of feeding. Moffat's views on these stories resonate closely with Davies' format specification that 'pure evil' should be avoided:

> I think it's boring to say that something is just 'evil' – it's bad writing. 'Evil' is just someone who has reasoning you don't understand, and ... the Doctor is able to decode the universe from the other guy's perspective and understand what it means from their point of view ... And you've got to give the Doctor an appropriate thing to fight – if it's just 'evil', then all you have is a war, and the Doctor isn't much of a warrior.[83]

Moffat's scripts do, however, adopt different approaches to 'progressive' horror. For example, in 'The Girl in the Fireplace' (2.4), the Doctor does not fully 'decode the universe' from the perspective of the Clockwork Droids. It is only the audience, in the episode's final shot, which is given a clear understanding of this.[84] And it could be argued that the Weeping Angels, a highly successful scary monster from the new series, are actually Moffat's least progressive creations. As statues that can move only when they are not witnessed, the Weeping Angels are almost entirely dehumanized and depersonalized; they have no language, and thus cannot be reasoned with, nor can they be understood in their own terms. Despite this, the Doctor offers a narrative account of their motivations: they steal energy from people's would-have-been lives. Quite how this explanation could have been arrived at, given that Weeping Angels appear not to be able to communicate, is never explored. There is an attempt at monstrous motivation, certainly, but it seems less integrated into the narrative than is the case for 'The Doctor Dances' (1.10), or 'The Girl in the Fireplace' (2.4). Instead of posing a *question* of monstrosity – i.e. a monster that can be sympathetically understood and offered a second chance – the Weeping Angels are implacable, silent, and virtually unstoppable, edging closer to Robin Wood's account of reactionary horror. More so than Moffat's other creations, they resemble conventional horror monsters, monsters who have no role *other than being monsters*.[85] Arguably, the Angels generate some ambivalence through the notion that they are 'lonely assassins', never able to see one another, but again this is characterisation produced solely via the Doctor's impossibly omniscient commentary. Analysis of 'Blink' (3.10) suggests that a strand of reactionary horror runs through new *Who*, despite its professed, progressive value systems.

As a result of the production process and series formatting, this progressive versus reactionary tension is also apparent in Paul Cornell's scripts, as well as in representations of how the Doctor ultimately deals with monstrous threats. I have already noted that, at Jane Tranter's request, monsters were added into 'Father's Day' (1.8). However, monsters were also added into Cornell's scripts for 'Human Nature' and 'The Family of Blood' (3.8–3.9), adapted from his novel *Human Nature*:[86] 'The scarecrows came from Russell. The aliens were shape-changers, and looked like people. So a monster was needed, so "how about some scarecrows?"'[87] Each instance indicates the production team's sense of format: a monster is 'needed'. Despite human-seeming villains being present in Cornell's draft series three scripts, this was judged to be insufficiently spectacular. Animate scarecrows, however, enabled the format of monster-as-spectacle to be preserved. Likewise, 'Father's Day' (1.8) had the Reapers added to it, time monsters who repair paradoxes by wiping people out. Such script additions, sometimes resisted initially by the writer,[88] begin to create difficulties for the show's progressive values. Seemingly by virtue of their bolted-on and less developed textual status, the Reapers and the Scarecrows are mute entities, again strongly dehumanised, and both are highly reminiscent of Wood's slime example; they simply *are*, operating as forces of nature, or metaphysical evils. Each story seeks to avoid this implication: the Reapers are performing a useful task, but as with 'Blink' (3.10) we have only the Doctor's omniscient account of this, whereas the creatures themselves are represented as traditional horror monsters. They do nothing other than circle and attack, and have no sympathetic connotations or communicative capacities. In short, they are monsters self-consciously designed to be monsters, even down to 'POV shots of ... Reaper attacks [which] seem very old-school *Who*'.[89] This is hardly surprising, given that they were added to the text under the format injunction of 'we need more monsters', therefore lacking the narrative space to be properly developed.

The Scarecrows of series three are similarly represented as pure monsters; again, they have no language and cannot be reasoned with. They can only be stopped by their violent destruction. Yet the text struggles against this reactionary status by depicting the Scarecrows' mowing-down as a metaphorical portent of what will happen to the youth of the era when they go 'over the top' in the coming World War. This metaphorical questioning of monstrosity is achieved partly through the counter-pointed use of hymnal music, and partly via the fact that the Scarecrows are felled by bullets.[90] This is a more effective re-contextualisation of reactionary horror than the omniscient accounts offered by the Doctor in 'Blink' (3.10) and 'Father's Day' (1.8). However, although the Scarecrows are metaphorically, progressively depicted at the moment of their demise, the fact remains that their monstrosity is narratively exterminated, rather than reasoned with, leaving them perilously close to the reactionary status of a metaphysical evil.

Despite the prevalence of 'monster-as-metaphor' double-coding, as Jack Graham has argued, sometimes new *Who* monstrosity is removed from all metaphorical interpretation:

> The thing about metaphor in *Doctor Who* ... is that even as it allows messages about all sorts of edgy subjects to be smuggled in, it also puts an ironic distance between those subjects and the viewer ... In 'Turn Left' [4.11] things are quite different.[91]

In this episode, Graham argues, human foibles are not transformed into visions of the alien. Rather than monsters coding us, we are the monsters:

> The nightmarish, decaying, dystopian Britain in this episode comes from terrifying faults in our own selves and ... our current political climate. The sci-fi elements might power the story, but the story is about human choices, personal and political. The 'Emergency Government' might exist because a Titanic-shaped spaceship fell on London, but there's no hint that their policy of 'England for the English' (and labour camps for the rest) is actually being fed to them by the evil, mind-controlling Zargoids.[92]

This unusual treatment, absolutely in line with Wood's view of progressive horror, does, however, hinge on the Doctor's diegetic absence. These monsters are never dealt with by the Doctor as hero. Real-world political issues are raised, without metaphorical distancing, but seemingly *only* where they are thoroughly detached from any possible Time Lord intervention. This again indicates one limit-point to the series' format. The Doctor's battles against monsters must not be too obviously about real-world, contemporary politics; generically, the show cannot, will not, genuinely tackle the territory of the political thriller.[93]

This limit-point also raises another formatting problem of new *Who*, following on from the perceived need to include spectacular, double-coded monsters: how are such monsters to be dealt with? If the Doctor's character is represented as progressively understanding monsters rather than exterminating them, then what narrative resolutions follow on from this? Robin Wood argues that horror's reactionary tendencies involve the monster's narrative destruction, with 'the happy ending ... typically signifying the restoration of repression' as monstrous, metaphysical evil is expelled from the narrative world.[94]

And whilst new *Who* frequently displays the ideals of progressive horror, its narratives nevertheless characteristically involve closure in which monstrous forces are destroyed. This means the show has to find devices through which monstrosity can be expelled without the progressive nature of the Doctor being compromised. As a result, monsters self-destruct ('Dalek', 1.6), or the Doctor is called upon to display out-of-character callousness ('The End of the World', 1.2) or an equally out-of-character punitive streak ('The Family of Blood', 3.9). Alternatively, others act to destroy monsters in his place – usually secondary characters sacrificing themselves for the greater good. Extreme narrative contortions are needed to square this format circle, as with, for example, the TARDIS regressing one monster back to the beginning of its life magically ('Boom Town', 1.11), as well as an alternative Doctor committing genocide in place of the diegetically 'real' Doctor ('Journey's End', 4.13).

Such is the tension introduced into the show's format between a progressive hero and reactionary narrative closure,[95] that this disjunction has become increasingly visible. By 'Journey's End' (4.13), the text reclaimed these formatting contradictions diegetically, with Dalek creator Davros alleging that the Doctor used his companions as 'weapons' against his enemies, hypocritically keeping his own hands clean. Yet there is seemingly no other way for the Doctor's progressive status to be preserved alongside horror genre discourses of reactionary narrative closure. Davros' interpretation of the Doctor's 'soul' can be read as lead writer, Russell T. Davies, adroitly transposing extra-diegetic format tensions into diegetic character tensions.

In this chapter, I have further explored the genre hybridities and formatting decisions of new *Who*. Focusing on production discourses and academic theories of monstrosity, I have argued that monsters are central to the new series because they offer a way of 'double-coding' content for imagined child/adult audiences. Monsters have also provided one textual element of visual spectacle, albeit augmented (and sometimes compensated for) by the SFX spectacle of alien environments and worlds. Furthermore, new *Who* has been disarticulated from horror genre discourses not merely through restrictions on showing blood and gore, but also through varied character reactions to monsters, and via the construction of sympathetic and brand-specific monster hybrids.[96] This has linked the series to 'progressive' horror, depicting monstrosity as a narrative puzzle and generally seeking to explain monsters rather than demonising them as metaphysical 'evils'.[97] However, the show's format has contained tensions here, with the perceived need to include visually spectacular monsters, such as Reapers, Scarecrows, Weeping Angels, or even the Macra, introducing reactionary elements of underdeveloped, uncharacterised and dehumanised monstrosity into otherwise progressive production/genre discourses. Progressive representations of the Doctor have also existed in tension with reactionary narrative closures (that is, the expulsion and destruction of the 'monster'), leading to a situation where secondary characters typically are made responsible for these repressive actions.

In the following chapter I want to relate new *Who* to a further debate that has been central to TV studies – how can 'quality' television be defined: by whom, and for whom? Part III of *Triumph of a Time Lord* moves away from addressing *Doctor Who*'s generic and formatting decisions (or its Foucauldian 'generic function') to take in broader levels of textual classification (quality/popular/mainstream/cult) that have circulated, discursively, as a 'text-function'[98] in and around the series. It may be hard for fans and some academics to believe, but is *Doctor Who* really now 'quality' television?

## NOTES

1    See Kim Newman (2005) *BFI TV Classics:* Doctor Who, BFI Publishing, London, p.22.
2    Tat Wood and Lawrence Miles (2006) *About Time 2: 1966–69*, Mad Norwegian Press, Des Moines, IA, p.165.
3    Ibid., p.169.
4    See James Chapman (2006) *Inside the TARDIS: The Worlds of* Doctor Who, I.B.Tauris, London and New York, pp.112–13.
5    Ibid., p.159.
6    Russell T. Davies in Gary Russell (2006) Doctor Who: *The Inside Story*, BBC Books, London, p.35.
7    Ibid., p.37, although 'The Next Doctor' (4.14) involves Rosita punching Miss Hartigan and leaving a small trickle of blood visible on her face. The Doctor promptly declaims his disapproval, emphasising the programme format's opposition to 'realist' violence.
8    Ibid.
9    Michele Pierson (2002) *Special Effects: Still In Search of Wonder*, Columbia University Press, New York, p.102.
10   See Andrew Pixley (2008) *Doctor Who Magazine Special Edition: The* Doctor Who Companion – Series Four, Panini Comics, Tunbridge Wells, pp.63–4.
11   Jason Mittell (2004) *Genre and Television*, Routledge, New York and London, p.17.

12 Helen Wheatley (2006) *Gothic Television*, Manchester University Press, Manchester, p.71; see also Matt Hills (2007) '"Gothic" body parts in a "postmodern" body of work? The Hinchcliffe/Holmes era of *Doctor Who* (1975–77)', *Intensities: The Journal of Cult Media* 4, available online at http://intensities.org/Issues/Intensities_Four.htm.

13 Justin Richards (2005) Doctor Who: *Monsters and Villains*, BBC Books, London, p.4.

14 See John Tulloch and Henry Jenkins (1995) *Science Fiction Audiences: Watching* Doctor Who *and* Star Trek, Routledge, London and New York.

15 Dave Owen (2007) 'The Lazarus experiment', *Doctor Who Magazine* 384, Panini Comics, Tunbridge Wells, p.60.

16 See, for example, Barbara Creed (2005) *Phallic Panic: Film, Horror and the Primal Uncanny*, Melbourne University Press, Melbourne, p.ix.

17 See, for example, Noel Carroll (1990) *The Philosophy of Horror*, Routledge, New York and London.

18 See also Robin Wood (1986) *Hollywood from Vietnam to Reagan*, Columbia University Press, New York.

19 Clayton Hickman (2004) 'Revolution number 9: the Christopher Eccleston interview', *Doctor Who Magazine* 343, Panini Comics, Tunbridge Wells, p.13.

20 Moffat in Benjamin Cook (2007) 'Favourite worst nightmares!', *Doctor Who Magazine* 384, Panini Comics, Tunbridge Wells, p.48.

21 Ibid.; see also Matt Hills (2005) *The Pleasures of Horror*, Continuum, London and New York; Wheatley: *Gothic Television*.

22 Rebecca Farley (2003) 'From Fred and Wilma to Ren and Stimpy: what makes a cartoon "prime time"?', in Carol A. Stabile and Mark Harrison (eds) *Prime Time Animation*, Routledge, London and New York, p.151.

23 Ibid.

24 Ibid.

25 Russell T. Davies (2005) 'Pitch perfect', in *The* Doctor Who *Companion: Series One*, Panini Comics, Tunbridge Wells, p.48.

26 Russell T. Davies (2005) 'The Long Game', in *The Shooting Scripts*, BBC Books, London, p.237.

27 See Davies in Russell: Doctor Who: *The Inside Story*, p.35.

28 Jonathan Bignell (2007) 'The child as addressee, viewer and consumer in mid-1960s *Doctor Who*', in David Butler (ed.) *Time and Relative Dissertations in Space: Critical Perspectives on Doctor Who*, Manchester University Press, Manchester, p.51.

29 Ibid.

30 Ibid.

31 Ibid., p.54.

32 Other brand-stretching aimed at the child audience has included interactive *Doctor Who* play (e.g. 'Attack of the Graske'), made available through the BBC's red-button service after transmission of 'The Christmas Invasion' (2.X).

33 Broadcast 25 May 2006.

34 Bignell: 'The child as addressee'. See also Dan Fleming (1996) *Powerplay: Toys as Popular Culture*, Manchester University Press, Manchester.

35    In Andrew Pixley (2006) *Doctor Who Magazine Special Edition: The* Doctor Who *Companion – Series Two*, Panini Comics, Tunbridge Wells, p.92.

36    Davies in Benjamin Cook (2008) 'Everybody's Talkin'', *Doctor Who Magazine* 398, Panini Comics, Tunbridge Wells, p.17.

37    Lawrence Miles and Tat Wood (2004) *About Time 4: 1975–79*, Mad Norwegian Press, Des Moines, IA, p.159.

38    Laura Mulvey (1999) 'Visual pleasure and narrative cinema', in Sue Thornham (ed.) *Feminist Film Theory*, Edinburgh University Press, Edinburgh, pp.62–3.

39    Linda Williams (1996) 'When the woman looks', in Barry Keith Grant (ed.) *The Dread of Difference: Gender and the Horror Film*, University of Texas Press, Austin, p.22.

40    Catherine Johnson (2005) *Telefantasy*, BFI Publishing, London, p.23.

41    See Dave Golder (2008) 'Midnight', Doctor Who: *The Special FX*, with *SFX Collection*, special edn 35, Future Network, Bath, p.21.

42    See Scott Bukatman (1995) 'The artificial infinite: on special effects and the sublime', in Lynne Cooke and Peter Wollen (eds) *Visual Display: Culture Beyond Appearances*, Bay, Seattle, p.270.

43    See John Urry (1990) *The Tourist Gaze*, Sage, London, and Chapter 3 in this volume on 'time-tourism'.

44    In particular see Tzvetan Todorov (1975) *The Fantastic*, Cornell University Press, Ithaca.

45    Carroll: *The Philosophy of Horror*.

46    Wood: *Hollywood from Vietnam*.

47    Carroll: *The Philosophy of Horror*, p.16.

48    Ibid., p.32.

49    Ibid., p.39.

50    Ibid., p.17.

51    Ibid., p.40.

52    Christopher Eccleston in Hickman: 'Revolution number 9', p.13.

53    Nicholas J. Cull (2006) 'Tardis at the OK Corral: *Doctor Who* and the USA', in John R. Cook and Peter Wright (eds) *British Science Fiction Television*, I.B.Tauris, London and New York, p.67.

54    Chapman: *Inside the TARDIS*, p.193–4.

55    In 'Evil of the Daleks' (1967).

56    As in Richards: Doctor Who, p.4.

57    See Davies in Nick Setchfield and Steve O'Brien (2006) 'The Lord of Time', *SFX Collection* special edn 24, Future Network, Bath, p.6; Piers D. Britton and Simon J. Barker (2003) *Reading Between Designs: Visual Imagery and the Generation of Meaning in* The Avengers, The Prisoner, *and* Doctor Who, University of Texas Press, Austin, pp.169–70.

58    Polycarbide is the fictional material from which Dalek casings are said to be made in *Doctor Who*.

59    See David Butler (2007) 'How to pilot a TARDIS: audiences, science fiction and the fantastic in *Doctor Who*', in David Butler (ed.) *Time and Relative Dissertations in Space: Critical Perspectives on* Doctor Who, Manchester University Press, Manchester, pp.19–42.

60    Todorov: *The Fantastic*; see Hills: *The Pleasures of Horror*, pp.33–45.

61  Todorov: *The Fantastic*, p.33.
62  Butler: 'How to pilot a TARDIS', pp.28–9.
63  Davies in Richards: Doctor Who, p.11.
64  Davies (2005) 'The End of the World', in *The Shooting Scripts*, BBC Books, London, p.56.
65  See Alan Stevens and Fiona Moore (2005) '*Doctor Who*: The Unquiet Dead', available online at *http://www.kaldorcity.com/features/articles/unquiet.html*, accessed 27 September 2008.
66  Dee Amy-Chinn (2008) argues that the series values the Doctor's agency over Rose's more 'limited form of empowerment' ('Rose Tyler: the ethics of care and the limit of agency', *Science Fiction Film and Television* i/2, p.246), suggesting that Rose's failure to identify horror monsters correctly, for example by initially caring for the last Dalek, is a narrative '*cause of trouble*' (p.242) and leads Amy-Chinn to argue that Rose Tyler's feminised ethics of care are devalued when set against the Doctor's ability to see 'the bigger picture' (p.241). However, 'The Unquiet Dead' (1.3) and 'Dalek' (1.6) both complicate this conclusion. Both narratives move back and forth between valorising the viewpoints (and monstrous interpretations) of the Doctor and Rose, hence my emphasis that audiences may not always automatically favour one identification figure over the other.
67  See John Ellis (2000) *Seeing Things: Television in the Age of Uncertainty*, I.B.Tauris, London and New York.
68  Matt Hills and Rebecca Williams (2005) '*Angel*'s monstrous mothers and vampires with souls: investigating the abject in "television horror"', in Stacey Abbott (ed.) *Reading Angel: The TV Spin-Off with a Soul*, I.B.Tauris, London and New York, p.214.
69  Gareth Roberts (2006) *I Am a Dalek*, BBC Books, London.
70  Hills and Williams: '*Angel*'s monstrous mothers', pp.215–16.
71  21–27 April 2007 edition.
72  Jonathan Bignell and Andrew O'Day (2004) *Terry Nation*, Manchester University Press, Manchester and New York, p.89.
73  See Paul Rixon (2008) '*Star Trek*: popular discourses – the role of broadcasters and critics', in Lincoln Geraghty (ed.) *The Influence of Star Trek on Television, Film and Culture*, McFarland, Jefferson and London, pp.153–69.
74  Wood: *Hollywood from Vietnam*, p.77.
75  Ibid., p.192.
76  Ibid., p.80.
77  Davies in Nick Griffiths (2006) '*Doctor Who* watch: talk of the devil', *Radio Times*, 10–16 June, p.10.
78  Wood: *Hollywood from Vietnam*, p.130.
79  Steve Couch, Tony Watkins and Peter S. Williams (2005) *Back in Time: A Thinking Fan's Guide to* Doctor Who, Damaris Books, Milton Keynes, p.168.
80  See Andrew Pixley (2005) 'Fact File: Aliens of London/World War Three', in *Doctor Who Magazine Special Edition: The* Doctor Who Companion – Series One, Panini Comics, Tunbridge Wells, p.33.
81  Russell. T. Davies (2005) 'Aliens of London/World War Three', in *The Shooting Scripts*, BBC Books, London, pp.126–99.

82    Justin Richards (2005) Doctor Who: *Monsters and Villains*, BBC Books, London.

83    Moffat in David Darlington (2007) 'Script doctors: Steven Moffat – "I had to change the entire script just because of the title"', *Doctor Who Magazine* 383, Panini Comics, Tunbridge Wells, p.26.

84    See also Moffat in Jason Arnopp (2008) 'Master of the macabre', *Doctor Who Magazine* 397, Panini Comics, Tunbridge Wells, p.33.

85    These monsters were added as part of the adaptation process. 'Blink' (3.10) drew upon elements of Steven Moffat's (monster-less) 2005 short story 'What I did on my Christmas holidays by Sally Sparrow' (in Clayton Hickman (ed.) *Doctor Who Annual 2006*, Panini Books, Tunbridge Wells, pp.53–9). The lonely assassins thus appear to have been self-consciously created to perform the role of '*Doctor Who* monster' rather than initially being integrated into Moffat's storyline. Other reactionary monsters in new *Who* seem, also, to have been added as part of a compliance with the show's format, contributing to their dehumanisation.

86    Paul Cornell (1995) *Human Nature*, Virgin, London.

87    Paul Cornell (2007) 'Adapting the novel for the screen', available online at *http://www.bbc.co.uk/doctorwho/classic/ebooks/human_nature/adaptation.shtml*, accessed 18 July 2007.

88    See Davies in Jason Arnopp (2007) 'Worlds apart' in *Doctor Who Magazine* 383, Panini Comics, Tunbridge Wells, pp.17–18.

89    Dave Golder (2007) 'Father's Day', *SFX Collection* special edn 28, Future Network, Bath, p.52.

90    See Stephen James Walker (2007) *Third Dimension*, Telos Press, Tolworth, p.209.

91    Jack Graham (2008) 'Not all unconvincing giant stag beetles sit on the back: reflections on "Turn Left"', available online at *http://www.freewebs.com/shabogangraffiti/turnleft.htm*, accessed 27 September 2008.

92    Ibid.

93    See Chapter 3 in this volume on 'consciousness-raising'.

94    Wood: *Hollywood from Vietnam*, p.75.

95    See Alan McKee (2004) 'Is *Doctor Who* political?', *European Journal of Cultural Studies* vii/2, p.215 n. 1.

96    *Contra* Carroll: *The Philosophy of Horror*.

97    Wood: *Hollywood from Vietnam*.

98    See Matt Hills (2007) 'From the box in the corner to the box set on the shelf: "TV III" and the cultural/textual valorisations of DVD', *New Review of Film and Television Studies* v/1, pp.41–60.

# PART III

# QUALITY AND MAINSTREAM TV

Foucault's discussion of authorship marginalises the question of 'what is a text?' ... Breaking the cultural world of signs and meanings into discrete texts requires symbolic work on the part of producers and consumers – and this work has been highly naturalised in contemporary media culture precisely because the selling and branding of texts requires that they be symbolically bounded and set apart from their surrounding [TV] 'flow' ... [W]hat I'm calling the text-function operates (akin to the author-function) as a discourse of ... value ... Some television is discursively characterised as merely a part of TV's undifferentiated, ceaseless daily 'flow', whereas ... 'forms of "quality television" ... make a great effort to establish the firmest textual borders they can'. (Corner 1999:67)

Matt Hills (2007) 'From the box in the corner to the box set on the shelf: "TV III" and the cultural/textual valorisations of DVD', *New Review of Film and Television Studies* v/1, pp.46–7.

# 5

# THE 'QUALITY TV' DEBATE ... AND THE
# VALUE OF *DOCTOR WHO*

What should be counted as 'quality' TV has been much discussed in cultural studies, the history of the discipline being one which has led to a suspicion of value judgements. Partly formed against views of capital-C 'Culture', cultural studies emerged out of a desire to contest what it saw as 'dominant', conservative norms of cultural value. It sought to diversify the range of cultural artefacts that could be taken seriously and studied academically – television amongst them. As a result of the cultural politics underpinning this interest in 'popular culture', definite value judgements became highly problematic.[1] Aesthetics was viewed as a tool for imposing, and naturalising, the cultural authority of elitist approaches to capital-C 'Culture':

> [T]here are always issues of power at stake in notions such as quality and judgement – Quality for whom?, Judgement by whom?, On whose behalf? ... 'Subjective factors', which propose an equality of subjectivity for all individuals, are mobilised within a culture or society in which there is a differential distribution of the possibilities and capacities for individuals to generalise about personal tastes. So some subjective factors seem more subjective than others.[2]

In this critical analysis, Charlotte Brunsdon identifies different discourses of 'quality' television, including 'traditional aesthetic discourse ... professional codes and practices ... realist and moral paradigms, and entertainment and leisure codes'.[3] Here, 'quality' is neither purely subjective nor objective, but is rather the outcome of competing discourses, working via a sort of 'text-function' akin to Foucault's author-function.[4] The 'text-function' covers all those discourses of textual classification which exceed authorship and genre but which nevertheless circulate around and through a text like *Doctor Who*. 'Quality' is one example: though its discourses may intersect with the 'author-function' and 'generic function' they also move through many other realms – the 'uniqueness' of a text or brand, the extent to which other media and markers of cultural value are drawn upon discursively, the extent to which discourses of 'politics' and 'social reality' are invoked, and so on. These classificatory discourses ('mainstream' and 'cult' being further instances) are not reducible to either authorship or genre, thus requiring their own specific Foucauldian terminology.

Brunsdon goes on to argue that totemic exemplars of 'quality' attempt to side-step the complexities of these discourses by implying that quality is something that we can all agree on naturally. Referring to 'specific programmes, which can then function as shorthand for taken-for-granted understandings of "quality"'[5] creates the illusion of objective 'quality' TV, with common examples being programmes such as *The Sopranos* or *The Singing Detective* (BBC, 1986). However, it has been suggested that TV is often 'marked by ... the lack of an agreed canon about what is good television'.[6] Bignell and O'Day observe that arguments over 'canon' have cropped up, rather differently, in academic and fan communities:

> Canon, a term deriving from the ancient Greek word *kanon* for a measuring rod and later acquiring the sense of 'rule' or 'law', operates according to a principle of inclusion and exclusion, setting up boundaries around what may be worthy of study. The word 'canon' is often used by fans of television programmes ... to authorise value judgements.[7]

Whilst scholars of cultural studies have sought to resist canons of 'valuable' television, fandom has used canon debates to enact value judgements over what 'is' and 'is not' proper *Doctor Who*. Discourses of quality therefore need to be expanded beyond the range examined by Brunsdon, to take in the interpretative community – the shared, communal interpretations – of fandom, as well as TV industry practitioners and professional scholars. In this chapter I explore how rival cultural discourses of 'quality' have been related (and denied relevance) to BBC Wales' *Doctor Who*. I will argue that self-conscious concerns over 'quality' have played a major role in the reinvention of the show, with fan-producers seeking to recontextualise *Who* as 'quality TV'. This has not been a univocal pursuit, however, given that professional codes of quality are 'highly internally differentiated'.[8]

Quality discourses tend to be relational, that is, 'good' TV is defined against 'bad' TV. This means that where *Doctor Who* is granted 'quality' status, it is likely to be valued against other, devalued genres or categories of television. Alternatively, where *Who* is denied 'quality' status, this may be in opposition to valued terms such as 'social realist' drama, or single dramas/serials. Jason Jacobs has suggested that 'it is perfectly possible to admire television drama ... without necessarily devaluing any other kind of programme. Criticism that wishes to understand ... excellence does not require a bad "other".'[9] *Contra* this, I will demonstrate how bids for, and against, *Doctor Who* as quality TV use discursive patterns of 'othering'. First, though, I want to examine how the programme's return to television screens was accompanied by a concerted effort to articulate it with 'quality' discourses.

## Quality for *Who*?
## Production Discourses and Popular Memory

Classic *Doctor Who* has rarely featured in 'quality TV' debates, though Tulloch and Alvarado argue that the show was conceptualised initially, within the BBC's public service ethos, as blurring 'the conventional "high/low culture" interface' via its use of science fiction, a genre that could incorporate both 'serious' social critique and 'mass entertainment' adventure.[10] Even by the 1980s, producer John Nathan-Turner remained 'keen to uphold the "quality" reputation of the series, and continued to encourage philosophical debate and literary references providing that they did not "get in the way" of the pace of the show'.[11]

TV scholar Jonathan Bignell has, unusually, pursued this notion of classic *Who* as 'quality TV'. Noting that academic and industrial 'justification of quality in British television drama has focused on its social realist tradition or on its relationship with literature', Bignell points out that this 'has reduced attention to ... popular genre series devised and authored by teams of contributors' such as *Doctor Who*.[12] Seeking to reclaim *Who* as 'quality TV',[13] Bignell notes that bids for quality may not always extend clearly into the programme's texts, being complicated by promotional discourses, merchandising activities, and audiences' understandings and memories of the show.[14] This rare focus on classic *Doctor Who* as quality television argues that 'the persistence of [audience] memories of the Daleks ... testifies to another kind of quality, measured by the enduring effect of television and its embedding in processes of identity-formation'.[15] Audiences seem to especially recall the first appearances of Daleks in stories, embracing the cliffhanger 'revelatory aesthetic' of the original series. Such Dalek remembrances can be described as 'popular memories' of the show. Lynn Spigel and Henry Jenkins have argued that audience memories of TV programmes tend not to be of specific episodes, but rather of recurring images that are blurred together as 'repisodic' (repeated, episodic) memories. This produces 'popular memory', constructing 'a prototypical text' out of remembered bits of repeated business, for example, the end-of-episode appearance of a Dalek.[16]

Nevertheless, the new series' production team appears to have found itself up against a very different 'popular memory' of *Doctor Who* — one entirely divorced from 'quality' discourses, and linked to notions of the show as camp, frivolous fare, marked by silly, dated special effects:

> The perception was that it was a light entertainment show and ... was always going to be a bit shoddy and silly. 'We all very quickly realised that whoever we were going to cast needed to be an actor with gravitas and stature and somebody who was primarily known for their drama work. We wanted people to see that this was a drama.' [said the producer of the new series, Phil Collinson][17]

This form of popular memory may be linked to 'television's tendency to treat its own history as camp nostalgia',[18] but work on 'straight' TV reruns has also argued that older shows tend to

> self-destruct into ridiculous stereotypes and clichés ... achieving heights of comedy that displace their original 'serious' intentions ... generic specificity dissolves as well, from drama to comedy ... [as] heretofore meaningless (implicit, unnoticed) production techniques ... become visible and take on meaning.[19]

Clips of old *Who* in shows such as *100 Greatest Scary Moments* (C4, 2003), as well as repeats of the programme on UK Gold, may have contributed to continued brand awareness as well as a sense of the show's obsolescence. Rather than being positioned as 'quality popular' public service edutainment,[20] or as a celebrated audience 'popular memory',[21] *Doctor Who* and quality discourses suffered a parting of the ways. As Robin Nelson has argued in *State of Play:*

> When, for example, it was suggested that I might include the new *Dr Who* (BBC) in this book, I recognised that the much-vaunted makeover and success of the series' revival made it a contender. But, immediately, it seemed to me to fall outside my conception of 'high-end', *given its history.*[22]

Series one represents a powerful bid for restored links between *Who* and TV industry concepts of 'quality', a return to the programme's roots, albeit in a radically changed industrial context. It was 'authored' TV for the first time in the show's history by virtue of being linked to the author-function of showrunner Russell T. Davies.[23] But it was also positioned as 'quality' TV through its casting of the two leads, Christopher Eccleston as the Doctor and Billie Piper as Rose Tyler. Furthermore, the show used high-cultural intertextualities, lending it 'literary' prestige, and, through a reliance on science fiction as social commentary, positioning it as 'political' drama. Given that series one won a BAFTA for best drama series (2005), such a text-function has been highly successful in industry terms. I will focus on these varied production discourses of quality – 'high-end' TV/high culture/politics – beginning with the involvement of Christopher Eccleston.

## The Ninth Doctor:
## Traditional Aesthetics For and Against *Doctor Who*

The casting of Eccleston formed one of new *Who*'s major bids for quality. As Russell T. Davies noted: 'he's a very, very high-end actor in drama and I would have assumed he wouldn't be interested in doing a series of thirteen parts, in Cardiff'.[24] And as a 'high-end' actor, Eccleston's star persona is linked strongly to prestigious, challenging and political drama such as Peter Flannery's *Our Friends in the North* (BBC, 1996) and Davies' own *The Second Coming*. An executive producer on series one, Mal Young, argued that Eccleston 'has his own brand'.[25] His casting could be described as analogous to that of Patrick Stewart in *Star Trek: The Next Generation* (Paramount 1987–94), having 'the advantage of association with "quality television" rather than with the somewhat down-market science fiction genre'.[26] The star persona involved here is not quite as straightforward: Eccleston has appeared in horror/SF/fantasy material such as *28 Days Later* (dir. Danny Boyle, 2002) due to his working relationship with Danny Boyle, whilst *The Dark is Rising* (dir. David L. Cunningham, 2007) reunited him with writer John Hodge. And he has taken minor roles in David Cronenberg's *Existenz* (1999) and Alejandro Amenabar's *The Others* (2001). He works repeatedly with favoured *auteur* figures, suggesting that he would equally well have done *Doctor Who* if Jimmy McGovern or Peter Flannery had written it,[27] and going on to work with writer-director Joe Ahearne after *Doctor Who*. The currency of Eccleston's 'quality TV' profile is evident in his discussion of McGovern and Flannery, as well as in his recourse to the author-functions of both Davies and Dennis Potter:

> Like Russell [T. Davies], I'm a huge fan of television, and I really took on board Dennis Potter's ideas about television, with it being the place where the nation talks to itself; a popular, quality medium for debate and feeling and entertainment. That's what we have an opportunity with here [in *Doctor Who*].[28]

However, Eccleston does not simply connote 'quality' through his intertextual articulations with a raft of TV *auteurs* such as McGovern, Flannery, and Paul Abbott.[29] He has also chosen roles that are not only politicised, but are also critical of representations of heroism, exploring tensions within performances of masculinity. Pamela Church Gibson suggests that his 'gaunt face ... replaces the soft features and floppy fringes of conventional heritage heroes'[30] in Michael Winterbottom's *Jude* (1996), and Michael Eaton recounts how Eccleston was drawn to the 'more complicated, anti-heroic part of Nicky' in *Our Friends in the North*.[31] Even in *Heroes* (NBC, 2006– ), Eccleston played a character, Claude, who literally wanted to disappear and disavow his 'heroic' superpowers. James Chapman has also commented on the unconventional casting of Eccleston for an iconic TV hero such as the Doctor: '[His] screen persona has been identified as that of a "damaged Everyman".'[32]

Along with a performative distance from 'the heroic', Eccleston's industry position as 'high-end'[33] carries the expectation of a thoughtful, 'studied' performance, albeit highly naturalistic. As James Stanton wrote in *Dreamwatch* magazine prior to the series' return: 'One suspects that Eccleston will have more of a performance-based approach to the role.'[34] Alan McKee has argued that:

> it is the performances in *Doctor Who* which are usually identified as its most outstanding contribution to television art ... Most notable is the performance of Tom Baker as the alien Doctor. Of the ten people who have played the lead role on television, Baker is not the best actor in the sense of performing a convincing character ... [T]he role offers a unique possibility to be an alien: to refuse conventions of how people behave ... naturalistically and instead simply to be *charismatic*.[35]

Eccleston approached the role in terms not dissimilar from those outlined by McKee: as a 'possibility to be alien'. However, this stress on performance was very much *not* interpreted as a licence simply to convey charisma. Instead, it was read through a specific SF, filmic pre-text, as explained by Eccleston:

> I happened to watch *Blade Runner* ... It was the Director's Cut, and although I'd seen the film, I'd never properly watched it, and I was very, very affected by it. The whole thing you get with Rutger Hauer's character longing to be human, and all the stuff about whether Harrison Ford's character is human or not. I thought that was very moving, and in some ways it complemented what I'd been thinking about the life of a Time Lord. So I emailed Russell [T. Davies] with my thoughts.[36]

This pre-text[37] resonates, again, with Eccleston's professional interest in the anti-heroic, given that Robert McKee describes *Blade Runner* (dir. Ridley Scott, 1982) in his book *Story* as a film where the 'centre of Good', that is, the main point of audience empathy, shifts from the assumed protagonist, Deckard (Ford), to the antagonist, Roy Batty (Hauer), making 'what should have been a huge success ... a cult film'.[38] Eccleston's emotional and intellectual reading of what it could really mean to be a Time Lord feeds into key performance areas of the science fiction genre identified by Christine Cornea:

> what amounts to the highly stylised acting repeatedly witnessed in science fiction frequently operates to defamiliarise aspects of supposedly 'naturalistic' acting, thereby making questions of human performance

or the performance of being human integral to the genre. This is perhaps most clearly affirmed in the way that the ... genre has consistently
questioned what stands for 'proper' human behaviour ... often established in a comparison between seemingly human and non-human
behaviour.[39]

Eccleston's work on the series can thus be read as an attempt to
produce 'quality' science fiction whilst also delivering a performance
that combines intense naturalism and disruptive moments of stylisation. Throughout all this, though, Eccleston does not play the Doctor as a generic hero. And nor is the character quite approached as
an angst-ridden, 'damaged Everyman' figure. Rather, the key to this
performance – partly as scripted, but also extended by Eccleston's embodied characterisation – is an emphasis on *performance of the heroic
as a mask*. The ninth Doctor can stand off against a Dalek fleet, for example, but first the character has to limber up and adopt a heroic persona. As scripted, this scene from the end of 'Bad Wolf' (1.12) indicates
only the following: '75. INT. FLOOR 500/INTERCUT WITH SPACESHIP
DAY ... THE DOCTOR steps forward, foreground, to face the Daleks...
"That's nice. Hello!" ... The Doctor stands forward, magnificent; por-
trait shot. "No, cos this is what I'm gonna do."'[40] We are given a sense
that the Doctor is 'magnificent', and should be the centre of our attention: the role as written seems resolutely, generically heroic. However, Eccleston's performance visibly subverts such a reading, as with a
shifting of his shoulders, he codes this dialogue as a performance that
his incarnation of the Doctor has to psyche himself up for. This reading is in line with later scripted content, such as scene 19 from 'The
Parting of the Ways' (1.13): 'INT TARDIS DAY, CU THE DOCTOR, as he
closes the door, leans against it. All his defiance gone. He's terrified.'[41]
Here, the script indicates that the Doctor's defiance in the face of the
Daleks is precisely a performance.

As Christine Cornea notes, 'melodrama ... often require[s] the flam-
boyant playing out of unrestrained or overstated human emotion'.[42]
There is certainly a melodramatic or 'histrionic code'[43] to the ninth
Doctor's displayed feelings. Switching non-naturalistically into such intense performance enables Eccleston to convey the Doctor's human–
alien duality: he feels emotions with flamboyance, but his alienness
involves rapid shuttling between emotional states, including the capacity to adopt a mask of heroic activity. Embedding emotion in cycles
of non-naturalistic switching means that the ninth Doctor is seemingly

stylised, rather than becoming a fully 'verisimilar' performance. In *Eloquent Gestures*, a study of historical acting styles in film, Roberta Pearson argues that histrionic performance codes work in the service of narrative, whilst 'verisimilar' performance codes convey character psychology in depth and are linked to 'realist' narrative.[44] 'Verisimilar' acting codes, I would argue, have been linked to 'quality TV', with histrionic acting codes being devalued as excessive, 'obvious' and rigidly coded acting. However, given that the ninth Doctor displays 'histrionic' or melodramatic outbursts within a pattern of suppression and release, it could be argued that this ultimately serves a 'verisimilar' agenda – that we, as an audience, come to understand the character's psychology. Despite the science-fictional non-naturalism of the Doctor's alienness and psychological oscillation, these operate ultimately in the service of emotional realism.

It might be assumed that Eccleston's casting worked univocally to construct the programme as 'quality' TV, but this was not the case. In some publicity material, rather than *Who* being recontextualised as 'quality', it was the programme itself that was 'othered' as low-cultural and non-quality. Here, the contrast was between 'serial' or one-off TV drama and *Doctor Who* as ongoing 'series' drama. And the proponent of this devaluing discourse – radically out of alignment with all other production discourses – was Christopher Eccleston himself. Drawing on his professional association with authored, prestige TV, Eccleston suggested that:

> There's a kind of madness when you essentially do the same thing in each episode ... the Doctor ... does the same thing every episode, he saves the world. And half way through this ... I found myself doing something very similar to the thing I'd done the episode before, and I got the fear 'cause you think 'am I simply repeating myself'. So, the previous work I've done, it's always been 'beginning, middle and end' drama, and this is a different animal.[45]

By nominating himself as a 'quality' actor in opposition to *Doctor Who*, rather than in support of the brand, Eccleston effectively inverted the show's discursive production bid for 'quality' as based upon his own star persona. For an actor to adopt such an oppositional discourse is highly unusual, and can be read as symptomatic of strained relations between Eccleston and the BBC. Two days after the final broadcast of *Project: Who*,[46] the Beeb issued a press release confirming that

Eccleston would be leaving the show, containing a supposedly direct quotation from the actor. On 4 April 2005, an apology was issued by the BBC on behalf of Head of Drama, Jane Tranter:

> The BBC regrets not speaking to Christopher before it responded to the press questions on Wednesday 30 March 2005 ... The BBC further regrets that it falsely attributed a statement to Christopher and apologises to him ... Contrary to press statements, Christopher did not leave for fear of being typecast or because of the gruelling filming schedule.[47]

Prior to this, Eccleston was already distancing himself from the role of the Doctor, drawing on the discourse of traditional aesthetics to do so. This discourse stresses the cultural value of 'stylistic coherence'[48] and textual cohesion in 'quality TV'.[49] *Contra* such 'coherence', Eccleston positioned *Who* as formulaic and repetitive, with the Doctor just repeating the same bits of behaviour. This apparently posed a challenge to him, as a 'quality' actor: 'to keep essentially doing the same thing, but keeping it fresh. To keep stepping into the TARDIS, delivering some pseudo-science ... Doing that thirteen times and trying to keep it original.'[50] As well as arguably being premised on sameness, rather than displaying the aesthetic development of 'beginning, middle, and end' drama, Eccleston also suggests that there is no organic whole or character consistency for him to latch on to: 'I learn things about the Doctor's character when the scripts land on my floor, through my letter-box, when I'm filming another episode ... Throw enough shit at the wall and some of it will stick.'[51] Again, this discursively assumed lack of textual unity violates the terms of 'traditional aesthetics', with Eccleston's profanity clearly devaluing *Doctor Who* as non-quality, 'popular' TV.

It has been argued by a number of TV scholars that television, especially cult TV, generates massive overlap between stars and characters, since 'subsidiary forms of circulation of cult television stars privilege the character over the actor'.[52] This 'character/actor join'[53] supposedly leads to typecasting, but Sara Gwenllian Jones has pointed out that publicity discourses can just as well involve constructions of difference, emphasising character/actor distinctions.[54] Eccleston's discursive separation of himself as a 'high-end' actor versus alleged script repetitions of *Doctor Who* is one extreme 'discourse of difference'. Tulloch and Alvarado ponder whether 'the frequent replacement of the star has laid stress on the *idea* of the character [of the Doctor] rather than on the star persona' of the actor playing him;[55] Eccleston's anti-quality discourse also implies that the Doctor is more of an 'idea' rather than a developing, psychologically real and consistent 'person' in line with the naturalism of 'quality TV'.[56]

Working against Eccleston's anti-quality discourses from *Project: Who*, Gareth Roberts has argued that the ninth Doctor was quite possibly the first to be realised via developed character psychology:

> the character of the Ninth Doctor ... feels all but complete ... This is, in no small part, down to the new series' emphasis on the characterisation of its two leads rather than the relentless pile-driving plot-driven nature of the original series, where characters – even the Doctor – often performed narrative functions in response to the stories rather than being part of them.[57]

In this argument, Eccleston's 'performance-driven approach' – despite his own, eventual anti-quality protestations – consistently embodied character psychology. For example, after his 'turn of the Earth' speech in 'Rose' (1.1), Eccleston's scripted behaviour runs as follows: '"That's who I am. Now forget me, Rose Tyler. Go home." He takes the plastic arm off her, turns and walks away.'[58] As performed in the final version, however, Eccleston adds in a verisimilar bit of business with the Auton arm, taking it from Rose and using it to wave goodbye in time with the dialogue 'Go home.' What the script gives as narrative information, that is, that the Doctor has to retrieve this alien artefact, is thus layered with additional performance detail. Here, the performed gesture gives emphasis to the Doctor's request, punctuating dialogue, but also serves to introduce a lighter moment (a prop-based instant of silliness and child-like play) into what is otherwise an earnest, dialogue-driven scene. As the sequence cuts to Eccleston walking away from Rose, the actor's face is set in a pensive expression, again marking rapid tonal variation and emotional switching.

Such visible moments of 'kidult' playfulness[59] link acting performance to 'quality TV' through psychological realism. Like Eccleston's performance decisions to stress the Doctor's performative adoption of heroism, and intensify the character's contrastive emotional undercurrents, such performance details draw on a 'quality tradition' of rapid shifts in tone, juxtaposing 'moments of comedy with scenes of high seriousness'.[60] Executive Producer Julie Gardner draws on this production discourse of quality TV when she notes that 'we thought it would be really interesting to take such a good actor and put him in situations that are often incredibly comic but can flip into something quite dangerous quite quickly'.[61] Tonal variation has also been viewed as part of the 'quality TV' status of *Buffy the Vampire Slayer*,[62] a show which, it has been argued, new *Who* draws on as part of the cultural interplay between the US and UK TV industries and constructions of 'quality'.[63]

In BBC Wales' *Doctor Who*, tonal variation is frequently realised not only through scripting but also through the 'serious acting pyrotechnics' involved in 'precise, very distinct change[s]' in emotional intensity/control, seriousness/comedy, and good/evil.[64] Guest stars such as Derek Jacobi in 'Utopia' (3.11) have also demonstrated this, following in a tradition of classic series' guest casting as part of a production bid for 'quality' and cultural value:

> This trend in *Doctor Who* guest stars we might call part of its 'edutainment' remit ... we see lurking throughout its history a desire to teach its audience about high culture: the Doctor is forever boasting about his meetings with Shakespeare and Leonardo da Vinci ... The Count's collection of 'priceless' artefacts [in 1979's 'City of Death'] includes Shakespeare's first draft of 'Hamlet', from which the Doctor reads ... In the same way, Shakespearean actors regularly guest star ... adding their cultural authority to the enterprise.[65]

New *Who*'s guest actors have also repeatedly been drawn from the arena of British 'quality TV', with a wide range of performers having previously appeared in the likes of *Blackpool* (BBC, 2004); *Clocking Off* (BBC, 2000–3); *Shameless* (C4, 2004– ); *Linda Green* (BBC, 2001–2); *State of Play* (BBC, 2003); and *The Street* (Granada/BBC, 2006–9). One might expect some overlap between these shows, but *Doctor Who* is now, in industry terms, very much on a level with social-realist BAFTA winners like *The Street* and *Shameless*, programmes that won the Best Drama Series award immediately before and after *Who*'s 2005 victory. Only in series three and four – with the show having already won a BAFTA and multiple Welsh BAFTAs – did casting start to become more star-led. Kylie Minogue's appearance in 'Voyage of the Damned' (4.X), and Catherine Tate's return in series four both represented a type of 'iconic' casting for the series, the implication being that *Doctor Who* was now an icon that could hold its own against other pop-cultural icons. This 'meeting of icons'[66] draws on a competing, differentiated industry discourse of 'quality', however, one which interprets the 'blockbuster' cultural omnipresence and reach of a TV show as a sign of its cultural value. Such an approach to 'quality' is more ratings-led, falling closer to quantitative 'measures' of 'the popular' rather than drawing on aesthetic concepts of quality.

For a SF-adventure series to reside in this TV industry 'high-end' and 'blockbuster' context is remarkable, and is not something one could readily observe of classic *Doctor Who*. There, as Alan McKee argues, guest casting formed part of a bid for 'quality'. New *Who*, however, typically carries this logic of 'quality' casting through into its lead roles. Although Billie Piper had formerly been a pop star, she also offered the new series an emerging 'quality TV' identity, rather than Eccleston's firmly established, consecrated position. Piper had previously appeared in the BAFTA-winning *Canterbury Tales* (BBC, 2003), and would go on to develop this 'high-end' TV drama profile by appearing in *Shakespeare Retold* (BBC, 2005) between *Doctor Who* series one and two. However, this Shakespearean construction of the show's 'literary' status was also developed further via its second casting of the Doctor.

## The Tenth Doctor:
## High-Cultural Value For and Against *Doctor Who*

David Tennant's hiring, like Eccleston's, was seemingly of a piece with production discourses of 'quality' based on securing 'the best of British acting'.[67] Tennant links the series more firmly to theatrical, Shakespearean high culture as an RSC-trained actor, whereas Eccleston's star persona had carried stronger connotations of 'high-end' TV. Interviewed in *DWM* in 2005, Tennant compared TV work to his RSC career, noting that 'if you're a fan of the RSC, you'd be aware of it', and leading his interviewer Clayton Hickman to playfully elide Shakespeare and *Doctor Who* fandom in the form of an invented '*RSCM*'.[68]

If David Tennant brought an emergent 'high-cultural'/RSC quality intertext to *Doctor Who* – something that in the past had been the function of guest stars rather than the lead actor – then his simultaneous cultural status as both 'the Doctor' and 'Hamlet' in 2008 seemingly posed a cultural threat to the RSC. Whereas Tennant developed the 'quality' profile of *Doctor Who*, he conversely appeared to bring discourses of 'TV celebrity', science-fiction fandom, and 'dumbing down' to the institution of the Royal Shakespeare Company. Interviewed by right-wing broadsheet the *Daily Telegraph*, the director of *Hamlet*, Gregory Doran, noted of *Who* that he had 'watched it as a child ... And I watched the episode about Shakespeare's lost play ['The Shakespeare Code' (3.2)], which was fantastic. But I stopped watching it when I was about 10, really, which is probably healthy.'[69]

*Doctor Who* is devalued here, positioned negatively as a childish text. Doran also disavows the programme's importance in his RSC casting of Tennant, arguing that the actor's appearance in a genealogical TV show *Who Do You Think You Are?* (BBC, 2004– ) was more influential.[70] Rather than downplaying a populist rationale for Tennant's casting, Doran directly refutes any such possibility, and represents himself, and *Hamlet*, against the devalued 'pop culture' of *Doctor Who*. This form of 'anti-quality' argument is, again, based on highly traditional aesthetic discourses: Shakespeare is the apotheosis of capital-C 'Culture', whereas *Doctor Who* is about TV celebrity and selling product. Rather than the RSC being implicated in any such commercial logic, the *Daily Telegraph* projects this onto an 'othered' low-cultural enterprise:

> The fish and chip shop just along the way from the Courtyard Theatre in Stratford-upon-Avon hasn't missed a trick: one of its windows is home to a giant poster of a Dalek – emblazoned with the words 'Exterminate Your Hunger'. Gregory Doran nods in recognition when I mention this, his expression wavering on the edge of a grimace before settling into a tense grin as he says: 'I went in and asked them, "Why have you got that up?" They said, "Don't you know? Doctor Who is in town!"'[71]

'Cashing in' on Tennant's link to the success of the show is, in this discursive frame, not an activity undertaken by the RSC. However, John Tulloch has argued that contemporary theatre, the RSC included, routinely markets itself to audiences through 'star-driven' approaches,[72] given that 'the RSC post-Thatcher is forced to think commercially, adding to its "company idea" what Sir Peter Hall has called "short-termism and ... one-off, TV-dominated casting"'.[73] Despite this theatre industry context, where the RSC is both 'cultural' and 'commercial', Gregory Doran is represented journalistically as being unconcerned with 'whatever motives may have driven punters to snap up all available tickets for *Hamlet*'.[74] His focus is purely artistic and Shakespearean, discursively devoid of commerce, and strongly defensive of a series of conservative binaries: quality versus popular; theatre versus TV; and Shakespeare versus *Doctor Who*.[75]

Shakespeare is conceptualised, in high-cultural terms, as a blocking-out of celebrity discourse, and as a 'haven' from 'sci-fi nutters'. *Daily Telegraph* arts journalist Dominic Cavendish curiously neglects to consider that David Tennant is himself a life-long *Doctor Who* fan. Such reportage draws on negative stereotypes of science-fiction fandom that cultural studies has spent the last 16 years or so challenging. Further press coverage of Tennant's RSC appearance announced that there was a '*Doctor Who* signing ban at *Hamlet*', implying that marauding hordes of *Who* fans might over-run the RSC, but also reinforcing the centrality of the RSC brand to the event, since 'only Royal Shakespeare Company or production-related memorabilia will be signed by members of the Company'.[76]

Despite Doran's 'anti-quality' devaluation of *Who*, his assessment of what Tennant brings to the role of Hamlet is closely related to the star persona established by the actor in both *Casanova* and *Doctor Who*. Tennant's 'estuary' vocal performance and several bits of character business, including theatrical exclamations of 'Oh yes!', and a cheeky clicking of the tongue, were carried over between these two TV texts – suggesting that his portrayal of the Doctor directly and intentionally reproduced elements of his energetic embodiment of Casanova. Crucially, though, each text also emphasised Tennant's delivery of speedy dialogue, displaying his rhythmic fluency with language.[77] Doran cites the following as key elements of Tennant's Hamlet:

> I knew he would be funny and charming ... and I knew he would get the speed of the language – those elements are crucial ... There are points when he makes you realise that all the wit is a front – an attempt to prevent Hamlet from seeing the abyss into which he's staring. At those moments, I think he has the potential to be truly great.[78]

Doran's account here would make just as much sense if you substituted 'the Doctor' for 'Hamlet' and misattributed the quote to Russell T. Davies, suggesting how closely intertwined Tennant's TV star persona and his 'high-cultural' theatrical career have become. Though Christopher Eccleston strongly detached himself from the Doctor, arguments regarding the (cult) TV overlap of character/actor in a hybrid 'charactor' seem to hold more weight in Tennant's case.[79]

The high-cultural 'Shakespeareanising' of new *Who* as a bid for 'quality TV' has not only been a matter of guest stars such as Derek Jacobi and Simon Callow, or of Tennant in the lead role: Shakespeare himself has appeared as a character, played by Dean Lennox Kelly in 'The Shakespeare Code' (3.2). Analysing Shakespeare's appearances in popular culture, Richard Burt argues that '[w]hen cited in television programs, Shakespeare is likely to be enlisted seriously as a sacred icon ... [this] might be adduced as ... evidence of television's conservatism'.[80] And Craig Dionne has offered a similar reading of *Star Trek*'s Shakespearean references:

> What is reproduced through *Star Trek*'s Shakespeare is a middlebrow audience attempting to distance itself even further from the popular lowbrow that defines mass culture generally, as a vaguely high-brow Shakespeare promises to help the series push its orbit even further from the aesthetic options located only a channel ... away.[81]

Where a genre is lent enhanced cultural value by the referencing of 'high culture', then the implicit 'other' in this process is that same genre – here, SF-adventure TV that is not 'elevated' through Shakespearean citation, and is merely 'popular' rather than 'quality' TV.[82] SF TV's use of Shakespeare has been criticised for reinforcing the playwright's conservative ideological position: 'the message we receive ... is that Shakespeare not only survives in the future but remains in untouched form as an icon of poetic truth and authority for all cultures'.[83] Science fiction tends to extend Shakespeare's cultural position as the ultimate arbiter of 'art' into the far future, if not into other fictional galaxies.[84] 'The Shakespeare Code' (3.2) is no exception to this tendency, with the Doctor affirming Shakespeare's status as a genius, and as 'the most human human' who has ever lived. In *The Romantic Cult of Shakespeare*, Peter Davidhazi argues that one of the major components of Shakespeare's culturally 'sacred' status has been an 'attitude of unconditional reverence ... so final and absolute that it precludes every conceivable criticism of its object',[85] and episode 3.2 represents this attitude repeatedly.

Nevertheless, in a range of ways, this story uses Shakespeare not merely as a source of cultural authority, but rather to 'popularise' his works. Its title intertextually cites Dan Brown's blockbuster novel *The Da Vinci Code*,[86] suggesting that Shakespeare is going to be recontextualised within a 'popular' discourse, whilst Shakespearean theatre in 1599 is described by the Doctor as 'popular entertainment for the masses'. Furthermore, Shakespeare is represented as if he were a contemporary celebrity, regardless of the historical fact that

> [w]hen he was still alive, Shakespeare was not much of a public figure. He seems to have avoided publicity, and ... preferred a relatively modest and retiring existence ... In Sonnet 65, Shakespeare writes of the 'miracle' of 'black ink' as the solution to the problem of 'sad mortality' ... As a private aspiration, fame is simply a wish to be remembered after one is dead ... Shakespeare's own desire for fame has been gradually transmuted into something radically different in the form of contemporary celebrity.[87]

To make Shakespeare relevant to a present-day mass audience, the episode projects posthumous celebrity back into his lifetime as a further popularising gesture. He thus tells the Doctor and Martha: 'no, you can't be sketched with me, and don't ask where I get my ideas from'. A similarly popularising approach was taken to Charles Dickens in 'The Unquiet Dead' (1.3), where the Doctor professed to be 'a big fan', whilst Dickens was heard to enquire, 'What the Shakespeare is going on?' High culture becomes the ground for playful (mis)quotation or 'commonplacing', with well-known quotes being drawn on[88] within a populist framing of 'Great Authors' as if they are contemporary media celebrities.

As Josh Heuman and Richard Burt have argued, the value of high-cultural citations in popular media can be

> difficult to assess, or one might even say 'undecidable' ... Are the literary references, mostly clichéd lines well known even to a public who has never read a play by Shakespeare, meant to be taken seriously ... or [are they] just another register of how Shakespeare gets reduced to familiar tag lines [in 'popular' rather than 'quality' discourses?]'.[89]

Though it might be suggested that Shakespeare's cultural value in 'The Shakespeare Code' (3.2) is 'undecidable' – Will is 'dumbed down' and Who is 'cultured up' – this neglects the centrality of the episode's 'unconditional reverence'. In comic book examples considered by Heuman and Burt, 'Shakespeare occupies one side of a stable binary opposition between hero and villain',[90] depending on whether heroes honour him, or villains threaten Shakespearean value. Indeed, this binary makes sense in relation to Gareth Robert's official *Doctor Who* comic strip 'A groatsworth of wit',[91] where the ninth Doctor and

Rose encounter an older Shakespeare – 'He ain't no Joseph Fiennes', mutters Rose.[92] In this tale, evil aliens demonstrate their lack of moral worth by threatening to alter history so that Shakespeare is forgotten in the twenty-first century. Of course, these despicable aliens must not upset Shakespearean cultural hierarchies of value, which are duly preserved by the Doctor, being naturalised as the order of things.

Where Shakespeare is reverentially celebrated by heroes, or his cultural value is threatened by villains, then a conservative discourse of 'timeless value' remains firmly in play. *Doctor Who* has, in fact, pursued critical rather than naturalising appearances of Shakespeare, but only in Big Finish's audio dramas that are branded as classic *Doctor Who*. *The Time of the Daleks* by Justin Richards directly attacks elitist conceptions of Shakespeare. [93] Its villain, one General Learman, is a Shakespearean devotee and Dalek collaborator who feels that Will's work is simply too good for the masses, dismissed as congenitally unable to appreciate it.[94]

There are no such critical readings in BBC Wales' *Doctor Who*. In fact, 'The Shakespeare Code' (3.2 ) doubles the 'unconditional reverence' accorded to Shakespeare within naturalisations of supposedly 'inherent value'. Both the Doctor and the villainous Carrionites are united in their affirmation of Shakespeare's 'genius'. His powers as a wordsmith are what the Carrionites require for their extraterrestrial plan, just as it is Shakespeare's literary dexterity which is called upon by the Doctor to defeat them. Oh, and a spell ('expelliarmus') from Harry Potter, in case the child audience remains in any doubt of Shakespeare's magical word-power. This citation of a rival popular fiction is unusual for new *Who*, though its presence seems less of a 'popular' recontextualisation of Shakespeare and more an attempt to partially pluralise the otherwise monocultural, and thoroughly conservative narrative conclusion – that Shakespeare's words alone can save the world. J.K. Rowling's concluding citation might disrupt the sense that this episode is an almighty paean to Shakespearean 'high-cultural' value, but it remains one moment in what is otherwise a consistent representation of Shakespearean cultural worth.[95] This places new *Who* in the arena of 'quality TV' by virtue of affirming conservative, dominant hierarchies of aesthetic value. Charlotte Brunsdon observes that there are 'conservative' and 'avant-garde' discourses of quality TV,[96] and at least one discursive strand of new *Who*'s bid for quality status falls squarely within the former camp.

Thus far, I have focused on production discourses of quality such as traditional aesthetics, 'high-end' TV casting and high-cultural referencing. I have argued that these are not without counter-discourses, evident in Christopher Eccleston's use of his own 'quality' profile to devalue *Doctor Who* as series drama, as well as in RSC director Gregory Doran's rejection of *Doctor Who* as popular culture. Such discursive struggle over *Doctor Who*'s textual classification demonstrates that its 'text-function' – that is, the classificatory discourse going beyond authorship/genre that circulates in and around the programme – will not always be coherent or without contestation. I want to conclude by focusing on a further discourse of quality that has been significant to producers and academics: politics.

## The Politics of a Time Lord:
## 'Will He Be Bothered by the Daleks Invading
## If There's Social Inequality'?

Whether or not TV drama is 'political' is a quality discourse that has arguably held greater sway in TV studies rather than the industry itself, though it does have a presence there in prestige 'political thrillers' tackling contemporary debates (e.g. *The Last Enemy* and *Burn Up*, both BBC, 2008). Frequently these thrillers are conspiracy and quest narratives.[97] *Edge of Darkness* (BBC, 1985) is a classic example of this type of 'quality TV', as is *State of Play*, which Robin Nelson takes as the title for his book on 'high-end' TV drama.[98]

Bignell and O'Day have pointed out that academic quality debates often invoke the 'criterion that quality involves engagement with political themes'.[99] And this has led to a series of otherings of 'non-quality' TV featuring

> a set of familiar oppositions: ... between television-as-flow and that which interrupts, anchors or 'penetrates' that flow; and between television-as-feminine, with its distracted viewer, and those 'authored' masculine interventions which invite a detached and critical engagement in the spectator.[100]

The original series of *Doctor Who* has not typically been viewed as 'political'. Although some stories can be interpreted as tackling 'philosophically subversive ideas',[101] and offering political messages,[102] the series has not usually been linked to quality discourses of 'the political': 'a number of *Star Trek* fans have written books in which they explicitly explore the political philosophical issues raised by that programme ... while nobody has written [books] on [classic series] *Doctor Who* in the same way'.[103]

In the responses of fans, then, drawing on what has been termed 'popular aesthetics' – the distinctions made by TV audiences rather than producers and scholars[104] – classic *Doctor Who* is about 'adventures' rather than 'politics'. It is this that leads fan-journalist James Stanton to ask, prior to Eccleston's appearance in the new series: 'Will [his] Doctor really be that bothered by the Daleks invading London if there's social inequality to be fought in Salford?'[105] Here, Eccleston's connection to highly politicised 'quality TV' threatens to upset the 'adventure' identity of the series. The apparent danger is that *Doctor Who* will somehow become worthy, 'unashamedly social realist ... TV drama'.[106]

'Social realism' represents another academically championed discourse of 'quality TV = the political', dealing less with the 'extraordinary' lives of political/corporate elites, as political thrillers tend to, and touching more on the ordinary lives of working class people. Jimmy McGovern's *The Street* and Paul Abbott's *Clocking Off* and *Shameless* all operate in and revitalise this tradition.[107] Social realism is not just about the details of ordinary life, however; as an explicitly political form of drama, it relates micro-structures of everyday life to macro-structures of economics, politics and the 'social inequality' cited by Stanton. Scholars such as Robin Nelson have continued to call for the twenty-first-century value of social realism.[108] Though reproducing a familiar binary of 'quality' versus the bad other of consumerist, 'feel-good' telly, Nelson's defence of social realism usefully points out another of its key elements: it seeks to represent socially excluded or culturally marginalised identities. Though this has frequently meant focusing on working-class characters, Russell T. Davies' *Queer as Folk* has been viewed as social realist, working progressively to normalise representations of gay life.[109]

Davies' involvement in new *Who*, and acute awareness of the 'quality = politics' discourse, has resulted in the series taking on a more directly 'political' status. Though it could not be described as 'social realism', the decision to have Eccleston play the Doctor in his own Salford accent links series one residually to social realist representations of

industrial, northern, working-class masculinity. Significantly, the series has also represented Downing Street, and state politics, more directly than ever before, using this within conspiracy narratives which,
though science-fictional, formally resemble the narrative structures of
political thrillers. Davies' working title for 'World War Three' (1.5) in
his series pitch was simply '10 Downing Street',[110] involving a scenario
where 'the Doctor goes to the heart of government to find out what's
been going on'. Given that the function of the pitch document was to
sell the series as a 'serious' proposition to BBC executives, it is perhaps
unsurprising that Davies would choose to highlight the political, gov-
ernmental setting of this episode strongly. Partially appropriating the
tone of a political thriller was again a strategy used in series three, with
the Master becoming the UK's Prime Minister in 'The Sound of Drums'
and 'Last of the Time Lords' (3.12–3.13). Echoing the programme's
discursive re-contextualisation, and its newfound text-function, books
analysing Doctor Who's politics have finally started to appear in the
wake of the 'Russell T. Davies era'.

Bids for politicised 'quality' status were compounded in series
one by the repeated use of science fiction as satire. The Doctor and
Rose travelled into the far future three times in this series – in 'The
End of the World (1.2), 'The Long Game' (1.7) and 'Bad Wolf'/'The
Parting of the Ways' (1.12–1.13) – and each occasion utilised science fiction as a political commentary on media society. 'The End of
the World' (1.2) is about spectatorship – groups of aliens gather on
Platform One to watch the Earth's demise through viewing screens
resembling a widescreen ratio. Echoing a version of contemporary
'dark tourism',[111] visitors to the viewing gallery assume they will be
able to witness a planetary explosion in perfect safety. Indeed, the
event is aestheticised: 'The Corporation ... move Platform One from
one artistic event to another', Jabe tells the Doctor, whilst the Viewing Gallery is described in the script as being 'like a private cinema
without seats',[112] and the Manchester Suite as having 'all the cool
and calm of an art gallery'.[113] Of course, the story's narrative threat
involves a failure in the Platform's shielding, with cracks appearing in
the protective screen between spectators and their 'art'. Spectatorial
detachment is critiqued by Davies: the implication is that, like Rose
Tyler, we should feel the emotional impact of Earthdeath rather than
decadently sipping cocktails. The episode's emphasis on feeling and
emotional engagement are moralised[114] as calls to action – having

seen the Earth's eventual fate, Rose is energised and given a sense of purpose.[115]

If 'The End of the World' (1.2) deals with media society metaphorically and moralistically, chastising decadent, insulated responses to what we see on our screens, then 'The Long Game' (1.7) and 'Bad Wolf' (1.12) tackle media culture more literally. The former critiques the 'other' of TV news as propaganda. This is explicitly commercialised news, designed to turn a profit on a 'long-term investment' by a 'consortium of banks', according to the Editor (Simon Pegg). One of the most infamous UK tabloid headlines from the Rupert Murdoch-owned *Sun* newspaper of 1982, 'Gotcha', is incorporated as part of the villainous Editor's dialogue.[116] And journalist Cathica's emphasis on the news being 'open and honest and beyond bias' recalls controversies over the use of 'Fair and Balanced' as a FOX News slogan. 'The Long Game' is thus science fiction as politicised commentary, attacking commercial news-gathering and defending a public service ethos of accurate, truthful information. Akin to Dennis Potter's *Cold Lazarus* (C4/BBC, 1996), the episode 'offers a deliberate and conscious critique of contemporary broadcasting'.[117] And similarly, Davies' *Doctor Who* positions SF not as a subversion of the 'truth' of human identity, but rather as a call for 'true' mediation:

> *Cold Lazarus* was an attempt ... to re-assert the very notion and possibility of 'truth' and 'reality' that so many contemporary science fiction dramas attempt to destabilise ... [O]ne can see Potter's final screenplay as offering a conscious subversion of a science-fiction dystopia like *Blade Runner* ... by providing, at its very centre, an actual and authentic sense of 'history' which Scott's 'replicants' (with their implanted memories) so conspicuously lack.[118]

Unlike Christopher Eccleston's cited pre-text of *Blade Runner*, this interpretation of *Cold Lazarus*, which I am suggesting makes just as much sense as a response to 'The Long Game' (1.7), positions it as a kind of 'anti-*Blade Runner*'. History is wrong in series one, and it is up to the Doctor to restore the truthful, 'authentic' Fourth Great and Bountiful Human Empire.

New *Who*'s use of SF as satire focuses again on media society in 'Bad Wolf' (1.12). Here, reality television and assorted game shows have enslaved humanity, and the Doctor is caught up inside a lethal, futuristic version of the *Big Brother* (Endemol, 1999– ) house. Dubbed

'Big Murder' in the series pitch,[119] this became *Big Brother* once rights clearance was secured and the actual *BB* theme along with a version of the eye logo could be used. Davina McCall also voiced 'Davinadroid', suggesting that the episode was seen by Endemol/Channel Four as a playful appropriation of their intellectual property rather than outright critique. Indeed, the Doctor is not opposed to reality TV per se. The script avoids having him attack this genre outright, as he is sidetracked into a paean to a (fictional future) reality show, *Bear With Me*.[120] Though he is a big fan of Charles Dickens, the ninth Doctor is evidently also an admirer of reality television. This non-elitist attitude mirrors Russell T. Davies' much-documented love of all television:

> One of the things that annoys me is that snobbishness about television, reality TV in particular. When I have that conversation with people, I have to sit there and painstakingly explain to them that I don't love it ironically, that I really genuinely find it enlightening and fascinating and maddening and beautiful. The relationship between Craig and Anthony [in *Big Brother 6*, 2005], a gay man falling in love with a straight man, I have never seen a drama portray that as convincingly ... So many cultural commentators ... assume that the millions of people who watch it are stupid.[121]

Despite Davies' professed views, and his positioning of the Doctor as a TV omnivore, 'Bad Wolf' (1.12) still hinges, narratively, on threats from a range of murderous, fictional game shows. J. Shaun Lyon describes it as 'more affectionate mocking than barbed allegory',[122] and one might observe that the version of *Big Brother* devalued here is a purely science-fictional, diegetic incarnation, implying no disrespect to the real-world *BB*. However, this strict separation of the fictional and the real, whilst technically accurate, ignores the extent to which devaluing a fictional *Big Brother* ('Big Murder') replays discourses of 'snobbishness' surrounding the show. Leading scholar of quality TV, Jane Feuer, has argued that in the twenty-first century:

> Reality TV is the great other to quality drama ... why should one form have so much more artistic status than the other? ... The reality show merges certain forms of documentary with the game show and the soap opera. Quality drama [has] merged soap opera with ... established genre[s] ... To the interpretive community that writes about TV, and who share a field of reference with those who create quality TV but not reality TV, only certain re-combinations matter.[123]

Like Davies, Feuer vehemently opposes elitist attacks on reality TV. However, given the prevalence of this quality/reality TV binary, it can hardly be seen as an accident that the returning *Doctor Who*, within its many bids for 'quality' status, just happened to posit reality TV as a further devalued other, that is, as a narrative threat to be morally overcome by the Doctor. 'Bad Wolf' (1.12) plays with, and seemingly invites, 'quality' discourses premised on a powerful othering of reality TV. And by using science fiction to pass judgement on an extrapolated instance of contemporary media, the episode again affirms a 'political', 'serious' textual identity for new *Who*. Media society is once more self-reflexively tackled, and this time the 'bad other' against which the critical, satirical text-function of *Doctor Who* can be contrasted is not decadent spectatorship, nor commercial news, but the game-show: a genre linked to moralising discourses of anti-commercialism across its history.[124]

Though I have focused on the ninth and tenth Doctors here, it is worth noting that production discourses of 'quality' TV remained firmly in play in the casting of the eleventh Doctor, Matt Smith. Incoming executive producers Steven Moffat and Piers Wenger successfully reinforced the place of *Doctor Who* as 'TV art' rather than 'TV commerce' by avoiding casting a 'household name'.[125] Disarticulating the title role from an established 'star persona',[126] Smith's emergence stressed acting credentials and social-realist/political intertexts rather than pre-sold audience recognition. Though news of his appointment occasioned headlines such as 'Who are ya' and 'Dr Who?',[127] Matt Smith had previously appeared in Jimmy McGovern's *The Street* ('Taxi', 2007) and political drama *Party Animals* (BBC, 2007). Like Eccleston, he had thus appeared in social-realist, 'authored' and politicised TV. The official BBC announcement of Smith's casting on 3 January 2009 stressed his difference from earlier Time Lords by emphasising his youthfulness. And though he is indeed the youngest actor to play the part, at the same time Smith is very much of a piece with both Eccleston and Tennant in terms of his positioning as a 'quality' TV actor. Where Tennant appeared in *Blackpool* and *Casanova* en route to *Who*, Smith's major role as geeky researcher and idealist Danny Foster in *Party Animals* effectively paved his way to the series. Though lesser known than Doctors nine and ten, it is doubtful whether Smith would have been judged sufficiently experienced as a TV actor were it not for this role in World Productions' take on *This Life*-meets-Westminsterpolitics. Focusing on his relatively tender age – as fans tended to in the immediate wake of the casting announcement – replays the BBC's preferred PR narrative of 'the young Doctor', neglecting the underlying fact that the eleventh TARDIS occupant strongly resembles his immediate predecessors in terms of 'quality TV' and theatrical intertexts rather than merely differing via youth, style, or appearance.

This chapter has examined discourses of quality that have been linked to new *Who*. I have argued that production discourses articulate *Doctor Who* with differentiated notions of quality (high-end TV/ high culture/ politics). Given these concerted bids for 'quality TV' status, the show's BAFTA successes have reinforced its industrial recontextualisation, and displaced negative 'popular memories' of the classic series. And yet, bids for 'quality' status have to continually ward off conservative discourses of high versus popular culture, and traditional aesthetics versus 'repetitive' genre TV. *Doctor Who*'s newfound cultural positioning thus remains relatively insecure. The discourses of quality drawn upon (high-end TV; Shakespearean high culture) have been used in contradictory ways to devalue *Who* without any disruption to underlying equations of cultural value with certain types of television and literature. As Michel Foucault has noted:

> Some contradictions are localized only at the level of propositions and assertions, without in any way affecting the body of enunciative rules that makes them possible ... the consequences that can be drawn from ... two theses [here, *Doctor Who* is/is not quality TV] are certainly very numerous ... but it can be shown that they originated in the same discursive formation.[128]

In the next chapter, I will consider another textual classification that has been discursively articulated with new *Who* – that of 'mainstream' television. In particular, I want to focus on the way that music has been used to downplay generic identifications of the series as purely 'science fictional'. In this instance, the generic function and text-function are interrelated, with 'mainstream TV' being defined in production discourse as 'anti-science fiction'. However, the mainstreaming text-function of *Who* goes beyond questions of music and genre, also incorporating discourses of 'the contemporary', which enter the programme via uses of popular music. Though music is frequently reflected on by fans, it tends to be de-prioritised in TV studies due to a focus on the tele*visual*. Chapter 6 aims to redress that balance by emulating fans' close readings of *Doctor Who*.

## NOTES

1   Christine Geraghty (2003) 'Aesthetics and quality in popular television drama', *International Journal of Cultural Studies* vi/1, pp.27–8.
2   Charlotte Brunsdon (1997) *Screen Tastes*, Routledge, London and New York, p.130.
3   Ibid., pp.134–6).
4   See Michel Foucault (1979) 'What is an author?', *Screen* xx/1, pp.13–33.
5   Brunsdon: *Screen Tastes*, p.139.
6   Geraghty: 'Aesthetics and quality', p.30; see also John Caughie (2007) *Edge of Darkness*, BFI Publishing, London, pp.2–3.
7   Jonathan Bignell and Andrew O'Day (2004) *Terry Nation*, Manchester University Press, Manchester and New York, p.4; see also Lance Parkin (2007) 'Canonicity matters: defining the *Doctor Who* canon', in David Butler (ed.) *Time and Relative Dissertations in Space: Critical Perspectives on* Doctor Who, Manchester University Press, Manchester and New York, pp.246–62.
8   Brunsdon: *Screen Tastes*, p.134.
9   Jason Jacobs (2006) 'Television aesthetics: an infantile disorder', *Journal of British Cinema and Television* iii/1, p.30.
10  John Tulloch and Manuel Alvarado (1983) Doctor Who: *The Unfolding Text*, Macmillan, London, p.178.
11  Ibid., p.179.
12  Jonathan Bignell (2005) 'Space for "quality": negotiating with the Daleks', in Jonathan Bignell and Stephen Lacey (eds) *Popular Television Drama*, Manchester University Press, Manchester and New York, p.76.
13  See, for example, ibid., p.82; see also James Chapman (2006) *Inside the TARDIS: The Worlds of* Doctor Who, I.B.Tauris, London and New York, pp.38–9.
14  Bignell: 'Space for "quality"', p.76.
15  Ibid., p.89.
16  Lynn Spigel and Henry Jenkins (1991) 'Same Bat channel, different Bat times: mass culture and popular memory', in Roberta E. Pearson and William Uricchio (eds) *The Many Lives of the Batman*, Routledge/BFI, London and New York, p.135.
17  In Gary Russell (2006) Doctor Who: *The Inside Story*, BBC Books, London, p.46.
18  Geraghty: 'Aesthetics and quality', p.31.
19  Jenny Nelson (1990) 'The dislocation of time: a phenomenology of television reruns', *Quarterly Review of Film and Video* xii/3, p.84.
20  See Tulloch and Alvarado: *Doctor Who*; Mark Jancovich and James Lyons (eds) (2003) *Quality Popular Television*, BFI Publishing, London.
21  Bignell: 'Space for "quality"'.
22  Robin Nelson (2007) *State of Play: Contemporary 'High-End' TV Drama*, Manchester University Press, Manchester and New York, p.2 (my italics).
23  See Chapter 1 in this volume.
24  Davies in *Project: Who?* (2005) BBC Audio, London.
25  In ibid.

26    Roberta E. Pearson (2004) '"Bright particular star": Patrick Stewart, Jean-Luc Picard and cult television', in Sara Gwenllian-Jones and Roberta E. Pearson (eds) *Cult Television*, University of Minnesota Press, Minneapolis, p.66.

27    In Clayton Hickman (2004) 'Revolution number 9: the Christopher Eccleston interview', in *Doctor Who Magazine* 343, Panini Comics, Tunbridge Wells, p.12.

28    Eccleston in ibid., p.12.

29    Lez Cooke (2005) 'The new social realism of *Clocking Off*', in Jonathan Bignell and Stephen Lacey (eds) *Popular Television Drama*, Manchester University Press, Manchester and New York, pp.185–6.

30    Pamela Church Gibson (2000) 'Fewer weddings and more funerals: changes in the heritage film', in Robert Murphy (ed.) *British Cinema of the 90s*, BFI, London, pp.118–19.

31    Michael Eaton (2005) *BFI TV Classics:* Our Friends in the North, BFI Publishing, London, p.27.

32    Chapman: *Inside the TARDIS*, p.190.

33    See also Nelson: *State of Play*, p.213 n.2.

34    James Stanton (2004) 'Will the new *Doctor Who* TV series be any good?', *Dreamwatch* 117, p.48.

35    Alan McKee (2007) 'Why is "City of Death" the best *Doctor Who* story?', in David Butler (ed.) *Time and Relative Dissertations in Space: Critical Perspectives on* Doctor Who, Manchester University Press, Manchester and New York, p.240.

36    Eccleston in Hickman: 'Revolution number 9', pp.10–11.

37    See John Tulloch (2000) 'Multiple authorship in TV drama' in Jonathan Bignell, Stephen Lacey and Madeleine Macmurraugh-Kavanagh (eds) *British Television Drama: Past, Present and Future*, Palgrave, Basingstoke, p.175.

38    Robert McKee (1999) *Story*, Methuen, London, p.379.

39    Christine Cornea (2007) *Science Fiction Cinema: Between Fantasy and Reality*, Edinburgh University Press, Edinburgh, p.217.

40    Russell T. Davies (2005) 'Bad Wolf/The Parting of the Ways', in *The Shooting Scripts*, BBC Books, London, pp.471, 473.

41    Ibid., p.482.

42    Cornea: *Science Fiction Cinema*, p.217.

43    Roberta E. Pearson (1992) *Eloquent Gestures*, University of California Press, Berkeley, Los Angeles and Oxford, p.52.

44    Ibid.

45    Eccleston in *Project: Who* (2005).

46    Aired on Radio 2 on 29 March 2005.

47    Cited in Stephen Brook (2005) 'BBC apologises to Eccleston over *Doctor Who* spin', *Media Guardian*, 5 April, available online at *http://www.guardian.co.uk/media/2005/apr/05/broadcasting.bbc*.

48    Sarah Cardwell (2007) 'Is quality television any good? Generic distinctions, evaluations and the troubling matter of critical judgement', in Janet McCabe and Kim Akass (eds) *Quality TV: Contemporary American Television and Beyond*, I.B.Tauris, London and New York, p.30.

49    See Sarah Cardwell (2006) 'Television aesthetics', *Critical Studies in Television* i/1, pp.72–80; Jason Jacobs (2001) 'Issues of judgement and value in television studies', *International Journal of Cultural Studies* iv/4, pp.427–47, and his (2006) 'Television aesthetics: an infantile disorder', *Journal of British Cinema and Television* iii/1, pp.19–33.

50    Eccleston in *Project: Who* (2005).

51    Ibid.

52    Pearson: '"Bright particular star"', p.62; see also Sara Gwenllian Jones (2000) 'Starring Lucy Lawless?', *Continuum: Journal of Media and Cultural Studies* xiv/1, pp.9–22.

53    David A. Black (2004) 'Charactor; or, the strange case of Uma Peel', in Sara Gwenllian-Jones and Roberta E. Pearson (eds) *Cult Television*, University of Minnesota Press, Minneapolis, p.105; see also Peter Kramer and Alan Lovell (1999) 'Introduction', in Alan Lovell and Peter Kramer (eds) *Screen Acting*, Routledge, London and New York, p.5.

54    See Gwenllian Jones: 'Starring Lucy Lawless?', p.15.

55    Tulloch and Alvarado: *Doctor Who*, p.179.

56    See John Caughie (2000) 'What do actors do when they act?', in Jonathan Bignell, Stephen Lacey and Madeleine Macmurraugh-Kavanagh (eds) *British Television Drama: Past, Present and Future*, Palgrave, Basingstoke, p.169.

57    Gareth Roberts (2005) 'Guess Who?', *Doctor Who Magazine Special Edition: The* Doctor Who *Companion – Series One*, Panini Comics, Tunbridge Wells, p.6.

58    Russell T. Davies (2005) 'Rose', in *The Shooting Scripts*, BBC Books, London, p.25.

59    Pat Kane (2005) 'Doctoring the Corporation', available online at *http://theplayethic.typepad.com/play_journal/2005/03/index.html*.

60    See Jane Feuer (2007) 'HBO and the concept of quality TV', in Janet McCabe and Kim Akass (eds) *Quality TV: Contemporary American Television and Beyond*, I.B.Tauris, London and New York, p.149; see also Russell T. Davies and Benjamin Cook (2008) *The Writer's Tale*, BBC Books, London, p.158.

61    Gardner in *Project: Who* (2005); see also Jim Collins (1992) 'Television and postmodernism', in Robert C. Allen (ed.) *Channels of Discourse, Reassembled*, Routledge, London, p.345; Kristin Thompson (2003) *Storytelling in Film and Television*, Harvard University Press, Cambridge and London.

62    Lisa Parks (2003) 'Brave new *Buffy*: rethinking "TV violence"', in Mark Jancovich and James Lyons (eds) *Quality Popular Television*, BFI Publishing, London, p.122.

63    See Nichola Dobson (2006) 'The regeneration of *Doctor Who*: the ninth Doctor and the influence of the slayer', *Flow* iv/4, available online at *http://flowtv.org/?p=227*, accessed 2 May 2006.

64    Graeme Harper with Adrian Rigelsford (2007) *Calling the Shots: Directing the New Series of* Doctor Who', Reynolds and Hearn, London, pp.198–9.

65    McKee: 'Why is "City of Death"...?', pp.241–2.

66    David Tennant in *Doctor Who Confidential* (BBC3, 25 December 2007).

67 Brunsdon: *Screen Tastes*, p.142.

68 '*RSCM*' jokingly refers to a fictional *Royal Shakespeare Company Magazine*, imagining the Bard being covered in the same way as *Doctor Who*, but for a readership of loyal Shakespeare 'fans'. In Clayton Hickman (2005) 'Perfect ten: the David Tennant interview', *Doctor Who Magazine* 359, Panini Comics, Tunbridge Wells, p.13.

69 In Dominic Cavendish (2008) 'Look Who's playing Hamlet', *Daily Telegraph*, 23 July, p.27.

70 Ibid.

71 Ibid.

72 John Tulloch (2007) 'Fans of Chekhov: re-approaching "High Culture"', in Jonathan Gray, Cornel Sandvoss and C. Lee Harrington (eds) *Fandom: Identities and Communities in a Mediated World*, New York University Press, New York and London, p.113; see also Barbara Hodgdon (2007) 'Shakespearean stars: stagings of desire', in Robert Shaughnessy (ed.) *The Cambridge Companion to Shakespeare and Popular Culture*, Cambridge University Press, Cambridge, pp.46–66.

73 John Tulloch (1999) *Performing Culture*, Sage, London, p.110, and his (2005) *Shakespeare and Chekhov in Production and Reception: Theatrical Events and their Audiences*, University of Iowa Press, Iowa City.

74 Cavendish: 'Look Who's playing Hamlet', p.27.

75 Ibid.

76 Caroline Briggs (2008) 'Doctor Who signing ban at *Hamlet*', available online at *http://news.bbc.co.uk/1/hi/entertainment/7523210.stm*, accessed 4 August 2008.

77 See Russell: Doctor Who, p.58.

78 In Cavendish: 'Look Who's playing Hamlet', p.27.

79 Gwenllian Jones: 'Starring Lucy Lawless?'; Black: 'Character; or, the strange case of Uma Peel'.

80 Richard Burt (1998) *Unspeakable ShaXXXspeares: Queer Theory and American Kiddie Culture*, Macmillan, London, pp.27–8.

81 Craig Dionne (2002) 'The Shatnerification of Shakespeare: *Star Trek* and the commonplace tradition', in Richard Burt (ed.) *Shakespeare After Mass Media*, Palgrave, London, p.176.

82 See Josh Heuman and Richard Burt (2002) 'Suggested for mature readers? Deconstructing Shakespearean value in comic books', in Richard Burt (ed.) *Shakespeare After Mass Media*, Palgrave, London, p.153; Joke Hermes (2005) *Re-reading Popular Culture*, Blackwell Publishing, Malden and Oxford, p.70.

83 Dionne: 'The Shatnerification of Shakespeare', p.176.

84 Terry Eagleton (1988) 'Afterword', in Graham Holderness (ed.) *The Shakespeare Myth*, Manchester University Press, Manchester, p.205.

85 Peter Davidhazi, (1998) *The Romantic Cult of Shakespeare*, Macmillan, London, p.9.

86 Dan Brown (2003) *The Da Vinci Code*, Doubleday, New York.

87 Michael D. Bristol (1996) *Big-Time Shakespeare*, Routledge, London and New York, pp.3–4.

88 See the arguments of Dionne in 'The Shatnerification of Shakespeare'.

89   Heuman and Burt: 'Suggested for mature readers?', p.153.

90   Ibid., p.154.

91   Republished in collected form in Gareth Roberts (2006) 'A groatsworth of wit', in *The Ninth Doctor Collected Comics*, Panini Comics, Tunbridge Wells, pp.87–104.

92   Ibid., p.97.

93   Justin Richards (2002) *The Time of the Daleks*, Big Finish Audio, London.

94   See also Nev Fountain (2006) *The Kingmaker*, Big Finish Audio, London, which uses Shakespeare as a character in an even more radical, iconoclastic way.

95   Davies and Cook: *The Writer's Tale*, p.192, suggests that Russell T. Davies considered writing an entire episode based around J.K. Rowling, though David Tennant felt the idea came dangerously close to a *Doctor Who*-meets-Harry Potter 'spoof' (p.202). This does indicate, however, that Davies has been keen to cite fantasy fiction intertextually which itself carries cultural values of 'mainstream' acceptability, as well as drawing on discourses of 'quality'. The choice of critically applauded fantasy author Philip Pullman to write a foreword to *The Writer's Tale* (p.7) resonates with this specific 'text-function': where *Doctor Who* does, unusually, borrow from other contemporary fictions/brands, it is often articulated with texts already associated with 'mainstream' and 'quality' textual classifications.

96   Brunsdon: *Screen Tastes*, p.134.

97   Liesbet van Zoonen (2005) *Entertaining the Citizen: When Politics and Popular Culture Converge*, Rowman and Littlefield, Lanham, MD, p.120.

98   See Caughie: *Edge of Darkness*; Nelson: *State of Play*.

99   Bignell and O'Day: *Terry Nation*, p.7.

100  Sue Thornham and Tony Purvis (2005) *Television Drama: Theories and Identities*, Palgrave-Macmillan, Basingstoke and New York, p.24.

101  Nicholas J. Cull (2001) 'Bigger on the inside ... *Doctor Who* as British cultural history', in Graham Roberts and Philip M. Taylor (eds) *The Historian, Television and Television History*, University of Luton Press, Luton, p.105.

102  Tulloch and Alvarado: Doctor Who, p.180.

103  Alan McKee (2004) 'Is *Doctor Who* political?', *European Journal of Cultural Studies* vii/2, p.214–15.

104  See McKee: 'Which is the best *Doctor Who* story?' and (ed.) (2007) *Beautiful Things in Popular Culture*, Blackwell Publishing, Malden and Oxford; S. Elizabeth Bird (2003) *The Audience in Everyday Life*, Routledge, London and New York; Matt Hills (2005) 'Who wants to be a fan of *Who Wants to Be A Millionaire?*', in Catherine Johnson and Rob Turnock (eds) *ITV Cultures*, Open University Press, Milton Keynes, pp.177–95; Jacobs: 'Television aesthetics'.

105  Stanton: 'Will the new *Doctor Who*...?', p.48.

106  Robin Nelson (1997) *TV Drama in Transition*, Macmillan, Basingstoke, p.245; Eaton: *BFI TV Classics*.

107  See Cooke (2005); Nelson: *State of Play*, pp.44–53.

108  Robin Nelson (1997) *TV Drama in Transition*, Macmillan, Basingstoke, pp.170–1.

109  See Chapter 1 in this volume.

110 Russell T. Davies (2005) 'Pitch perfect', in *The* Doctor Who *Companion: Series One*, Panini Comics, Tunbridge Wells, p.46.
111 See John Lennon and Malcolm Foley (2000) *Dark Tourism: The Attraction of Death and Disaster*, Continuum, London and New York.
112 Russell T. Davies (2005) 'The End of the World', in *The Shooting Scripts*, BBC Books, London, p.51.
113 Ibid., p.53.
114 See McKee: 'Is *Doctor Who* political?'.
115 Davies: 'Pitch perfect', p.45.
116 The *Sun*, 4 May 1982.
117 Glen Creeber (2004a) *Serial Television: Big Drama on the Small Screen*, BFI Publishing, London, p.72.
118 Ibid.
119 Davies: 'Pitch perfect', p.49.
120 Davies: 'Bad Wolf/The Parting of the Ways', p.454.
121 Davies in Cathy Pryor (2006) 'Russell T Davies: one of Britain's foremost television writers', *Independent*, 22 October, available online at http://www.independent.co.uk/news/people/russell-t-davies-one-of-britains-foremost-television-writers-421182.html.
122 J. Shaun Lyon (2005) *Back to the Vortex*, Telos Press, Tolworth, p.364.
123 Feuer: 'HBO and the concept of quality TV', pp.156–7.
124 See Hills: 'Who wants to be a fan...?'.
125 Casting director Andy Pryor discusses the fact that it is not 'absolutely necessary for the Doctor to be a household name' in Russell: Doctor Who, p.57.
126 Tulloch and Alvarado: Doctor Who, p.179.
127 See, for example, Caroline Davies and David Smith (2009) 'Dr Who? Big names lose out to Matt Smith', available at http://www.guardian.co.uk/media/2009/jan/03/doctor-who-matt-smith, and Grant Rollings (2009) 'Who are ya', available at http://www.thesun.co.uk/sol/homepage/showbiz/tv/article2094236.ece.
128 Michel Foucault (2002) *The Archaeology of Knowledge*, Routledge, London and New York, p.170.

# 6

# MAINSTREAMING *WHO*:
# THE IMPORTANCE OF MUSIC

**M**y focus in this chapter is on an aspect of television that TV studies has neglected frequently: music.[1] Indeed, it is common for books and articles on the subject to begin with just such an admonishment, as Robynn Stilwell demonstrates: 'the position of sound within the field ... is still marginal ... Even more narrowly focused studies of genres or individual [texts] ... may omit sound and/ or music while still making some claim to comprehensiveness.'[2]

However, if sound typically has been left out of media studies' analyses of representation, then television's sound and music have been ignored twice over, both as a result of this general absence, and as a result of the notion that sound/music design for television are marked by paucity of ambition or redundancy. Even the leading theorist of film sound, Michel Chion, has argued – he claims with 'with no pejorative intention' – that 'television is illustrated radio. The point here is that sound, mainly the sound of speech, is always foremost in television. Never offscreen, sound is always *there*, in its place, and does not need the image to be identified.'[3] For Chion, contemporary TV has taken on a more and more 'radiophonic nature ... The image here no longer touts itself as the essential ingredient ... it's more like an unexpected gift.'[4] Though music video channels and rolling news may approximate to this idea, the 'radiophonic' nature of a drama such as *Doctor Who* is questionable in the extreme, as is the prejudice that its sound will always be on-screen, never needing the image to be scrutinised. Celebrated moments of *Doctor Who*, including the BBC's 'Golden Moment of 2005',[5] resoundingly give the lie to this type of approach: 'Are you my mummy?', along with the tick-tocking of the very first clockwork droid encountered by the Doctor and young Reinette in 'The Girl in the Fireplace' (2.4), are both instances of sound shifting from on-screen to off-screen in order to produce threatening diegetic moments. Suddenly, what we and the characters have assumed is a safe and identifiable sound – a tape recording or a clock shown on-screen – is revealed to have its source elsewhere. Temporarily off-screen, and a matter of narrative threat, these sounds are transformed into harbingers of monstrosity.

In what follows, I focus on how production discourses have positioned new *Who*'s music as a key element of textual identity. The discursive 'text-function' surrounding and entering the programme – made up of classificatory discourses aiming to position *Doctor Who* as 'quality' and 'mainstream' TV – operates through sound and music just as much as through narrative/representation. Although individual music scores are composed for stories, these are all created by one composer, Murray Gold, and make considerable re-use of leitmotifs, or music 'cues'. Rather than specific stories differing vastly in terms of their musical presence – as tended to be the case for the classic series – Gold's work contributes to the consistency and 'semiotic slimness' of new *Who* by reinforcing connotations of 'adventure' and marginalising genre discourses of the science fictional. 'Regenrifying' the series at an audio level,[6] Gold's input semantically stresses melodrama *not* science fiction, fantasy-horror *not* science fiction, and action-adventure *not* science fiction. As former producer Philip Hinchcliffe noted whilst watching 'Planet of the Ood' (4.3) for *The Stage*: 'This type of action music heightens the chase ... It's bringing a big-screen personality to the drama. You're getting a bigger dramatic experience ... They grab you and they keep you.'[7]

The use of 'big' music works to 'mainstream' *Doctor Who* discursively, articulating its textual identity with 'Hollywood' fantasy-epic and thoroughly exnominating – writing out – any assumed science fictionality. SF coding is assumed to threaten new *Who*'s bid for inclusiveness and mass-audience accessibility, alienating audiences who equate science fiction with 'niche' TV. The SF genre identity is *imagined*, in production discourse and the associated 'text-function', as an obstacle to 'mainstream' cultural acceptance. However, as Mark Jancovich and Nathan Hunt have argued, the 'inconsistent and contradictory way in which the mainstream is imagined'[8] indicates that the term has no stable meaning. Instead, it tends to fluctuate between different discourses, here taking on the connoted meaning of 'anti-science fiction'. Sarah Thornton similarly observes that 'the mainstream' often displays 'exaggerations of an imagined *other*',[9] that is, it is not based on empirical evidence, but shifts to suit whatever binaries of cultural identity are in play. I will argue that new *Who* imagines 'the mainstream' as an audience identity strongly opposed to SF, and thus seeks to bring its textuality 'down to Earth' symbolically, not only narratively via Earth-based story settings but also through 'big' action-adventure and melodramatic music.

Though music's powerful impact on 'viewers' is often ignored in TV studies,[10] the soundtrack to *Doctor Who* evidently requires close attention in terms of its textual strategies. It is an attribute of the show that fandom has debated in detail, with many long-term fans celebrating the 'special sound' in the classic series.[11] *Doctor Who*'s fans have focused just as intently on the show's music and sound effects as they have on its performers, producers, visuals and storylines. Kevin Donnelly's contribution to *Time and Relative Dissertations in Space* reminds readers that so 'distinctive and foregrounded were [classic] *Doctor Who*'s sound effects that several recordings were available commercially'.[12] The importance of audio FX in the series even leads Donnelly to describe sound as a 'star':

> [S]ound 'starred' rather than simply being there to convince audiences of the veracity of screen representations. In addition to this, certain sounds were reused constantly and thus had more status than simply 'sound effects'. The relaunched 2005 series of *Doctor Who* has demonstrated great awareness and respect for these 'sonic stars', with returning effects including the TARDIS materialisation/dematerialisation ... and the throbbing ambience created for the Dalek control room.[13]

However, the classic series has also been criticised by fans for its rather uneven use of non-diegetic music (the score accompanying a narrative but not occurring within its events). As *DWM* reviewer Vanessa Bishop has remarked:

> *Doctor Who*'s incidental music has traditionally been something of a hit-and-miss affair, up and down as much as the programme's own production values ... The decision to give all the [new] series' music to just one composer has not only meant the programme can exploit the use of recurring themes ... but that the show has finally attained a consistent standard.[14]

The selection of Murray Gold to compose all incidental music – and to rearrange the programme's theme music – generates new-found textual consistency. This production decision also enables the reuse and retooling of character or event-specific music cues, further achieving branded standardisation. Donnelly argues that this style of music deployment is economically useful for TV series, as '[t]elevision music has ... suffered from another severe constraint, that of cost limitations, particularly when compared with its more ... opulent cousin of film music'.[15] One cost-cutting efficiency involves the

> use of repeated blocks of music [rather] than commissioning an underscore to fit the dynamics across the whole programme ... Indeed, its economical and comprehensive format is probably most suited to long-form television drama ... The effect of this is to provide musical cohesion for the programme through the regular repetition of the same pieces of music.[16]

As Donnelly points out, the repetition of blocks of incidental music offers coherence and a strong sonic identity for any given TV show. It has often been assumed that the musical identity of a TV series persists in its aptly named 'signature tune' or theme music, but as the BBC Radiophonic Workshop maestro Dick Mills thoughtfully points out in Doctor Who: *The Unfolding Text*, *Doctor Who*'s wide variation of story locales and time frames poses problems for any such encapsulation by theme tune:

> It would be very difficult to imagine how to devise a signature tune that would encompass all the time scales through which the Doctor travels ... I think really to help this time travel business the incidental music plays a far bigger part ... All the signature tune could do was give an unearthly feel, a sort of space feel, give a bit of mystery and spookiness, but not necessarily time travel.[17]

Rather than just following an economic diktat, the reiterated use of Murray Gold's themes such as those for the Doctor's companions ('Rose's Theme'/'Martha's Theme'/'Donna's Theme'), the Doctor ('The

Doctor Forever') and action sequences ('All the Strange, Strange Creatures') creates a musical signature through tuneful incidental music as well as via the show's theme. Classic *Who* never consistently worked in this way via reinforcement of a musical identity, though it did feature occasional incidental music echoes of its infamous signature tune.

The first piece of Murray Gold's *Doctor Who* music that a 'viewer' is likely to encounter is, indeed, his rearrangement of the main theme. As he recounts in the liner notes to the series one and two soundtrack CD:

> ...in October 2004, the first episode of the new series was on my desk with Delia Derbyshire's original recording of the Ron Grainer classic playing over the end credits. And it didn't feel right. It just didn't seem to suit the ebullient clatter and chaos of 'Rose' [1.1].[18]

In fact, Gold has rearranged the *Doctor Who* theme for series one, created a full orchestral arrangement for 'The Christmas Invasion' (2.X) onwards, and come up with a further new arrangement for the 2007 Christmas special, 'Voyage of the Damned' (4.X), which simultaneously cites the early 1980s electronic version of the theme by Peter Howell and re-emphasises the 'action-adventure' dynamics and insistent drum rhythms of the 2005 incarnation.

Gold's condensed account of his initial realisation of the Grainer/ Derbyshire theme stresses the resonance between the 'clatter and chaos' of the series opener and his own musical additions, constructing a view of his signature tune rendition as a mirror for the new series: 'I added string lines, a booming horn, and some clatter and chaos of my own, and it stuck.'[19] In a more detailed description of how he worked with the digitised, isolated parts of the original theme, Gold takes a slightly different tack, this time emphasising how his version draws on the original significantly, to the extent of starting and ending with direct samples: 'I used the electronic "scream" at the start, the famous swooping top line, the organ harmony underneath, the bass line, and the "time tunnel whoosh" at the end.'[20] *Sound on Sound* journalist Matt Bell concludes that the 2005 theme and its additional 'sampled instrumentation including cellos, timpani, horns and snares ... worked superbly with the energetic new series title sequence'.[21]

Displacing the 'electronic SF music' effect and otherworldly feel of the original,[22] Gold's newly augmented theme, particularly through its use of strings and drums, emphasises the adventure or even thriller genre more than earlier versions. It is also a very 'full' sounding mix, reflecting the sense that, by 2005, the key element to bringing *Who* back was 'the opposite of minimalism ... [m]aximalism ... The first idea about how to deal with the sound on *Doctor Who* was "Sensory overload – chuck everything at them!"'[23] This apparent anxiety – that grabbing and holding the attention of a twenty-first century audience called for aural 'sensory overload', a 'big' full sound and a frenetic pace – was also very much carried through from the 2005 theme into the opening moments of 'Rose' (1.1), as I will now go on to argue via a more detailed focus on new *Who*'s non-diegetic music.

## Murray Gold's Non-Diegetic Music:
## 'We Just Want Big Tunes'

As episode 1.1 commences, a techno-influenced incidental music track plays over the character of Rose Tyler waking up and going to work. Though the visuals here – after an SFX 'swoop' from space down to London – are entirely mundane, allowing for the show's setting-up of an identificatory and 'ordinary' present-day female lead, the incidental music races along as if a fully-fledged chase sequence is occurring. The show's reformatting requires that episode one *not* begin with obvious visual spectacle, alien invasion, or some other action-adventure staple, since Rose's everyday human life needs to be established prior to the intrusion of the Doctor and his spectacular world. A sped-up montage sequence of picture-postcard London serves this introductory purpose. Accompanying the pacey editing, it is effectively Murray Gold's incidental music that sells the show as thrilling action-adventure.

Indeed, this mismatch between non-diegetic music and visuals occurs elsewhere in expository sequences during 'Rose' (1.1) (such as the Doctor's assertion, 'This is me, swanning off!') and I would argue that this is a result of the 2005 production team's anxiety not to lose their audience despite starting with depictions of Rose's ordinary, everyday life. The opening incidental music track of episode 1.1, despite being dipped and raised in volume, continues through to the first scene of menace in Henrik's basement, playing over all of the material establishing 'contemporary London'. In one of the most influential academic studies of non-diegetic (film) music, *Unheard Melodies*,

Claudia Gorbman argues that incidental music such as 'the orchestral grandeur of the theme in *Star Wars* that plays as spaceships speed through the galaxy' can help to

> *make a spectacle* of the images it accompanies; it lends an epic qual-
> ity to the diegetic events. It evokes a larger-than-life dimension which,
> rather than involving us in the narrative, places us in contemplation
> *of* it. Intimate 'identification' music ... and epic 'spectacle' music have
> different codes and functions ... the spectator is more apt to notice the
> latter kind, which [... works to ...] bond the spectator not to the feelings
> of the characters but to his/her fellow spectators.[24]

Though Murray Gold's music frequently serves both of these functions, what is so unusual about the opening incidental music in 'Rose'
(1.1) is that it appears to be noticeable *not* for the way that it self-
consciously makes images 'spectacular', but rather for the manner in
which it substitutes for, and works strenuously in place of, spectacular
imagery.

As new *Who* has progressed, its use of non-diegetic music has become less hysterically anxious, moving towards the conventions of film
scoring whilst generally suppressing codes of science-fictional music in
favour of orchestral sounds and styles linked to epic fantasy. Donnelly
points out that 'in television drama, the production values of film music
have provided an optimum model, even if rarely met ... In certain television programmes ... a small repertoire of musical pieces ["cues"] provided the essential character of the programme'.[25] Donnelly goes on to
discuss the original series of *Star Trek* here as an instance where repeated incidental music served to convey the 'character' of the show. And
though *Doctor Who's* fans may often contrast it with *Star Trek*, I would
argue that, in its use of incidental music, new *Who* approximates more
closely than ever before to the musical patterns and procedures of *Star
Trek: The Original Series*. David Darlington has suggested that new *Who*,
unlike *Trek*, does not have a 'musical "house style", [and uses] no library of cues',[26] but whilst technically true this downplays the extent
to which cues have been reworked between 2005 and 2008. And given
that 'the themes from *The Next Generation* and *Voyager*, etc., all have
triumphant French horn and trumpet elements, which are highly reminiscent of music normally associated with pioneering Westerns [sug-
gesting a kind of] brass triumphalism',[27] this connection may also carry
though into the new series' theme tune, which is more imbued with

'brass triumphalism' than every previous rendition, perhaps bar the 1996 *Doctor Who* TV movie.

However, the use of Murray Gold's work does not just help non-diegetic music to become the 'symbolic internalisation ... of ... the "aura of the programme"',[28] thus giving incidental music almost as strong a branding role as the show's theme tune. Gold's sonic presence also lends the programme a 'name' composer and the prestige of a film-score-like accompaniment:

> Prestige dramas, such as BBC costume dramas, use large numbers of musicians, significant amounts of music and expensive 'name' composers, who come together to produce highly evident 'prestige' music that is now more often a star than a bit-part player ... these programmes use film-like underscores ... More recent serial costume dramas such as *Vanity Fair* (1998, BBC/WGBH Boston) ... included scores that in their sumptuousness and sheer volume [i.e. quantity] of music could have been film scores.[29]

By intriguing coincidence, the 'quality' non-diegetic TV music chosen to exemplify the turn to 'film-like underscores' is *Vanity Fair*, which was in fact Murray Gold's first TV commission. Interviewed for *Sound on Sound* magazine in 2007, Gold described his approach to *Vanity Fair* as being 'really expressive, but messy and anarchic too, with loads of woodwind and brass', suggesting that his use of an orchestra for *Doctor Who*'s second Christmas Special – 'The Runaway Bride' (3.X) – goes 'back to where I was with *Vanity Fair* to some degree ... [using] *exuberantly* orchestral ... music'.[30]

Gold has also commented on the reception his demo tape got from one of the producers of *Vanity Fair*: 'I realised ... what I was doing was writing "music with jokes in". That became a bit of a trademark.'[31] By 'music with jokes in', Gold means practices of pastiche and knowing citation. He carries this through into his *Doctor Who* work, whether it is echoing 1980s synthesiser-led music from the Peter Davison era in the 2007 Children in Need Special 'Time Crash' featuring Davison himself, or citing Dudley Simpson in 'Rose' (1.1):

> There are actually little quotes from [1970s *Doctor Who* composer] Dudley Simpson in there, in the Mickey scene with the bin for instance. There are things like that which I thought were almost a gift to the fans ... There's a knowingness about my music which probably isn't there with the composers of the past so much.[32]

Through this approach, Gold's TV work recalls what has been termed 'post-classical' film scoring;[33] a return to wall-to-wall modes of classical Hollywood underscoring linked to giants of film music such as Max Steiner (e.g. *King Kong*, dir. Merian C. Cooper and Ernest B. Schoedsack, 1933) and Erich Wolfgang Korngold (e.g. *Anthony Adverse*, dir. Mervyn LeRoy and Michael Curtiz, 1936), but with the added twist of ironic quotation and musical intertextualities.[34] Gold compares his work to that of Korngold and, coming more up-to-date, Danny Elfman:

> I think in the first series, I still owed a lot to Danny Elfman and his score for the first *Batman* film. It has a lot of what people would casually refer to as a big movie sound; they call it the Korngold sound in Hollywood. There was a lot of that in the first series, and lots of four-to-the-floor drum loops and sequences, because I didn't have an orchestra, and I had to create some excitement somehow.[35]

In another instance of TV economising, Gold was instructed to achieve 'the sound of an orchestra'[36] in his series one compositions, without actually using one as this would have been prohibitively expensive. As a result, he was forced to use sampled orchestral instrumentation. It was only after the success of the 2005 series that the show's music budget was increased, enabling the partial use of an actual orchestra, and hence moving the production a step closer to the 'optimum model' of a 'film score for TV':

> I got one day with the National Orchestra of Wales to record the 45 minutes of music I needed for the [2005] Christmas special, and used the afternoon of that day to re-record some of my favourite cues from Series One, which I also used in the second series.[37]

Gold's work approximates to archetypal, Elfman-style Hollywood film scoring in another manner: it eschews significant use of 'electronic' synth-led or ambient, textural sounds. As the composer says of his initial brief, there 'was only one type of music they specifically didn't want, and that was Radiophonic Workshop-style electronic stuff'.[38] Early demos containing more abstract and less tonal material were 'immediately dispatched ... "We just want Big Tunes!" Russell [T. Davies] and Julie [Gardner] both said ... it was felt that strings, brass, woodwind was the best way to go.'[39] This music appears to have been chosen precisely for its mainstreaming qualities, connoting 'Hollywood fantasy' and action-adventure 'epic' rather than 'science fiction',[40] not to mention 1980s *Doctor Who*. David Darlington has questioned Gold's approach here, observing that it lacks a science-fictional edge:

> [Darlington:] I think one thing you're missing is that it [music in classic *Who* – MH] very much established the 'otherness' of the show, that this was science fiction melodrama, rather than just melodrama. [MG:] And now the 'otherness' is just not there. This show belongs to Earth, its concerns are with the decisions taken by men and women.[41]

Courting the displeasure of long-term fans, Gold explicitly positions the semantics of his music as being about pure 'melodrama' untainted by science fiction. *Doctor Who Magazine*'s review of the commercially available series three soundtrack pursues this opposition:

> Some of Gold's views can be quite surprising ... He chooses *The Shakespeare Code* [3.2] as a favourite score, but ... to this reviewer at least, it sounds like the standard and overcrowded fantasy fare of a latter day *Star Wars* or *Harry Potter* film. While that might be appropriate, it doesn't feel as unique or distinctive as many of his other pieces.[42]

This criticism exhibits the same value system, and the same fan viewpoint, as Darlington's earlier enquiry. For these *DWM* contributors, Gold's music has participated in shifting *Doctor Who* away from science fiction and towards 'overcrowded fantasy fare'. It feels simply too standardised, too mainstream, rather than quirky, offbeat, or eccentric, hence striking at the heart of a long-held fan-cultural justification for *Doctor Who*'s exceptionalism, that is, that its titular character is *not* merely a conventional fantasy hero, and that the show carries a spark of science-fictional 'otherness'. By seeking to reproduce the 'prestige' sound of 'Korngold'-type non-diegetic music – whilst also knowingly pastiching other compositions – Gold's style brings the show down to earth, rooting its latter-day musical identity in the 'wall-to-wall ... absolutely *massive* music' of Hollywood fantasy epic.[43]

It is evident that Murray Gold works very much to a brief from the show's executive producers and guarantors of brand consistency. Though his *Vanity Fair* style of energetic, playful composition already, to an extent, fits with the requirements set out, we cannot conclude that new *Who*'s music is purely the outcome of individual, romanticised creativity. As Gold has pointed out: 'I think in the minds of the production team, they've settled on a way that they want to use music, and they've settled on it being "abundant", and "grand", and "all-pervasive". That's come from 'the top', that directive.'[44] Nor can it be concluded that *Doctor Who*'s current non-diegetic music has securely achieved the quality of film-like underscoring, as along with budget constraints there are also considerable time constraints in TV production. Gold has been known to work from scripts as he is composing, not having visuals to which he can compose:

> Writing the music itself, I've got down to about a week ... and if scoring it for an orchestra takes another two weeks, you just can't do it [in the time allocated]! So I have to just guess; compose on the basis of the script and hope that we can make it fit. That's why we recorded a whole load of 'get-out' chords.[45]

Nor does Gold participate in how his music is integrated with other elements of the show's soundtrack: 'It's hard because I never hear the finished effects track, and often there are competing frequencies which I'd really rather weren't there.'[46] As such, his work is subject to re-contextualisation by executive producers, something he has occasionally brought into public discourse with comments such as 'Producers ... move in mysterious ways'[47] in the liner notes for 'Track 10, Hologram' on the first soundtrack CD. And in the notes accompanying the series three release, Gold observes of the track 'Only Martha Knows' that the use of 'whistling was voted out 2 to 1 by the execs. I voted it back in 1 against 0 for the CD.'[48] The genre of the DVD commentary, however, appears to work against musical analysis. Perhaps because such commentaries are conceptualised as adding new audio to pre-existent pictures, participants tend to comment on what's happening visually on-screen.[49] In each of his series three DVD box set commentaries, Gold does not speak in detail about his non-diegetic music, even stating that 'I never talk about music, I just do it',[50] although his detailed self-analyses elsewhere imply that this reticence is perhaps due to the demands of informal DVD chatter.

Generic 'science-fictional' incidental music may largely have been downplayed in the new series, but the show has not so vigorously resisted using conventions of music linked to the horror genre. Film music of this type has been analysed usefully by Donnelly in *The Spectre of Sound*[51] and by Peter Hutchings in *The Horror Film*.[52] Donnelly points out that horror's music relies on a 'small selection of musical devices ... the "stinger" or "sting", which manifests a physical shock in a musical blast, and the tension ostinato, a loop of music that provides tension through cumulative effect'.[53] However, despite these distinct musical functions, as Hutchings has argued:

> music for horror films tended to be fairly conventional ... throughout the 1930s and 1940s ... [T]here is nothing here that substantially challenges the general conventions of film music, nothing that could not easily be recycled as music for films in other genres.[54]

Unlike the electronic ambiences linked semantically to science fiction, horror music does not threaten to send out 'off-message' connotations that may damage the new series' pursuit of a mainstream, allegedly anti-SF audience. Horror's music, whilst serving generic roles, is paradoxically not immediately hearable as generic in ways which might work against the melodramatic 'Hollywood epic' formulations of *Doctor Who*'s new aurality. In Hutchings' terms, horror music does not challenge all-purpose Hollywood scoring and its musical languages.[55] As such, it offers a more workable palette for Murray Gold's music, given that this has suppressed 'otherness' in pursuit of coding *Who* as an essentially human drama suitable for a mass, 'mainstream' imagined audience.

Though BBC Wales' *Doctor Who* may not use non-diegetic music to follow all the strictures of the horror genre, it has used one key device recurrently that Donnelly[56] and Hutchings[57] both highlight – representing the presence of the off-screen (about to be on-screen) monster through a specific musical cue. Perhaps the most infamous horror monster of all time, Dracula, had a three-note theme structured like 'Drac-u-la' in the 1958 Hammer film. Possibly representing another of Murray Gold's knowing pastiche moments, the reborn Master (John Simm) has his own theme: 'the Saxon motif which sounds like it's singing The *Ma*-ster'.[58] And whilst each of the major old series' returning monsters – Daleks, Cybermen and Sontarans – now have their own sound bite catchphrases, they also have distinct musical markers of their presence, which cut through textual soundscapes (including diegetic chanting in the third case). The Daleks frequently appear along with non-diegetic 'stinger'-like bursts of choral voices, whilst the Cybermen have a six-note theme which 'can't really be separated from the clump of their marching ... This, as much as the music, signalled their ominous advance.'[59] Associating the Daleks with a choral sound intertextually recalls Jerry Goldsmith's Oscar-winning score for

*The Omen* (dir. Richard Donner, 1976),[60] which Hutchings analyses as

> an important vehicle for the film's systematic counter-pointing of a
> contemporary world's rational scepticism with pre-modern beliefs ...
> [C]horal music... [in *The Omen*] helped to give a sense of an ages-old
> conflict between good and evil that predated the drama of the films
> and which gave narrative events a portentous resonance.[61]

Likewise, the reappearance of the Daleks in the *Doctor Who* universe is linked to a portentous 'ages-old conflict between good and
evil' involving the Doctor's own people. It has also been linked to a
range of religious meanings, given that the Daleks of 'The Parting of
the Ways' (1.13) are identified as fundamentalists. By the time of 4.13's
Dalek finale, however, Murray Gold's non-diegetic music is more insistently rhythmic and led by percussion rather than a choral tone, positioning these Daleks, and their creator Davros, within an escalating
scale of ever-more-epic connotation. Whereas series three culminated
with 'The Sound of Drums' (3.12) present in its diegesis, series four
ends with drumming sounds dominating Gold's non-diegetic music,
still strongly coding the series as 'mainstream' action-adventure rather
than SF.

However, it is not just the headline acts of Daleks, Cybermen and
the Master who are given intriguing musical themes. As the werewolf
of 'Tooth and Claw' (2.2) chases the Doctor, Rose and Queen Victoria,
highly rhythmic techno-flavoured incidental music is deployed, which
uses extreme stereo separation, seeming to bounce from speaker to
speaker. On a home cinema-style set-up this has the effect of physically moving the non-diegetic music rapidly and rhythmically from
place to place around the viewer's room; even on a standard stereo
TV, the soundtrack pulses metronomically from left to right channel.
As Robynn Stilwell notes, television sound is now capable of reproducing a reasonably 'naturalistic acoustic picture which has direction'.[62]
In this case, the non-locatable threat of the werewolf – which remains
menacingly offscreen and hence un-placed for much of the episode's
library sequence – is captured by the use of stereo separation and
literal sonic movement within the soundtrack's acoustic picture. Incidental music and sound effect are blurred together here.[63]

If the placing of stereo sound can form part of *Doctor Who*'s use
of horror music stylings, then so too can the unusually marked absence of music and indeed all sound: '[i]n horror's world of sounds
... sometimes the most unnerving sound is no sound at all'.[64] This

disruption of both diegetic sound (within the narrative world) and non-diegetic music (on the soundtrack) tears a hole in the sonic fabric of the programme, especially given the frequently 'wall-to-wall' presence of non-diegetic music. It occurs in '42' (3.7), when the Doctor and Martha are separated in outer space by the fact that Martha has become trapped in a jettisoned escape pod. The cessation of diegetic and non-diegetic sound emphasises the unbridgeable separation of the characters; even communication of the most basic sort has become a physical impossibility. It also calls up a science-fictional intertextuality: the 'realist' outer-space silences of *2001: A Space Odyssey* (dir. Stanley Kubrick, 1968). We might expect a melancholic incidental theme marking the loss and emptiness of such a moment, but by opting for stark silence, director Graeme Harper achieves a rare, ominous punctuation in the soundscape's clatter and 'epic fantasy' template. The irony here, of course, is that having studiously avoiding branding *Doctor Who*'s music as science-fictional, where SF audio *is* strongly intertextually referenced, then it is essentially only present via absence. The one sound of hard-edged science fiction that is seemingly allowed to leak into the text without damaging its brand identity as 'mainstream' is the sound of silence.

If new *Who* has very occasionally been cut adrift from non-diegetic music, then Murray Gold's music has also taken on an independent, extra-textual existence via concert performances such as those on Sunday 19 November 2006 (for Children in Need) and Sunday 27 July 2008 (the Proms). The notion of using *Who*, as a 'mainstream' family TV series, to widen access to classical music was embraced by the latter event – a *Doctor Who*-themed Prom at the Royal Albert Hall. Russell T. Davies' programme notes offer a character-based justification for the Doctor's appearance in the Proms, displaying detailed intratextual fan knowledge:

> Way back, the First Doctor ended up in the court of Emperor Nero, disguised as Ancient Rome's most famous lyre-player ... while the Ninth was seen to dance with Rose Tyler in the TARDIS, to the music of Glenn Miller! But when I realised that the Tenth Doctor hadn't yet shown any aptitude for music, I decided that this special Proms concert was my chance to put things right.[65]

The articulation of *Doctor Who* and the BBC Proms – two BBC brands acting in synergy and in support of a 'public service' elevation of 'cultured' good taste – is thus presented and justified narratively.

This is 'naturally' how the character of the Doctor is. Davies' character justification ultimately segues into a parallel between *Doctor Who* itself and 'music': '[M]usic can go anywhere, reach anyone, and make better people of us all. Just like the Doctor.'[66] Declining to identify this music as Wagner, Prokofiev or Holst, it is left discursively open, unidentified by genre and type, despite the fact that the event is about promoting the conservative, civilising value of the Proms specifically, and not the music of the Prodigy, for instance, or *High School Musical*. Press coverage, for example in the *Independent*, was quick to cry 'dumbing down' in response to the collision of new *Who*'s non-diegetic music and classical pieces:

> The concert ... was part of the drive to make the annual Proms season more inclusive, [c]ombining popular pieces including parts of Holst's Planets Suite and Wagner's The Ride of the Valkyries with scores from the TV series ... Hosting a concert using the popular appeal of such a ... programme has left the BBC open to accusations of dumbing down, a charge vehemently denied by festival director and BBC Radio 3 controller Roger Wright[:] ... 'It's hard to talk about dumbing down when we're hosting a concert for families that include[s] pieces by Holst, Wagner and Prokofiev.'[67]

Whether undecidably 'dumbing down' the Proms or 'culturing up' *Doctor Who*,[68] this event nevertheless links *Who*'s non-diegetic music with brand values of mainstreamed 'accessibility' and inclusiveness. Murray Gold's work on new *Who* was required to be 'easily assimilable',[69] and the Prom event emphasises this very accessibility as a 'nice "in" for kids to see classical music live'.[70] *Doctor Who Magazine*'s coverage of the event also notes the 'stated aim' of the Proms: 'to encourage an audience for concert hall music who, though not normally attending classical concerts, would be attracted by the low ticket prices and informal atmosphere'.[71] New *Who* and the BBC Proms resonate as brands, and cultural texts, precisely because both are focused so intently on connoting inclusivity.

Thus far, I have focused predominantly on the non-diegetic or 'incidental' music added over *Who*'s narratives, but what of its diegetic relative, that is, music which occurs within narrative events and settings? In the following section, I will move on to consider how diegetic music has been used to further defuse the programme's associations with 'niche' science fiction and position it as 'mainstream' TV. This forms another way in which the 'text-function' operates discursively

in new *Who*. 'Mainstream' TV, like 'quality' TV, is not a naturally occurring thing, but rather a classification that emerges through (extra-)
textual and discursive bids for categorisation, as, for example, with the
use of pop music to call up discourses of 'the contemporary'. Though
Murray Gold has described some of his non-diegetic music, such as
'Doomsday' and 'This is Gallifrey' as having a 'soft-rock ... beat ...
quite driving ... [with] a melodic, rock 'n' roll ... feel',[72] it is as diegetic
music that pop has made its presence most strongly felt.

## Pop–Rock Diegetic Music:
## A Time Lord Brought Down to Earth

New *Who* does make use of music that's shown to be occurring within
its narratives, but it does so sparingly, for example in several Christmas
specials where 'Love Don't Roam' (3.X) and 'The Stowaway' (4.X),
both written by Murray Gold, are integrated into scenes of celebratory
dancing and partying. Gold also wrote the show tune 'My Angel put
the Devil in Me', featured diegetically in 'Daleks in Manhattan' (3.4).
These compositions fit into *Doctor Who*'s format precisely because
they are linked to 'special' episodes and to stories dealing with Earth-
based or derived celebratory rituals (weddings, Christmas) as well as
relevant periods of history, in the case of 'Daleks in Manhattan'.

Arguably, the new series' episode that pushes most at the established format of *Doctor Who* is also the episode containing the most
diegetic popular music: 'Love & Monsters' (2.10).[73] This episode was
filmed at the same time as another, meaning that it could only briefly
feature the Doctor and Rose. The problem posed by this production
wrinkle is what to substitute for the presence of the Doctor – a greater
focus on the story's monsters than usual? Or the creation of surrogate
Doctor/companion characters?

'Love & Monsters' puts a connotative version of *Doctor Who* fandom centre-stage, featuring a group of people ('LInDA') who are
aware of the Doctor's interventions in Earth affairs, and who appreciate and analyse his actions. But it is not just fandom that moves into
the space vacated by the Doctor; popular music also fleshes out this
present-day episode, whether it is Il Divo as a sign of Jackie Tyler's
tastes, or ELO as loved by the character of Elton Pope (Marc Warren). The episode even makes the Doctor and ELO's music curiously

interchangeable in a number of ways; both are objects of fixation for Elton, both are linked to his childhood and images of his mother, and both are shown as assisting in the bonding and companionship of the LInDA group.

However, it remains the case that BBC Wales' *Doctor Who*, on the whole, makes relatively little use of diegetic popular music. This can be contrasted with the rise in TV drama's use of popular music, which Robin Nelson and others have argued has become 'a dominant feature of television drama'.[74] Nelson sees this as an especially prevalent phenomenon in dramas aimed at youth audiences:

> This whole approach resonates with the omnipresence of popular music as a soundtrack to contemporary life ... Young people in particular carry their music with them (on ... iPods) such that everything they do is set to music and the sounds are inscribed within memories.[75]

Whilst new *Who* has been targeted successfully at a 'family', 'mainstream' audience, there is an apparent obstacle to its diegetic use of popular music. Analysing the employment of pop music in film soundtracks, Jeff Smith notes that 'science fiction and historical epics ... [involve] problems of musical appropriateness posed by each genre's treatment of setting', since narratives in the distant past or remote future make it 'difficult to motivate popular songs' within their diegetic settings.[76] In short, *Doctor Who*'s time-travelling scenarios greatly reduce possibilities for using pop music diegetically. Having said that, Russell T. Davies' opening scripts for series one immediately invert such a logic, refraining from using pop music and iPod references in the present-day London of 'Rose' (1.1), whilst deploying both within the science-fictional, far-future setting of 'The End of the World' (1.2). Here, the character of Cassandra mistakes a jukebox for an iPod, and both Soft Cell's electro-pop 'Tainted Love' and Britney Spears' 'Toxic' are used diegetically.

Davies' screenplays recognise that when the visual imagery and *mise-en-scène* of a story are highly science-fictional, then it is via recognisable popular music that such settings can be symbolically 'brought down to earth' for a mainstream audience imagined to be prejudiced against science fiction. Such a device – the musical recoding of SF settings – occurs again in the diegetic music of Matt Jones' 'The Impossible Planet' (2.8) (with Ravel's *Boléro* playing whilst alien creatures, the Ood, troop from their workplace). Back in series one, the futuristic version of *Big Brother* in 'Bad Wolf' (1.12) is given cultural verisimilitude and a contemporary, non-SF flavour by the pumping use of the *Big Brother* theme tune. And in spaceship-bound '42' (3.7), the SF *mise-en-scène* is supplemented by pub-quiz-style questions involving the pop music of Elvis and the Beatles. Viewed as science fiction, such dialogue may seem jarring, odd, and even generically unconvincing – as might the existence of *Big Brother* in the far future of 'Bad Wolf'. However, to criticise the inclusion of pop trivia and diegetic pop music as 'bad' science fiction misses the point that these are precisely about the making-contemporary of what might otherwise be too far removed from the experiences and tastes of audiences imagined as hostile to science fiction. Diegetic pop thus serves to discursively 'mainstream' new *Who*, acting as part of its classificatory text-function.

As well as being used as a counterpoint to the conventions of science fiction, pop has also been introduced diegetically as part of a strategy of aestheticisation. This is apparent in 'The Sound of Drums' and 'Last of the Time Lords' (3.12–3.13), where the Rogue Traders' track 'Voodoo Child' ('Here come the drums, here come the drums') and the Scissor Sisters' 'I Can't Decide' are both played by the Master, a psychotic Time Lord with a taste for high-energy pop. In one sense, this again defuses science-fictional conceits; the invasion of Earth by future-human death-spheres is set to a bouncing, synth beat, whilst the Doctor's aged, incapacitated self is wheeled around to a Scissor Sisters' neo-disco accompaniment. But the counterpoint here is not simply that of 'contemporary' diegetic sound versus science-fictional visuals. For, in these two cases, diegetic music more precisely re-contextualises the narrative's bleakness. As showrunner Russell T. Davies intimates in a moment of self-critique, the conclusion of series three moved into territories that were about as dark as the format could support, such as the transformation of humanity into Toclafane monsters: 'it's not a slip-up as such ... but it does get very dark, Series Three, as it progresses, and I think there's a little element of fun missing'.[77]

If Murray Gold's non-diegetic music substituted for spectacle at the beginning of 'Rose' (1.1), then here the use of diegetic pop music substitutes for the 'fun', the lightness of touch, and the optimistic, feel-good verve that are all so markedly absent in depicted narrative events. This diegetic music is not only anti-science-fictional but also compensatory in tone, working as a conservation of narrative energy and a promise of the Doctor's return to potency. 'Voodoo Child', of course, simultaneously demarcates the cliffhanger high-point of series three, and the pop song's thumping high-energy is an effective marker point for this:

> television is dominated by moments of climactic drama among its fragmentation within a continuous 'flow'. This requires that certain moments are emphasised, noted as significant, monumentalised and aestheticised. Pop music has proved adept at all of these.[78]

It should also be noted that the lyrics of both pop songs featured in the final two episodes of series three are directly relevant to narrative events, providing a further motivation for their inclusion. 'Here come the drums' refers to the drumming sound which has mentally plagued the Master, whilst the Scissor Sisters' lyrics 'I can't decide/Whether you should live or die' reflects the ambivalent relationship between the Doctor and the Master, as well as mirroring the fact that the Doctor is, at this point, the Master's prisoner.

After the extreme integration of narrative and diegetic pop music represented by 'The Sound of Drums' and 'Last of the Time Lords' (3.12–3.13), series four resisted repeating this equation. Unusually, the 2008 run of episodes refrained from mainstreaming *Who* through the use of diegetic pop–rock, though by featuring Catherine Tate as companion, the episodes instead took on a more 'star-led' strategy to position *Doctor Who* as a 'mainstream' and connotatively anti-SF text. If music was less frequently called upon to diegetically and non-diegetically 'regenrify' the show across series four, this may have been because its light entertainment credentials were more directly represented through Tate's casting and performance: 'Catherine Tate makes it very accessible ... *Doctor Who* is a part of that landscape of light entertainment now.'[79]

Elsewhere in the series, diegetic pop music has been used as a tool for 'softening' the narrative representation of dark and perverse actions, as well as substituting for visuals that would be unacceptably gory or violent in an early-evening 'family' TV show. 'The Lion Sleeps Tonight' by Tight Fit (1982) is utilised in 'Rise of the Cybermen' (2.5) in this way. Here, the song plays over the conversion of homeless people into Cybermen, covering up this wrongdoing and distracting from horrifying narrative implications via its attention-grabbing incongruity. The realisation of this sequence works in three sonic stages: when the music track first comes in, it is vibrantly present, mixed high and clear, the implication being that Mr Crane (Colin Spaull), his eyes closed, is personally blocking out the grim reality of the Cyber conversion. We then fade to empty long-shots of the conversion factory and its machinery, with the music receding in the mix, becoming more distant, emptier, and akin to the thinner, tinnier sound of a workplace radio. Finally, over a shot of the night skyline, the music track fades out altogether, echoing into the distance. Audible human screeching continues, *sans* diegetic music.

As a result of sounds of human suffering being maintained throughout, and outlasting the diegetic music, the ultimate effect is one of a failed cover-up: we, the audience, can still bear aural witness to John Lumic's Cyber-conversions. By using the soundtrack alone to convey both suffering and its attempted drowning-out, highly unpleasant visual imagery is evaded, whilst narrative darkness is lightened, at least to a degree. As Helen Wheatley has observed of 'gothic television', a category into which she places new *Who*,[80] the notion of 'showing restraint' for the TV audience often 'refers to visual, not aural, restraint'.[81] Sound supposedly delivers what would otherwise be too threatening or distressing for visualisation. As I have suggested here, however, sound – and diegetic music especially – can also run counter to, and ameliorate, narrative or visual unpleasantness.

To conclude, I have argued that *Doctor Who*'s distinctive aural identity has been a key component in the success of its twenty-first century makeover. Using diegetic and popular music far less than many other contemporary TV productions, it has employed 'wall-to-wall' non-diegetic music modelled on classical Hollywood film scoring and associated with 'prestige' TV. As such, Murray Gold's contribution to the show's re-conceptualisation and genre-shifting towards 'epic fantasy' should not be underrated. Whilst common sense might suggest that it is greatly enhanced CGI and effects work that has single-handedly brought about this change, I would suggest that Gold's anti-science-fictional and post-classical incidental music has been just as instrumental, to excuse the pun. Gold's non-diegetic music has even substituted for visual spectacle on occasion, and has grounded the series in a consistent sense of 'mainstream' melodrama and fantasy-horror. Meanwhile, other diegetic and non-diegetic popular music has sometimes gone so far as to substitute for the character of the Doctor, as well as, more commonly, modifying the darker tone of certain narrative events and visuals. New *Who*'s music has become an efficient, standardised point of branding and a marker of the series' newfound textual consistency, unlike the 'hit-and-miss' variations of the classic series.

The textual classification of 'mainstream' TV has, like 'quality' TV, usually been a relational term, that is, it has been defined against assorted 'others'. This chapter has explored how new *Who's* music has evaded connotations of science fiction – conceptualised as a 'niche' genre – in favour of 'Hollywood fantasy-epic' and emotive 'human drama', with these being culturally positioned and imagined as 'mainstream'. In Chapter 7 I want to analyse the variability of mainstream discourses in more detail, addressing how *Doctor Who's* status as 'cult' television has been strongly opposed in production and publicity discourses. Resembling author-functions and generic functions, what I have termed the 'text-function' acts as an attempted discursive fixing of textual classifications, seeking to police and box-in specific textual identities (such as 'quality' and 'mainstream' TV) by appropriating relevant discourses – here 'big music', 'wall-to-wall' scoring and 'contemporary' pop. But the discursive operations of the 'text-function' also ward off unwanted textual classifications, as Chapter 7 will further explore. Just why has 'cult' status become so problematic for *Doctor Who's* fan-producers?

## NOTES

1   See Caryl Flinn (1992) *Strains of Utopia*, Princeton University Press, Princeton, p.6.

2   Robynn J. Stilwell (2001) 'Sound and empathy: subjectivity, gender and the cinematic soundscape', in K.J. Donnelly (ed.) *Film Music: Critical Approaches*, Edinburgh University Press, Edinburgh, p.168.

3   Michel Chion (1994) *Audio-Vision: Sound on Screen*, Columbia University Press, New York, p.157.

4   Ibid., p.165.

5   See *http://www.bbc.co.uk/tvmoments/vote/* and Matt Hills (2008) 'The dispersible television text: theorising moments of the new *Doctor Who*', *Science Fiction Film and Television* i/1, pp.25–44, on '*Doctor Who* moments'.

6   See Rick Altman (1999) *Film/Genre*, BFI Publishing, London, p.78, on 're-genrification', though he approaches it as extra-textual. Here, I am arguing that new *Who* uses music to intratextually regenrify other narrative and visual elements, thereby seeking to position the programme as 'mainstream'.

7   Hinchcliffe in Charles Norton (2008) 'Evolution of a monster hit', *The Stage*, 15 May, p.52.

8    Mark Jancovich and Nathan Hunt (2004) 'The mainstream, distinction, and cult TV', in Sara Gwenllian-Jones and Roberta E. Pearson (eds) *Cult Television*, University of Minnesota Press, Minneapolis, p.40.

9    Sarah Thornton (1995) *Club Cultures*, Polity Press, Cambridge, p.101.

10   See K.J. Donnelly (2005) *The Spectre of Sound: Music in Film and Television*, BFI Publishing, London, pp.8–9.

11   See K.J. Donnelly (2007) 'Between prosaic functionalism and sublime experimentation: *Doctor Who* and musical sound design', in David Butler (ed.) *Time and Relative Dissertations in Space: Critical perspectives on Doctor Who*, Manchester University Press, Manchester and New York, pp.190–203; Louis Niebur (2007) 'The music of machines: "special sound" as music in *Doctor Who*', in Butler (ed.): *Time and Relative Dissertations in Space*, pp.204–14.

12   Donnelly: 'Between prosaic functionalism', p.197.

13   Ibid.

14   Vanessa Bishop (2007) 'Original television soundtrack', *Doctor Who Magazine* 379, p.65.

15   Donnelly: *The Spectre of Sound*, p.112.

16   Ibid., p.119.

17   Dick Mills in John Tulloch and Manuel Alvarado (1983) Doctor Who: *The Unfolding Text*, Macmillan, London, p.20.

18   Gold, Murray (2006) 'Music notes' on the inlay card for Doctor Who: *Original Television Soundtrack*, BBC, Silva Screen Records.

19   Ibid.

20   In Matt Bell (2007) 'Doctor's notes – Murray Gold: composing for *Doctor Who*', *Sound on Sound* (June), p.45.

21   Ibid.

22   Tulloch and Alvarado: *The Unfolding Text*, p.19.

23   Gold in David Darlington (2005) 'Murray Gold: incidental hits', *Doctor Who Magazine* 362, p.40.

24   Claudia Gorbman (1987) *Unheard Melodies: Narrative Film Music*, BFI Publishing, London, p.68.

25   Donnelly: *The Spectre of Sound*, p.122.

26   David Darlington (2006) 'Murray Gold', in Doctor Who: *A Celebration*, BBC Wales, Cardiff, p.5.

27   Jan Johnson-Smith (2005) *American Science Fiction TV: Star Trek, Stargate and Beyond*, I.B.Tauris, London and New York, p.243.

28   Niebur: 'The music of machines', p.210.

29   Donnelly: *The Spectre of Sound*, p.117.

30   Gold in Bell: 'Doctor's notes', pp.41, 46.

31   Gold in Darlington: 'Murray Gold: incidental hits', p.36.

32   Ibid., p.39.

33   See K.J. Donnelly (1998) 'The classical film score forever? *Batman, Batman Returns* and post-classical film music', in Steve Neale and Murray Smith (eds) *Contemporary Hollywood Cinema*, Routledge, London and New York, pp.142–55.

34   See also Kathryn Kalinak (1995) '"Disturbing the guests with this racket": music and *Twin Peaks*', in David Lavery (ed.) *Full of Secrets: Critical Approaches to* Twin Peaks, Wayne State University Press, Detroit, pp.82–92.

35    Gold in Bell: 'Doctor's notes', p.43.
36    Ibid., p.42.
37    Ibid., p.44.
38    Ibid., p.42.
39    Gold in Darlington: 'Murray Gold: incidental hits', p.38.
40    See Jeff Smith (1998) *The Sounds of Commerce: Marketing Popular Film Music*, Columbia University Press, New York, p.218.
41    In Darlington: 'Murray Gold: incidental hits', p.42.
42    Vanessa Bishop (2007) 'Original television soundtrack: series three', *Doctor Who Magazine* 390, p.66.
43    Gold in Darlington: 'Murray Gold: incidental hits', p.40.
44    In David Darlington (2006) 'Gold bars', *Doctor Who Magazine* 373, p.54.
45    Ibid.; see also Murray Gold (2007) Liner notes for *Doctor Who: Series 3 Music*, BBC National Orchestra of Wales, conducted by Ben Foster, BBC, Silva Screen Records on 'The Master Tape' theme.
46    Gold in Darlington: 'Murray Gold: incidental hits', p.39.
47    Gold: 'Music notes'.
48    Gold: 'Liner notes'.
49    See Matt Hills (2007) 'From the box in the corner to the box set on the shelf: "TV III" and the cultural/textual valorisations of DVD', *New Review of Film and Television Studies* v/1, pp.41–60.
50    See 'Human Nature' (3.8), DVD commentary track.
51    Donnelly: *The Spectre of Sound*.
52    Peter Hutchings (2004) *The Horror Film*, Pearson Education, Harlow.
53    Donnelly: *The Spectre of Sound*, p.91.
54    Hutchings: *The Horror Film*, p.142, referring partly to Max Steiner's classical score for *King Kong*, 1933; the type of film score approvingly cited by Gold.
55    See also Theodor Adorno and Hanns Eisler (1994 [1947]) *Composing for the Films*, Athlone Press, London and Atlantic Highlands, pp.16, 36–7.
56    Donnelly: *The Spectre of Sound*, p.93.
57    Hutchings: *The Horror Film*, p.141.
58    Gold: 'Liner notes'.
59    Gold: 'Music notes'.
60    See Donnelly: *The Spectre of Sound*, p.101.
61    Hutchings: *The Horror Film*, p.145.
62    Stilwell: 'Sound and empathy', p.173.
63    See Donnelly: 'Between prosaic functionalism'; Niebur: 'The music of machines'; and David Burnand and Miguel Mera (2004) 'Fast and cheap? The film music of John Carpenter', in Ian Conrich and David Woods (eds) *The Cinema of John Carpenter: The Technique of Terror*, Wallflower Press, London, p.65.
64    Hutchings: *The Horror Film*, p.147.
65    Russell T. Davies (2008) 'Russell T. Davies introduces "Music of the Spheres"', in *Doctor Who Prom Programme*, BBC, p.15.
66    Ibid.
67    Jerome Taylor (2008) 'Daleks invade the proms (while earthlings pay £250 for a ticket)', *Independent*, 28 July, available online at *http://www.*

*independent.co.uk/arts-entertainment/music/news/daleks-invade-the-proms-while-earthlings-pay-163250-for-a-ticket-878691.html.*

68    See also Chapter 5 in this volume.

69    Darlington: 'Murray Gold', p.5.

70    Ben Foster in David Darlington (2008) 'Music to your spheres', *Doctor Who Magazine* 399, Panini Comics, Tunbridge Wells, p.36.

71    Ibid.

72    In ibid., p.37.

73    See J. Shaun Lyon (2006) *Second Flight*, Telos Press, Tolworth, p.288.

74    Robin Nelson (2007) *State of Play: Contemporary 'High-End' TV Drama*, Manchester University Press, Manchester and New York, p.118; see also Donnelly: *The Spectre of Sound*.

75    Nelson: *State of Play*, p.119.

76    Smith: *The Sounds of Commerce*, p.218.

77    Davies in Benjamin Cook (2007) 'Leader of the gang', *Doctor Who Magazine* 386, Panini Comics, Tunbridge Wells, p.14.

78    Donnelly: *The Spectre of Sound*, p.134.

79    Hinchcliffe in Norton: 'Evolution of a monster hit', p.52.

80    Helen Wheatley (2006) *Gothic Television*, Manchester University Press, Manchester, p.71.

81    Ibid., p.41.

# 7

# A MAINSTREAM CULT?

The reimagined *Doctor Who* has been positioned as 'quality' TV through a 'text-function' comprising a range of industry discourses (see Chapter 5), whilst also seeking to avoid associations with science fiction via its use of pop music and Murray Gold's 'action-adventure' compositions (Chapter 6). In this final chapter I will explore a further textual classification, previously articulated with *Who*, which the new series has sought to disavow – the issue of 'cult' status. Whether a TV show is 'cult' or 'mainstream' has been viewed by scholars as a binary, an either/or, with the two categories being defined against one another. As Mark Jancovich and Nathan Hunt suggest:

> There is no single quality that characterizes a cult text; rather, cult texts are defined through a process in which shows are positioned in opposition to the mainstream, a classification that is no more coherent as an object than the cult and is also a product of the same process of distinction that creates the opposed couplet mainstream/cult.[1]

I will argue that production discourses have represented 'mainstream' versus 'cult' in this manner, leading to the disparagement of oppositional sections of online fandom positioned as a 'cult' audience. 'Proper' fandom has thus been disciplined discursively and partly brought into line with a vision of new *Who* as 'mainstream' TV.[2] At the same time, however, a series of mainstream/cult distinctions have continued to operate, with fans supposedly wanting long-term textual continuity, versus the mainstream audience wanting clearly told stories, and fans wanting technobabble and SF trappings versus the mainstream audience appreciating contemporary relevance. The couplet mainstream/cult has been drawn on in fan and production discourses, with fan cultures seeking to define their distinctiveness from the 'general viewer' at the same time as fan-producers have sought to discipline *Doctor Who*'s long-term fandom discursively.

I will further argue that *Who* fans do not always position 'mainstream' status as an imagined, bad other to cult status. 'Mainstream' acceptance can represent a positive affirmation of fans' tastes, and fandom partly celebrates the mainstreaming of *Doctor Who* as well as adopting a discursive distance from it. It is production discourse, rather than fandom, which most rigorously polices difference and distinction between 'mainstream' and 'cult' TV. Previous scholarship has characterised *Doctor Who* fans as a 'powerless elite' structurally 'situated between producers they have little control over, and the "wider public" whose continued following of the show can never be assured'.[3] But how, if at all, has the new series altered the positioning of this 'powerless elite' in relation to cult/mainstream distinctions?

In the second section of the chapter I consider how 'cult' and 'mainstream' textual classifications may be increasingly intersecting due to changes in the contemporary TV industry, especially the move towards 'transmedia storytelling'.[4] Producers' antagonistic 'text-function' of 'mainstream' (valued) versus 'cult' (devalued) may be heading for technology-driven obsolescence. And I will argue that through a variety of narrative strategies – high-concept; 'the narrative special effect'; Dalek-centric storytelling; technobabble-as-performance – new *Who* successfully unites 'cult' and 'mainstream' readings. Here, rather than cult and mainstream constituting an either/or binary, cult becomes simply one grouping *within* a 'consensus' audience defined as mainstream by the BBC's public service remit.[5] First, though, how have battle lines from *Doctor Who*'s history been drawn up around the latest incarnation?

## Cult versus Mainstream:
## 'It's High Time We Dropped the Cult Thing'

For UK *Doctor Who* fans, the term 'cult' is not necessarily something to be embraced, having taken on a specific meaning in the show's history. Cult status has been equated with *Who's* ratings decline across the 1980s, and its eventual cancellation in 1989:

> The trend in the 1980s ... was towards an increasingly segmented and compartmentalised view of audiences ... the family audience was dissipating ... Thus it was that in its final years, *Doctor Who* became a marginal series made for a 'cult' rather than a mainstream audience.[6]

An influential fan-cultural narrative of the original series' decline focuses on the notion that *Who* became too self-referential, and too focused on its own history, until the 'general audience' were alienated from continuity-heavy stories. In 1996, when selecting a classic series story to screen to a non-fan audience of 10- and 11-year-old children, then-editor of *Doctor Who Magazine* Gary Gillatt included only one story from the 1980s as a possible choice, 'The Visitation' (1982). All others were ruled out by the condition that the selection should 'Have a comprehensible and rewarding storyline ... [n]ot requir[ing] too much "pre-knowledge" of the main characters or a detailed understanding of *Doctor Who* continuity.'[7] This perspective on the 1980s series is not absolute within fandom, especially as different generations of fans grew up with different eras of the show. However, it has been commonly reproduced in academic accounts from scholar-fans, such as Kim Newman's description of 'decline into niche cultdom',[8] or Neil Perryman's account of the show's 2005 return as a transformation from 'niche cult, aimed at a minority of hardcore fans ... [to] flagship franchise.'[9] Such analyses assume that 'mainstream' and 'cult' are essentially opposed terms – *Doctor Who* cannot be both things simultaneously, but instead has veered between the two across its history.[10] 'Cult', for long-term fans, hence carries the taint of the programme's failure in the 1980s rather than necessarily being viewed positively as an anti-mainstream discourse. It has a specific fan-cultural meaning rather than fitting into academic generalisations.[11]

By contrast, 'subcultural' accounts of cult status assume that the term is valued positively by media fans seeking to distinguish themselves from a devalued 'mainstream'. Joanne Hollows has argued that

this binary is gendered, with 'cult' being linked to cultural constructions of masculinity, whereas the 'mainstream' is feminised as a space
of distracted consumerism.[12] Sarah Thornton's work on subculture
also supports this concept of the 'mainstream' as a culturally feminised space devalued by male subculturalists.[13] Jancovich and Hunt
relate these arguments directly to cult television:

> Cult TV fandom claims that the industry's commercial considerations
> lead to a lack of originality in the development of shows and a tenden-
> cy to ruin established shows in the pursuit of the mainstream audience
> ... executives, associated with mainstream consumerism by virtue of
> their supposed adherence to the profit motive and interest in numbers,
> are placed in stark contrast with fandom's appreciation of ... shows.[14]

Cult is again connotatively masculinised, being contrasted to
'mainstream consumerism' and TV 'commerce'. In Jancovich and
Hunt's account, cult TV fans also construct distinctions between cult
and mainstream *audiences*:

> The widening popularity of what were originally deemed cult TV shows
> threatens to blur the line between the authentic subcultural insider and
> the inauthentic outsider. This produces a policing of the boundaries of
> the subculture ... Related to policing is the search for a new authentici-
> ty. The exclusivity that gives value to a cult text may not be sustainable.
> As others come to appreciate the text, fans must either find new forms
> of exclusive appreciation or relegate the text to the passé.[15]

*Doctor Who* fandom has recurrently shown an interest in demarcat-
ing distinctions between fans and non-fans, cult and mainstream,
but not purely along the axis of authentic/inauthentic. Thanks to the
show's cancellation, and the 'interregnum' where it was off-air as
an ongoing, new TV series,[16] fans have sought to reduce cult/main-
stream distinctions, arguing that 'their' show could once again be a
popular success (as, indeed, it now is). The 'imagined other' of the
non-fan has thus been an object of fascination for fandom as well as
an opposed identity, with both *Doctor Who Magazine* and fanzines
attempting to 'assess the defining traits of the fan and casual audiences of *Doctor Who*, and how the two groups may differ from each
other'.[17] Before, and upon, *Doctor Who*'s return in 2005 this was a
far from academic question for fandom: answering it meant assess-
ing whether the show could achieve widespread popularity in the
noughties.[18]

Though fan magazine articles might be assumed, in scholarly terms, to 'police' the line between insider *Who* fans and outsider non-fans, they rarely work directly in such a way. Fan distinctions are reproduced, but 'non-fan' responses are depicted simultaneously as resembling elements of fan identity:

> what have we learnt from [our panel of 10 students aged 10 and 11 from] class 4G [of Ibstock Place School]? ... They have championed the importance of a good story above all other factors, including special effects and such gimmickry. They have shown that *Doctor Who* – when it takes care to cater for the general viewer and not bury its head in its own mythology – still has a place on teatime television.[19]

By indicating that non-fans actually care about the same things as long-term fans – for example, the fan-cultural narrative that 'good' *Doctor Who* has traditionally revolved around storytelling rather than glossy production values[20] – fan interpretations of the classic series are validated. Likewise, after the 1996 TV movie, the non-fan audience could again be demonstrated to mirror fan readings: [Jo, age 11 years and 3 months, said] 'The 1970s *Doctor Who* had a brilliant story and good-enough special effects, but this new one had brilliant special effects and a good-enough story.'[21] Stressing fan and non-fan sameness rather than policing fan-cultural difference is a strategy that recurs in Mark Wyman's *DWM* article dealing with the 2005 series. Here, 21 students aged between 11 and 14 years old from Patcham High School wrote diary entries about the new series, as well as being visited for focus group discussions.[22] Wyman playfully stresses that this youthful audience does not always use the 'correct' fan-cultural terminology for Christopher Eccleston's Doctor, calling him 'the *first* Doctor',[23] and light-heartedly apologises for their lapse: 'Sorry, should have told old hands to look away.'[24] He also quotes another respondent from Year 7: 'Brad, like a true *Who* fan of the old school, felt one thing was lacking – gratuitous continuity. "If that was meant to be the last time the Daleks would be shown, there should have been lots of flashbacks with the Doctor and the Time Lords."'[25]

Discursively, 'old school' fandom and supposed 'non-fan outsiders' are united in a shared response to the text, again affirming fan readings. This construction of fan and non-fan sameness rather than a rigid policing of authentic/inauthentic audiences is also strongly evident in unofficial fanzines. Screening 'The Awakening' (1984) to members of a *Doctor Who* Appreciation Society Local Group, and to a group made up of family and friends outside socially organised fandom, the *Doctor's Recorder* argued:

> Perhaps the biggest difference between the two groups is that casual viewers would be more inclined to remember icons such as the Daleks, and to exaggerate their significance in the series as a whole, whereas the fans are more knowledgeable about the minutiae of the series's history ... When it comes down to ... actually watching the programme, our exercise seems to demonstrate that there is actually very little difference between what the fans appreciate and that which is sought by casual viewers.[26]

A follow-up article dealing specifically with the new series went even further by inverting assumptions over how 'old school' fans and the new audience might react. Here, it was a lifelong male fan who 'glanced at the "off" switch on my remote' during 'Bad Wolf' (1.12), whilst a new 13-year-old, female viewer 'loved the the *Big Brother* part and the *Weakest Link*. Trinny and Suzanna was one of the best. It was a brilliant idea.'[27]

Matt West's study for fanzine *Time Space Visualiser* involved screening 'Rose' (1.1) to 30 students between the ages of 11 and 16.[28] Distinctive fan readings are recognised through West's commentary, for example, '[t]he bin got a laugh I'm afraid'.[29] This assumes a common frame of reference, that is, that readers of the fanzine will not approve of the episode's belching wheelie bin sequence. What the fan community assumes as a consensus reading is based on 'othering' this humour as puerile and lacking the 'intellectual' values of 'good' *Doctor Who* storytelling. But West's write-up of viewer responses also stressed how '[o]ne of the media students observed that there was no set-up for Rose's gymnastic skills and so her ability at the end seems implausible'.[30] This non-fan comment appears partially analogous to fan-cultural criticisms of the new series' use of narrative, given that fans have debated what are seen as unsatisfactory *deus ex machina* plot devices:

> The literal *deus ex machina* plot of the final episode ['The Parting of the Ways' (1.13)] is only the most lamentable example [of poor plotting]. Giving one of your protagonists previously unannounced god-like powers in order to save the day is perhaps number two in the list of rancid plot devices (number one being that it was all a dream).[31]

Media scholar S. Elizabeth Bird, studying television fans' readings, argues that 'one of the key elements in aesthetic appraisal of narrative is a consciousness of the "appropriateness of narrative developments"', suggesting that this is '[l]ike any traditional English literature analysis'.[32] And *Doctor Who* fans do occasionally seem to be engaged in English Lit debates, as they analyse narrative constructions of 'Boom Town' (1.11), 'The Parting of the Ways' (1.13), 'New Earth' (2.1), 'Last of the Time Lords' (3.13), 'Journey's End' (4.13) and others for allegedly involving *deus ex machina* resolutions.[33] This style of fan discussion has even been parodied in fanzine *Tachyon TV*'s review of 'The Girl in the Fireplace' (2.4): 'I initially thought the convenient Deus Ex Fireplacea was a cop-out solution.'[34] And the *SFX Collection* magazine enters fan debate by arguing that although many 'have criticised *NuWho* for using *deus ex machina* ... in fact this ['Boom Town' (1.11)] is the only time it's been used [in the first two series]'.[35] Frequently depicted as a weakness in episodes by Russell T. Davies,[36] this fan-cultural reading works to distance fans from 'mainstream' audiences, or what is sometimes called the 'Not-We' within fandom,[37] creating fan distinctions[38] at the same time as discursive mirrorings of fan and non-fan response are also enacted.

Evidently, *Doctor Who* fandom has not been concerned merely with 'policing' the distinction between fan insider and non-fan outsider, but has also been invested in closing the gap symbolically between 'cult' fans and 'mainstream' audiences by uncovering fan-like readings outside fandom. This forms part of a project aimed at disavowing 'cult' distinction due to negative connotations and histories (the 1980's 'hiatus' and cancellation) that the term possesses specifically for *Who* fandom. The show's triumphant 2005 return allowed fans to further develop this symbolic project by appropriating the programme's cultural omnipresence as an even stronger validation of their fan tastes. Whereas *The Phantom Menace* (dir. George Lucas, 1999) was deemed inauthentically 'mainstream' by some *Star Wars* fans because of its extensive marketing,[39] hype surrounding *Doctor Who*'s TV comeback was instead affirmatively described by fan and writer Lance Parkin: 'It was the greatest week *Doctor Who* has ever seen ... Constant trailers ... Billboards, magazine covers ... *Doctor Who* ... made the front page of the British papers three times that week.'[40] Due to the 1989 loss of 'their' show, rather than seeking to distinguish themselves from new audiences fans were overjoyed to have *Who* restored to 'mainstream' success:

> *Doctor Who* is everywhere, it's cool ... If I'd have written this six months ago, as a prediction of what would happen, my editor would have rejected it as mad fanboy nonsense. *Doctor Who* fans may never see a week like it again. But ... wow. *Doctor Who* is ... bigger and better than even we could have imagined.[41]

In fact, the week between 'The Stolen Earth' (4.12, 28 June 2008) and 'Journey's End' (4.13, 5 July 2008) almost rivalled the UK impact of 'launch week' in 2005, this time involving massive media speculation over David Tennant's possible regeneration, and being capped by the programme's first ever UK number one weekly TV rating. Rather than being a 'cult' TV show threatened with 'mainstream' status,[42] *Doctor Who* has had a more complex textual history in which 'mainstream' status, according to fan lore, declines into 'cultdom' before being restored by BBC Wales: 'It was the seventies all over again ... you could admit to enjoying [*Doctor Who*] ... without feeling a social outcast!'[43] The new series

> transformed *Doctor Who* from its previous image of ... a bit of a joke of a show just watched by spoddy nerds *back in to a mainstream success*, popular with all sections of the community ... A couple of days after the ... episode ['Rose' (1.1)] was screened, I kept on overhearing conversations in town with people singing its praises, and it just filled me with a sense of joy.[44]

This 'mainstream' status is embraced by *Who* fandom, almost as if it represents the restoration of a prelapsarian condition – reversing the programme's 1980's fall into 'niche cultdom'. Far from entry into the 'mainstream' requiring *Who* fans to defensively 'find new forms of exclusive appreciation or relegate the text to the passé',[45] this shift has provoked widespread celebration within fandom. *Doctor Who Magazine* editor, Tom Spilsbury, argues that *Who* should no longer be described as a 'cult' show, though his suggestion replays the binary of 'cult' versus 'mainstream':

> there's something about the word ['cult'] that somehow implies it's a *minority* interest. You wouldn't call football 'a cult sport', would you? Or The Beatles 'a cult band'? ... So does 'being a bit spacey' automatically qualify a TV series as 'cult'? ... Last Christmas Day, *Doctor Who* was watched by over 13 million viewers ... That's more people than watched anything else on TV [in the UK] last year, bar the immediately following episode of *EastEnders* ... So ... it's high time we dropped the whole 'cult' thing.[46]

Here, it is not 'the mainstream' that acts as a 'bad other' at all, but rather cult status that is denigrated. Such a powerful othering of cultdom by a professionalised TV fan may seem counter-intuitive, but Spilsbury's 'official' fan discourse – appearing in a *Doctor Who Magazine* editorial – echoes very strong anti-cult production discourses. Whereas the fan community has, by and large, embraced 'mainstream' status, bridging 'cult' and 'mainstream' textual classifications, the BBC Wales production team has insistently othered cult fandom in extra-textual publicity discourses contributing to the show's 'text-function'. It could be argued that the taint of failure that 'cult' carries within *Who* fan culture is a discourse shared by fan-producer Russell T. Davies, being intensified by his position as showrunner responsible for the programme. But Davies' extra-textual denigrations of 'cult' suggest that the mainstream/cult binary is more discursively powerful, and delimiting, for producers seeking to open out the appeal of the show than it is for fans seeking to validate communal distinction.

Interviewed for the *Observer* on 6 March 2005, Davies mused that 'diehard fans' of the show were 'like members of the Flat Earth Society. It would be mad to take them too seriously.'[47] New *Who* was very much represented as being for all rather than just for the fans. As Davies has reiterated more recently: '*Doctor Who* is absolutely designed to be seen by everyone.'[48] This was a deliberate textual and publicity strategy, fitting with the BBC's public service discourse of primetime Saturday night TV as 'mainstream':

> In the US, the popularity of mainstream television drama is defined through reference to specifically economically valued audiences. By contrast, in the UK it is measured [by the BBC] in relation to appeal across a ... consensus audience ... a consequence of a continuing understanding of the need for public service broadcasting to appeal to a broad ... audience.[49]

Catherine Johnson argues that *Randall and Hopkirk (Deceased)* (BBC, 2001–2), commissioned as Saturday night TV just a few years before *Doctor Who*'s return, was deemed a failure precisely because it did not accord with the public service discourse dictating that BBC1's Saturday-night schedule was about 'catering for everyone'.[50] However, *Randall and Hopkirk*'s producer Charlie Higson had defended the show initially as having the potential to regenerate the 'family audience'.[51] In the event, *Randall and Hopkirk* failed to deliver on this potential promise of cult-as-transgenerational.[52] This failure at the start of the twenty-first century seemed to imply that telefantasy – even reimagined shows with established cult followings and nostalgic audiences – could not carry a 'mainstream' audience, as this was defined within the BBC's public service remit. 'Cult' was not just a dirty word for *Doctor Who* fandom, it was also a badge of failure for the early noughties BBC1 Saturday night line-up. And it was within this industry context that BBC Wales was tasked with remaking *Doctor Who*. As Johnson has observed, 'in the US in the 1990s, telefantasy has become equated with the economic and aesthetic value of mainstream drama, [yet] its status in Britain is more problematic',[53] being articulated with 'cult' status and restricted audience reach. As film critic Danny Peary has suggested, 'the word cult implies a minority',[54] and it is this meaning that production discourses have drawn on, along with official fan discourses such as those of *DWM* editor Tom Spilsbury. However, meanings of 'cult' have developed and shifted in the context of contemporary US television, arguably leaving the 'cult = minority' equation in place only as an outmoded assumption.[55]

Davies' mission as showrunner was to demonstrate that *Doctor Who* could deliver on the failed promise of *Randall and Hopkirk (Deceased)* by converting telefantasy-as-'cult' into telefantasy-as-'consensus' audience grabber. However, it should be noted that this broadcasting model is not strictly defined against cult. Quite to the contrary: using audience nostalgia for a show that people may have loved as children, as well as drawing on an established fanbase, is actually about *incorporating and assimilating cult status* – with 'cult' fans becoming just one audience fraction amongst others. However, the perceived need to shift *Doctor Who's* text-function from that of a 'niche cult' show to a 'mainstream' BBC hit seems to have strongly driven the textual and extra-textual strategies of BBC Wales. And so, rather than the industry reality that it was being co-opted, 'cult' status was instead discursively othered:

> Julie Gardner ... talked about how [though] ... they appreciated how keen the hardcore fans were about the series, they are not making it for that cult audience ... [She] was also quite clear that there was a definite distinction between 'fans' and audience ... Julie felt that fans in chatrooms could appear to be 'louder' than they actually are, and stressed that her job was to enable R[ussell] T. D[avies] to write what he wants to write, not write what fans ... want him to write.[56]

Conceptualised as 'not for the cult audience', the cult/mainstream binary runs through production and publicity discourses surrounding new *Who*. *Contra* the 'subcultural' account of Jancovich and Hunt, fan-producers police cult/mainstream difference by valorising 'the mainstream' and devaluing 'cult' imagined audiences. Interviewed by *SFX* magazine before series one had transmitted, Davies asserted that the programme was 'absolutely' not about continuity of the type assumed to be favoured by long-term fans:

> 'Children like mythology', he says ... 'What you don't want is lots of, oh, I don't know, the Cybermen came from Telos and Mondas, you don't want the complication of it. You have to distinguish between mythology and continuity ... there is a difference. Mythology is simple and *emotional*! Mythology makes you feel something. Continuity is like, "I come from the constellation of Casterborus" [sic], which is *absolutely* irrelevant. You can discover that later on.'[57]

This particular binary is structurally homologous with mainstream/cult: where 'mainstream' mythology TV is simple and has emotional impact, 'cult' TV continuity is complicated and crammed with 'irrelevant' unemotional detail.[58] Davies has also drawn more directly on 'cult' versus 'mainstream' discourses: 'I wanted *Doctor Who* to have a genuine simplicity ... I've seen too many sci-fi story arcs disappear up their own back-reference, forcing the audience into the groves of the cult, far away from the glittering lights of primetime.'[59] Again, 'cult' is equated with detailed continuity and audience knowledge, allegedly alienating the 'primetime' audience. The phrasing equates cultish 'back-references' with scatological detail, paraphrasing the saying 'to disappear up their own fundament'. 'Back-reference' is hence discursively positioned with the lower bodily stratum, being devalued through Davies' recoding of an insult. Otherings of the 'cult' audience have also, however, taken the form of direct insults:

> 'It's a drama, he's a character with a full emotional range. It is a very science fiction thing to separate the plot off and dissect a story and talk about, I don't know, the 57 emotional lines spoken by the Doctor.' [Davies] has been ... critical of a tiny but vocal minority of Whovians ... calling them 'mosquitoes' ... 'They are not real fandom, though, they are a core of mostly men who like to complain. Fandom is bigger and richer than that, and they are only about 1,000 people who give everyone else a bad name.'[60]

These fans, gendered by Davies in a way that resonates with Hollows' arguments on the 'masculinity' of cult,[61] have also been labelled 'ming-mongs' by the showrunner: 'That's not proper fans, just a small corner of fandom, the ming-mongs.'[62] Dismissed as 'not proper' fans, this section of the audience is resolutely othered by Davies, despite himself being a fan of the series, and a regular contributor to the official *Doctor Who Magazine*. The term 'ming-mong' stems from a 1987 Victoria Wood sketch lampooning *Doctor Who*, where it is used as a parody of the show's technobabble, or invented science-fictional language. The Doctor's companion tells him 'Doctor, we don't have the ming-mongs', a problem which means their plan to defeat the evil 'Crayola' has to be rapidly rethought. Whilst the villain's name, also a brand of crayons, links the programme to notions of childishness, 'ming-mongs' represent an absent signified – the words are meaningless, as we never learn what 'they' actually are. It is nonsense language; the comedy sketch implying that *Doctor Who* of the late 1980s was childish and full of meaningless gibberish. To adopt the term 'ming-mongs' for 'cult' fans therefore suggests that such people are childish, if not mentally deficient, since the invented compound term also draws problematically on 'mong' as in 'mongoloid'.[63] Shot-through with a discursive history of playground insults, 'ming-mong' is very much an anti-cult term as used by Russell T. Davies.[64] By contrast, his successor as showrunner, Steven Moffat, has sought to include himself in the category, thereby blunting its self/other binaries: 'It's only us ming-mongs that care' about leaked storylines, he suggests.[65] And after public news of his appointment as showrunner had broken, Moffat developed this 'inclusive' approach:

> I'm going to be honest and fans may hate me for it but they have to remember that I am a fan myself. A proper list-making-borderline-autistic fan. I am head mingmong. I'm King Ming. But I don't do anything for the fans. I honestly don't think that the fans want me to do anything for them. Except maybe for the odd little line now and then. Some little thing somewhere. Russell does that. I do that ... But we don't do anything for the fans. There aren't enough fans. There's the whole audience.[66]

Moffat's approach closely replays the positioning of fans as a 'powerless elite'.[67] *Doctor Who*'s established fan culture has, historically, been placed between the 'general audience', which does not share its investment in fan cultural capital, and the show's producers, who have previously lacked the textual knowledge displayed by fandom. Fans have thus been 'experts', but 'with little control over either the conditions of production or reception of "their" show'.[68] The discursive othering enacted by Russell T. Davies asserts that fandom still has no control over the direction that he, as a media professional, chooses for the programme. And Steven Moffat's more inclusive stance still ultimately gives way to a similar argument that fans are not important – the 'whole' audience, counted in millions rather than thousands, is what matters. Fandom seems to find itself back in the role of powerless elite.

Nevertheless, John Tulloch argues that the 'powerless elite' concept has to be qualified differently in different national contexts: 'each national fan club [in the 1980s was] contextually positioned and determined ... there ... [were] important differences between the "powerless elites" of England, the USA, and Australia'.[69] Fans in Australia may have been fighting to get the show back on air, whereas 'Society' fans in the UK were arguably far more 'on side' with the show's producers.[70] And just as the concept needs to address national specificity, so too does it need to be modified to take in the differences between 1980s *Doctor Who* and the new series. The expertise of fans is, in this instance, shared by showrunners, who themselves possess very high levels of fan knowledge, as witnessed by Russell T. Davies' 'Production Notes' column for *DWM*. Whereas former producer John Nathan-Turner used a fan, Ian Levine, as an unofficial advisor to the programme, *Doctor Who* (2005– ) needs no such additional fan input. Its long-term fandom paradoxically is both represented by fan-producers, yet simultaneously marginalised by industry requirements and discourses aimed at winning a 'mainstream' audience. Not quite a 'powerless elite', fandom is recontextualised here as a sort of ambivalent 'powerless duality', sometimes catered for by producers in official niche media such as *Doctor Who Magazine*, or BBC podcasts, and sometimes powerfully othered as part of a text-function bidding for 'mainstream' status. Losing its 'elite' identity by virtue of fan-producers' shared levels of fan knowledge, *Doctor Who* fandom has been addressed partly as a target market and partly as an atavistic embarrassment.

This situation resonates with Derek Johnson's work on 'fan-tagonism'. It is through this process, Johnson argues, that fandom is disciplined discursively by contemporary media producers. As a vocal, unruly audience, whose textual criticisms can be intensified by online, communal responses,[71] fans become something of a headache for producers, especially where their readings challenge the value of a 'brand', denigrating plots or characters:

> Because copyright law cannot curb consumer dissent, alternative strategies must rejoin the challenges represented by fans' discursive power to construct aesthetic histories of corporate production. To this end, the television text itself has been mobilized to narratively construct 'acceptable' fan activity ... building critiques of unruly fans directly into the text.[72]

Johnson argues that producers use what authority they do have – power over the text itself – to construct images of 'good' and 'bad' fandom:

> representations of fans themselves have been deployed ... as a discursive means of disciplining fan activity, inscribing it in relationship to textually represented categories of normativity/deviance ... the character operating as a kind of 'fan representative' has become a standardized part of many ensemble casts. *Lost*'s Hurley, for example, is frequently legible as a stand-in for the series' fans, parroting questions and theories.[73]

Derek Johnson goes on to suggest that 'proper' fandom is represented positively by specific stand-in diegetic characters, with 'bad' resistant fandom being negatively depicted via geeky villains (in *Buffy*) or characters unable to distinguish between fantasy and reality (in *Star Trek: The Next Generation*). The not-so-implicit textual meaning is that the fan audience should know their place, and refrain from vocally contesting production decisions. Where new *Who* is concerned, this discursive struggle between fans and fan-producers over the text-function (i.e. how the text should be classified) has occurred in promotional discourses as much as in the text itself. But *Doctor Who* has also made use of diegetic fan stand-ins. Episode 1.1 represented over-weight, middle-aged Clive (Mark Benton) connotatively as a fan of the Doctor – a conspiracy and Internet 'nut' tracking the Doctor's movements. Clive's fellow fan 'nuts' were predominantly men, as witnessed by his wife's astonished comment that 'She's a she!' when Rose Tyler visited. Mark Benton had previously appeared in Russell T. Davies' *The Second Coming*, where he played a seedy, desperate, lonely man possessed by the Devil. In terms of intertextual associations, Benton's casting as Clive sends a powerful signal as to Davies' view of 'old' fandom, and the discursive need to reposition the show. The episode 'Rose' (1.1) represents a connotative handover from the 'cult' old guard; the Doctor is no longer just an object of fascination for middle-aged men, but belongs to Rose rather than Clive, who is seemingly killed off by marauding Autons.

By series two, fandom was not just being killed off by monsters, however, it had diegetically *become* the monster. Cult fandom as powerless duality rather than powerless elite is represented textually in 'Love & Monsters' (2.10). Marc Warren plays Elton Pope, standing in for a positive, affectionate view of good fandom, which follows the Doctor amongst other pop-cultural interests (such as ELO). Victor Kennedy (Peter Kay) stands in for bad, deviant fandom – seeking to control fellow fans and obsessively pursuing the Doctor. Fandom is connoted rather than denoted throughout the story, with the Doctor being treated as a real figure rather than a fictional character. In a sense, though, this is 'metacult' television: TV about cult TV audiences. As Shaun Lyon noted: '[this] shows us who we are, rather than who the Doctor is ... [representing] *Doctor Who* fans and their experiences'.[74]

Yet both types of fan representative are shown to be damaged emotionally and marked by loss. Elton is fascinated by the Doctor because he saw him on the night his mother died, whilst Kennedy is an alien trapped on Earth unless he can locate the Doctor, unable to physically touch people around him, and thus also represented as emotionally deficient. Equally, neither Victor Kennedy nor Elton Pope actively resolve their narratives – it takes the Doctor's last-minute intervention to defeat Kennedy, or the 'Abzorbaloff', as he is christened. Fan culture is figured as a powerless duality within the narrative, as despite different characters allegorically representing 'good' and 'bad' fandom, all are shown to be subordinated to the narrative power of the Doctor-as-hero. And in 'Fear Her' (2.11) by Matthew Graham, there is a remarkable diegetic statement of *Doctor Who's* newfound mass appeal, with the tenth Doctor seizing the 2012 Olympic Torch and saving the Olympics in front of a global audience. Connotatively, this image implies that the character now belongs not to Fan Local Groups but to the masses, with the Doctor's insertion into a populist 'media event' self-reflexively commenting on the ratings success of series one.

From this point on, new *Who* features more textual connotations of mass popularity. Rather than being represented, 'old' fandom is predominantly displaced in series three and four in favour of images of worldwide crowds chanting 'Doctor' in 'Last of the Time Lords' (3.13) and massed phone lines calling the Doctor's number in 'The Stolen Earth' (4.12). These series-finale spectaculars have used such imagery to code 'mainstream' popularity – representing literal and connotative masses 'calling out' for the Doctor's help. Such populist narrative scenarios were unheard of in the original series, but from 'Fear Her' onwards, they have found a textual home in the new series. Where fandom sometimes decries such textual moments,[75] it may be that fans are implicitly recognising their diegetically coded irrelevance. Such representations can, nonetheless, be thought of as a further type of 'fan-tagonism', in Derek Johnson's terms, seeking to discipline 'cult' fans by installing diegetic images of the programme's 'mainstream' popularity. By 2008, the Doctor seemingly belongs diegetically to the crowd, and not to the individual, Internet fan (Clive in 1.1) or even the small-scale fan group (in 'Love & Monsters', 2.10). Fan representatives in series three and four have typically appeared in Steven Moffat's scripts; Lawrence in 'Blink' (3.10) repeatedly watches the DVD 'Easter egg'[76] of the Doctor like a 'good' fan, happily consuming what is industrially provided for him. On the other hand, 'Silence in the Library' and 'Forest of the Dead' (4.8–4.9) caution against reading 'spoilers', implying that this is an activity pursued by 'bad' fandom seeking information in advance of its official release. The disciplining implications of these 'metacult' storylines are that 'proper' fandom should follow the pathways allocated to it by the TV industry.

Thus far, I have argued that new *Who*'s textual strategies and promotional discourses have sought to other 'cult' fans, textually depicted via nerdish, middle-aged masculinity, which gives way to Rose Tyler's affection for the Doctor, and extra-textually denigrated as 'ming-mongs'. The 'cult/mainstream' binary occurs in production discourses of the 'cult' fan as 'obsessed with complicated continuity' and 'anti-emotion', versus 'mainstream' audiences assumed to be focused on 'mythology', 'emotion' and textual simplicity. Whilst fans have celebrated *Who*'s mainstreaming as an affirmation of 'their' show, it is fan-producers (reproducing BBC public service discourses) who have far more rigidly policed boundaries between 'cult' and 'mainstream' viewers as part of the new series' text-function. However, in the next section I want to contest this relational binary, and address cult status as something that has been absorbed into new *Who*'s consensus audience. The irony here is that the Abzorbaloff, the connotative fan-villain from 'Love & Monsters' (2.10), may be a more accurate image for the BBC's public service construction of 'mainstream' TV – seeking to assimilate as many different audiences as possible, cult included – than it is for elements in *Doctor Who's* fan culture.

## Cult *Within* Mainstream:
## 'In Its Soul, *Doctor Who* Isn't Cool'

Rather than viewing cultishness purely as 'a strategy of "anti-mainstream" cultural distinction',[77] here I want to address 'cult' as a multiple set of differential reading strategies. Instead of cult/mainstream forming a clear binary, this means that 'cult' status can entirely predate a text, being residually brought to it by an established cult audience, *and* can simultaneously emerge within a text's new, cult-like and 'mainstream' following.[78] *Doctor Who* has its own residual/emergent cult audience equivalents to the *Lord of the Rings* films (2001–3), but rather than Tolkien cultists transferring their attentions to film adaptations, here 'old school' fandom of the classic TV series acts as a residual cult, with fan affect being carried over to the reimagined television series. And what I have termed emergent cult(-like) status belongs to 'new fandom', where audiences become fans of BBC Wales' *Doctor Who* wholly without back-reference to the classic show (like fans of the *LOTR* films who have never read Tolkien).

Reducing processes of residual and emergent cult fandom to a cult/mainstream binary misses differences within cult consumption by trying to fix a logical separation of categories in place. In what follows, I will consider how 'cult' and 'mainstream' classifications can intersect thanks to a variety of textual strategies in new *Who*, with residual cult fans bringing their distinctive reading strategies to the show's mainstreaming, and emergent fans within 'the mainstream' responding in 'cult-like' ways to elements in the new series. For the purposes of analysis, I will split these textual strategies into five separate areas – transmedia storytelling; high concept; 'narrative as special effect'; Dalek-centric storytelling; and technobabble-as-performance – each of which I will examine in turn. These complex interactions of 'cult' and 'mainstream' discourse illustrate the reductive nature of the text-function and its attempts to stabilise textual classifications discursively – for example, that of 'quality', 'mainstream' television.

First, then, there is the matter of new *Who's transmedia storytell-ing*. This has been analysed by both Charles Tryon and Neil Perryman. Tryon views transmedia storytelling as a tactic for 'cultivating the fan relationship'[79] via podcasts and the 'Tardisodes' that accompanied se-ries two. These were shorts available online and on mobile phones, mini-dramas that extended the diegesis of each televised episode. Some mimicked news broadcasts ('Doomsday', 2.13), others crime-show appeals ('Fear Her', 2.11) and still others corporate videos ('New Earth', 2.1). This integrated transmedia development of the *Doctor Who* brand across mobile phones and websites – usually extending textual continuity without violating it, and sometimes even repairing continuity lapses in spin-off shows such as *Torchwood*[80] – appealed to 'residual' cult fandom by presenting long-term fans with a con-sistent, multi-platformed hyperdiegesis, or narrative world.[81] At the same time, such multi-platforming also appealed to emergent cult-like fans, who could follow *Doctor Who* across platforms as a matter of interactive 'tele-participation', without necessarily even thinking of themselves as traditional 'cultists':

> industry trends suggest a need for historicized understandings of 'cult', 'cult fandom', and 'fandom'. If the primary consistent factor across varying understandings of 'cult' is tele-participation in the service of exploring all aspects of a show's fictional world, then it becomes im portant to examine how [US TV] networks are building environments to support this – but aiming for a larger audience than most cult shows garner.[82]

In *Beyond the Box*, Sharon Marie Ross argues that a range of US TV shows, most especially *Lost*, have provoked puzzle-solving specula-tion amongst online audiences without attracting any of the previous 'stigma' of cultdom,[83] and without any loss in ratings (the proverbial 'decline into niche cultdom'). Ross argues that tele-participation, pre-viously assumed to be specific to 'cult' TV, is now reaching outside conventional cult shows and audiences and is becoming industrially normalised.[84] By embracing the cutting-edge use of BBC podcasts (even ahead of an assessment exercise by the BBC Trust[85]) and extend-ing its brand into online and mobile phone content, new *Who* has embraced the possibility of 'emergent' fandom given that 'social audi-ences today engage in activities and relationships with non-cult TV programs in very cult-like ways'.[86] Transmedia storytelling thus unites 'residual' and 'emergent' cults, catering for the desire of 'old-school' cult fans for brand consistency (see Chapter 2) as well as inciting new 'cult-like' fan practices in relation to non-stigmatised, 'mainstream' and high-rating TV shows. In marked contrast to these historicised, technological shifts, rigid cult-versus-mainstream production dis-courses appear to belong to a dematerialising media context. There is a strong disconnect between the broadcast-centric, 'Saturday night BBC1' model of text and audience evident in Russell T. Davies' anti-cult stance, and the transmedia storytelling model through which 'cult' and 'mainstream' become unproblematically co-existent, if not coterminous.

Second, new *Who* has been textually positioned as *'high-concept'* TV. This would appear to be a resolutely 'mainstream' gambit, since it is premised on a 'marketing-driven' view of the medium,[87] where each story can be summarised in a 'hook' sentence for publicity purposes:

> the stories should be strong. Well, obviously. But I mean unashamedly high-concept. ... [E]very bloody week there should be something to grab a new viewer. Something irresistible. Big, cheeky headlines: Rose sees the end of the world! The Doctor meets Charles Dickens! Aliens invade Downing Street! The return of the Daleks![88]

It is this emphasis on a one-line marketable hook that defines 'high-concept'[89] along with the use of pre-sold properties and highly recog-nisable 'generic icons' such as the mad scientist (as, for example, with 'The Lazarus Experiment', 3.6) or the Beast ('The Impossible Planet'/ 'The Satan Pit', 2.8–2.9). 'High-concept' tends to use these generic icons in altered contexts – Dr Lazarus reverses the ageing process and cites T.S. Eliot; the Devil is trapped under an alien planet's surface.[90] Russell T. Davies has consistently envisaged *Doctor Who* as 'high-con-cept' television. This targets a 'mainstream' audience through its sim-plicity, but it also caters for the residual cult audience by harking back to the Philip Hinchcliffe and Robert Holmes producer/script editor era in the 1970s.[91] At that time, *Doctor Who* was similarly driven by *avant la lettre* 'high-concept' tendencies: for example, 'Planet of Evil' (1975), 'The Brain of Morbius' (1976) and 'The Hand of Fear' (1976) were all strongly concept-driven by one-liners ('a living planet story'/'a Fran-kenstein story'/'a scary disembodied hand story'). Though Holmes and Hinchcliffe's work has been described as 'high gothic',[92] it is no more or less 'high-concept' than Russell T. Davies' version of *Doctor*

*Who*. Indeed, when Hinchcliffe commented on 'Planet of the Ood' (4.3) in *The Stage*, he singled out its 'good, clear concept' for praise.[93] As an unintended consequence, then, Davies' 'high-concept' approach can be read intratextually through related approaches in the programme's history, opening up its apparent mainstream 'simplicity' to distinctive 'residual' cult readings. Via 'high-concept', cult and mainstream responses can again co-exist, united in valuing the same textual aspects rather than adopting divergent value-systems.

Third, new *Who* can be thought of as displaying what US scholar Jason Mittell has dubbed the *'narrative special effect'*.[94] Though the series may strive for conceptual clarity, its storytelling is sometimes very intricate, especially in Steven Moffat's scripts. Mittell argues that much contemporary US TV stresses its 'written-ness' by constructing plot twists that massively alter audiences' understanding of previous events, as well as offering discrete episodes with 'starkly limiting storytelling parameters' and 'shifts in perspective (telling an adventure from the vantage point of an habitual bystander)' or the 'foregrounding [of] an unusual narrator'.[95] Whilst Mittell's examples of these 'narratively spectacular episodes'[96] are from *Buffy*, new *Who* has also engaged in such narrative play, particularly through 'Doctor-lite' episodes hardly featuring the lead character.

Mittell terms the emphasis on plotting, twists and varied narrative parameters an 'operational aesthetic' where audience pleasure is 'less about "what will happen next?" and more concerning "how did ... [the writer] do that?"'[97] And, as he argues, this 'operational aesthetic is on display within online fan forum dissections of the techniques that complex ... dramas use to guide, manipulate, deceive, and misdirect viewers, suggesting the key pleasure of unravelling the operation of narrative mechanics'.[98] This certainly captures the narrative dissections of online *Who* fandom. And episodes such as 'Love & Monsters' (2.10), 'Midnight' (4.10), and 'Turn Left' (4.11) (all by Russell T. Davies) represent excursions into extreme narrative parameters, unusual narration, and shifts in perspective – prime characteristics of the 'operational aesthetic'. Moments of narrative 'akin to special effects' which 'pull us out of the diegesis to marvel at the technique required'[99] are evident in Steven Moffat's 'Blink' (3.10) where the same sequence of DVD dialogue is replayed in different contexts, as well as in the final reveal of 'The Girl in the Fireplace' (2.4), which 'ties up everything in a nice, neat bow. Brilliant!'[100] Such 'moments push the operational aesthetic to the foreground, calling attention to the constructed nature of the narration and asking us to marvel at how the writers pulled it off'.[101]

Despite this narrative complexity, Mittell points out that:

> these programs can be quite popular with a mass audience (*Lost, Seinfield, The X-Files*) or have narrow appeals to cult viewers willing to invest the efforts into the decoding process (*Arrested Development, Veronica Mars, Firefly*) ... the striking popularity of some complex programs suggests that a mass audience can engage with and enjoy quite challenging and intricate storytelling.[102]

Narrative as 'special effect' is thus a textual strategy which again appears to cut across 'cult' and 'mainstream' audiences, rather than playing into audience distinctions. The success of repeated memes such as 'Bad Wolf', 'Torchwood', 'Saxon' and the 'Medusa Cascade/ Shadow Proclamation' from series four also testifies to this cult/mainstream unity rather than opposition, with narrative complexity's 'interplay between the demands of episodic and serial storytelling'[103] allowing new *Who* to become a kind of puzzle-solving text inciting both residual and emergent fan audience attention. As Ross has argued: 'many survey respondents offered the explanation that shows which could capture viewer loyalty ... "had to" have elements ... that would prompt viewers to approach the program like a puzzle or game'.[104] And more than ever before in its history, new *Who* is just this sort of ludic text, playing games with residual cult fan anticipation and emergent cult-like speculation within the 'mainstream' audience, but nevertheless balancing its narrative designs strongly in favour of episodic closure rather than fully serialised, 'story-arc' openness.

Another narrative device that unites 'cult' and 'mainstream' audiences rather than conceptualising them as opposed audience fractions has been the *Dalek-centric storytelling* of new *Who*. As the fanzine exploration of 'general audiences' versus 'fans' in the *Doctor's Recorder* pointed out, the biggest difference between the two groups was that 'casual viewers would be more inclined to remember icons such as the Daleks, and to exaggerate their significance in the series' whereas residual cult fandom was 'more knowledgeable about the minutiae of the series's history'.[105] BBC Wales' *Doctor Who* has imported that general audience expectation back into the text, making the Daleks more narratively central than they ever were in the classic series. Being revealed as the Time Lords' Time War enemies, these monsters are granted a diegetic pre-eminence that fits the casual viewer's 'narrative image'[106] of *Who*. A non-fan misperception is read back into the series, and literalised. The re-imagining of *Doctor Who* has also refrained from altering radically the appearance of icons such as Daleks, Cybermen and Davros, both leaving them recognisable as 'mainstream'/nostalgic audiences would remember them, and avoiding upsetting fans invested in the designs: 'You're daft to fiddle with those things. You can improve them, gloss them up, but they're visual icons ... The moment you tamper with those, you're in trouble.'[107] By focusing on Daleks as recognisable icons and self-consciously playing up to their 'general audience' perception as the 'number one monster', new *Who* again implicitly unites 'cult' and 'mainstream' audiences rather than its textual strategies favouring one imagined group versus the other (i.e. the text-function aimed at fixing 'mainstream' status is occasionally fissured and multivalent).

Finally, I want to consider how the series addresses the matter of *technobabble*. This is invented language for imagined technologies and aliens, and has been assumed to distinguish science fiction from 'mainstream' media content. Technobabble has been mocked as part of science fiction's anti-mainstream incomprehensibility, as in the sketch featuring 'ming-mongs'. Analysing science fiction's use of language, Peter Stockwell argues:

> it is not that science fiction is packed full of neologisms, but it is the case that it has more than are encountered in mainstream literature ... if you take the opening page of a few mainstream texts, the only new words you are likely to encounter will be new characters' names or invented new places. The paraphernalia of everyday life in mainstream fiction is simply there with its familiar terms attached.[108]

Davies' pitch document for series one was extremely direct in its 'othering' of SF technobabble, asserting that: 'If the Zogs on the planet Zog are having trouble with the Zog-monster ... who gives a toss ... Every story, somehow, must come back to Earth.'[109] The 'paraphernalia of everyday life', seen as characteristic of 'mainstream' fiction by Stockwell, is given due place in Davies' vision of *Doctor Who*, in a powerful cult-versus-mainstream binary.

Science fiction terminology was indeed avoided assiduously in 'Rose' (1.1), which offered simple explanations of the TARDIS,[110]

avoided naming the Autons in dialogue, and had the Doctor battling sentient plastic with 'anti-plastic'. One fanzine article, featuring
long-term fans watching the episode, had a respondent clamouring
for '[m]ore technobabble',[111] whilst another fanzine audaciously argued that:

> As a word, 'cool' is an example of something that we *Doctor Who* fans
> are quite familiar with: bafflegab, technobabble (or, in this instance,
> culturebabble). It fulfils the same basic function as 'I've reversed the
> polarity of the neutron flow'. It's used as a substitute for a concept too
> fundamentally unreal to be explained.[112]

Here, fan writer Jack Graham deconstructs the technobabble-as-cult/
mainstream-as-cool binary by suggesting that cultural concepts at
the heart of *Doctor Who*'s mainstreaming – is it now 'cool' to like the
show? – are themselves akin to science-fictional words with an absent
signified, having no established referent. Effectively making 'cool' and
the planet 'Zog' interchangeable signifiers forms part of Graham's thesis that 'in its soul, *Doctor Who* isn't cool' because 'Cool is about elitism, complacency, profit, media doublespeak, vanity and conformity.
*Doctor Who* is, fundamentally, about fighting evil ... that, very often,
involves elitism, complacency, profiteering, media doublespeak, vanity and conformity.'[113] Though this critical reading may seem to recu-
perate (radical) 'cult' versus (reactionary) 'mainstream' oppositions,
it challenges the notion that 'technobabble' somehow separates cult
and general audiences.

In any case, the minimisation of technobabble did not prove to be
a sustainable textual strategy for new *Who*, given its genre hybridities,
and in this regard 'Rose' (1.1) (and its hysterical, exaggerated text-
function of 'mainstream' rather than 'cult' TV) stands out in relation
to almost all later episodes. Instead, Davies developed a different approach to the naming of alien races, planets and technologies – he
anticipated and incorporated criticism of technobabble into his own
creation of neologisms, making them deliberately baroque, for example, 'Raxacoricofallapatorius' or the 'Mighty Jagrafess of the Holy
Hadrojassic Maxarodenfoe'. The nonsensical nature of such invented
language is also emphasised textually: the Doctor invents 'triplicate
the flammability' as a bluff in 'World War Three' (1.5), for example.
Davies' neologisms were self-conscious tongue-twisters: performance
challenges to younger viewers and residual and emergent fans alike.

By stressing the materiality of language, and representing technobabble-as-performance, Davies has sought to ward off the 'othering' of SF neologisms. His scripts have used technobabble-as-performance to depict the Doctor's intellect and energy, or to gloss over SF plot points by converting them into comedic bits of business. For example, when the DoctorDonna defeats the Daleks in 'Journey's End' (4.13), her Time Lord mind is represented via the rapid-fire delivery of exaggerated technobabble: 'closing all Z-Neutrino relay loops with an internalised synchronous back-feed reversal loop ... Oh, bioelectric dampening field with a retrogressive arc inversion?' and so on.[114] Technobabble is maximised rather than kept to a minimum, but it is performed as Catherine Tate impersonating David Tennant playing the Doctor, and has the heightened, stylised quality of a sketch or skit. The modality of the text is momentarily moved towards comedy, self-consciously drawing attention to technobabble as nonsense. 'Serious' scientific language is recurrently undercut, as in Steven Moffat's description of the Doctor's lash-up in 'Blink' (3.10): 'it goes ding when there's ... stuff', and the infamous 'wibbly wobbly timey wimey' to gloss over time paradoxes. And lengthy, almost unpronounceable invented names are comedically contrasted with their terse cousins, such as the twin planet of Raxacoricofallapatorius being called 'Clom' in 'Love & Monsters' (2.10). Though all this borderline self-parody betrays an anxiety that the 'mainstream' audience will be alienated by SF technobabble, it actually unites 'cult' and 'mainstream' audiences by anticipating and incorporating critiques of science fiction 'nonsense'. Residual and emergent fans are challenged to learn such terms, through what Sharon Marie Ross calls an 'obscured' invitation to audience activity,[115] whilst non-fans can laugh at the self-mocking modality.

In the previous chapter, I noted that text-function classifications such as 'the mainstream' tend to be imagined in inconsistent ways,[116] being constructed as anti-SF in textual strategies regarding non-diegetic and diegetic music. This chapter has explored variant discourses of 'the mainstream', defined instead as anti-cult. Fan-producers have repeatedly othered cult audiences, seeking to secure *Doctor Who* within public service BBC discourses of 'mainstream-as-consensus'.[117] As a result, the cult/mainstream binary has been policed rigorously in production discourses, albeit via an inversion of typical 'subcultural' fan discourses – here, valuing the 'authentic' mainstream over inauthentic niche cultdom. However, *contra* academic generalisations,[118] *Doctor Who*'s fan culture has not always sought to distinguish itself from 'general viewers', instead frequently seeking to minimise rather than exaggerate fan-cultural difference. Discursively mirroring fan and non-fan readings has formed one way for *Who* fandom to validate its tastes and identities, arguing for the show's return after its 1989 cancellation. And post-2005, established *Who* fandom has celebrated the new series' 'mainstream' success rather than constructing 'cult versus mainstream' as an authentic/inauthentic binary.

Anti-cult production discourses, meanwhile, are radically out of alignment with technological, industrial shifts whereby 'cult-like' fan practices have entered the normative activities of mainstream, convergence-culture TV.[119] Despite extra-textual attacks on cult fandom, the texts of new *Who* have sometimes blurred together 'cult' and 'mainstream' imagined audiences. I have argued that a range of narrative strategies (transmedia storytelling; high-concept; narrative-as-special-effect; Dalek-centric storytelling; technobabble-as-performance) have all contributed to *Doctor Who*'s assimilation of 'cult' readings within a broader consensus audience. Fan-producers' anti-SF, anti-cult 'text-function' has, therefore, acted in partial tension with specific production strategies, representing a situation where discursive conflict has surrounded fandom as a powerless duality rather than a powerless elite. Sometimes targeted, sometimes disavowed or insulted, in actuality assimilated into a coalition audience, *Doctor Who*'s residual cult fandom has been subjected to discursive industry disciplining.

There can be no doubting the success of BBC Wales' *Doctor Who*. Cemented in public discourse, multi-award-winning, and breaking ratings records even after four years on air, it really has represented the triumph of a Time Lord. For the first time in the series' long history, *Doctor Who* has become 'authored' TV (see Chapter 1), bringing a generation of *Who* fans into the official television production of the very programme they love (see Chapter 2). And new *Who* has utilised time-travel narratives within a distinct, multi-generic format of 'intimate epic' drama (see Chapter 3), creating spectacular, brand-specific monsters as 'TV horror' (see Chapter 4). At the level of the text-function, or textual classification, it has achieved 'quality' status, 'culturing up' via diegetic appearances from Dickens and Shakespeare (see

Chapter 5). Murray Gold's music has also been 'cultured up' through brand synergy with the BBC Proms, as well as participating in an anti-SF textual 'mainstreaming' (see Chapter 6). Despite fans becoming textual 'gamekeepers', discursive and cultural struggles between fan-producers and *Doctor Who's* wider fan culture have not disappeared from view (as in this chapter), returning us to the info-war examined in Part I.

By variously exploring the Foucauldian 'author-function', 'generic function' and 'text-function' of BBC Wales' *Doctor Who*, I have examined this particular text as a 'node' of many different discourses, constructed discursively as: 'quality' television art; a TV brand; a labour of fan love; a multi-generic format; a mainstream show 'for everyone'; an extension of fan discourse; and a professional product opposed to fan poaching. These different discursive positions may act as a 'unity' underpinning new *Who's* episodes, but they are open to contradictory statements (or counter-discourses) as I have shown, especially in this chapter and Chapters 2 (for and against fandom) and 5 (for and against quality). Nor, as a result of these differential discourses, can scholarship isolate one definitive power relationship between fans and (fan-)producers. Instead, specific contexts and particular discursive practices need to be explored empirically when we think about fandom less as a powerless elite within contemporary media culture, and rather more as a powerless duality.

As James Chapman asks rhetorically: 'The Doctor may have conquered Daleks, Cybermen, and Ice Warriors, but would he survive an encounter with Foucault?'[120] *Triumph of a Time Lord* has proffered an answer of sorts – and, as my title suggests, the Doctor will always find a way to win out at the last moment. *Doctor Who* may, accordingly, have undergone many trials across its cultural career, but the 'Russell T. Davies era' must surely be counted, by fans, critics and scholar-fans alike, as a golden age for the series. I am already looking forward to fan and scholarly analysis of the 'Steven Moffat era' featuring the eleventh Doctor, Matt Smith, but that will be another set of stories altogether. And though academic writing might sometimes be criticised by fans for its excessive quotation – 'why doesn't the writer just say what *they* think?' – I shall end with one final quote. In the words of my favourite Doctor, and speaking as a long-standing fan and professional academic: '*Fantastic!*'

## NOTES

1    Mark Jancovich and Nathan Hunt (2004) 'The mainstream, distinction, and cult TV', in Sara Gwenllian-Jones and Roberta E. Pearson (eds) *Cult Television*, University of Minnesota Press, Minneapolis, p.27; see also Jonathan Blum (2002) '50 essential questions: TV', *Doctor Who Magazine* 312, Panini Comics, Tunbridge Wells, p.7.

2    See Derek Johnson (2007) 'Inviting audiences in: the spatial reorganization of production and consumption in "TVIII"', *New Review of Film and Television Studies* v/1, pp.61–80, and his (2007) 'Fan-tagonism: factions, institutions, and constitutive hegemonies of fandom', in Jonathan Gray, Cornel Sandvoss and C. Lee Harrington (eds) *Fandom: Identities and Communities in a Mediated World*, New York University, New York and London, pp.285–300.

3    John Tulloch and Henry Jenkins (1995) *Science Fiction Audiences: Watching Doctor Who and Star Trek*, Routledge, London and New York, p.145.

4    See Henry Jenkins (2006) *Convergence Culture*, New York University Press, New York and London; Neil Perryman (2008) '*Doctor Who* and the convergence of media: a case study in "transmedia storytelling"', *Convergence: The International Journal of Research into New Media Technologies* xiv/1, pp.21–39; and Charles Tryon (2008) 'TV Time Lords: fan cultures, narrative complexity, and the future of science fiction television', in J.P. Telotte (ed.) *The Essential Science Fiction Television Reader*, University Press of Kentucky, Kentucky, pp.301–14.

5    See Catherine Johnson (2005) *Telefantasy*, BFI Publishing, London.

6    James Chapman (2006) *Inside the TARDIS: The Worlds of Doctor Who*, I.B.Tauris, London and New York, p.162; see also Tat Wood (2007) *About Time 6: The Unauthorized Guide to Doctor Who 1985–1989*, Mad Norwegian Press, Des Moines, IA, p.171.

7    Gary Gillatt (1996) 'First impressions', *Doctor Who Magazine* 235, Marvel Magazines, London, p.6.

8    Kim Newman (2005) *BFI TV Classics: Doctor Who*, BFI Publishing, London, p.4.

9    Perryman: '*Doctor Who* and the convergence of media', p.22.

10   See also Francesca Coppa (2006) 'A brief history of media fandom', in Karen Hellekson and Kristina Busse (eds) *Fan Fiction and Fan Communities in the Age of the Internet*, McFarland, Jefferson, p.51.

11   See, for example, Cornel Sandvoss (2005) *Fans: The Mirror of Consumption*, Polity Press, Cambridge, p.41.

12   Joanne Hollows (2003) 'The masculinity of cult', in Mark Jancovich, Antonio Lázaro Reboll, Julian Stringer and Andy Willis (eds) *Defining Cult Movies*, Manchester University Press, Manchester, pp.36–7.

13   Sarah Thornton (1995) *Club Cultures*, Polity Press, Cambridge, p.104.

14   Jancovich and Hunt: 'The mainstream, distinction, and cult TV', pp.30–1.

15   Ibid., p.28; see also Nathan Hunt (2003) 'The importance of trivia: ownership, exclusion and authority in science fiction fandom', in Jancovich, Reboll, Stringer and Willis (eds): *Defining Cult Movies*, p.190.

16    Perryman: 'Doctor Who and the convergence of media', p.22.

17    Andrew Hardstaffe (2002) 'Watching them watching Who', the Doctor's
      Recorder 30, p.4.

18    See Gillatt: 'First impressions', and Gary Gillat (1996) 'Second sight', Doc-
      tor Who Magazine 242, Marvel Magazines, London, pp.6–11; Andrew
      Hardstaffe (2005) 'Watch with others', the Doctor's Recorder 43, pp.10–
      18, 27; Mark Wyman (2005) 'Class of 2005', Doctor Who Magazine 361,
      Panini Comics, Tunbridge Wells, pp.12–21; Matt West (2005) 'Kids today:
      when even getting kids to watch TV is a struggle', Time Space Visualiser:
      The Journal of the New Zealand Doctor Who Fan Club 71, pp.22–3.

19    Gillatt: 'First impressions', p.9.

20    See Tulloch and Jenkins: Science Fiction Audiences, pp.122–4.

21    Gillatt: 'Second sight', p.11.

22    Wyman: 'Class of 2005', pp.15, 18.

23    Ibid., p.21.

24    Ibid.

25    Ibid., p.20.

26    Hardstaffe: 'Watching them watching Who', p.10.

27    In Hardstaffe: 'Watch with others', pp.18, 27.

28    West: 'Kids today', p.22.

29    Ibid.

30    Ibid., pp.22–3.

31    Alistair Pegg (2005) 'Saturday night, Sunday morning', Black Scrolls 8
      (winter), p.46.

32    S. Elizabeth Bird (2003) The Audience in Everyday Life, Routledge, London
      and New York, p.131.

33    See also Victor Costello and Barbara Moore (2007) 'Cultural outlaws: an
      examination of audience activity and online television fandom', Television
      and New Media viii/2, p.131.

34    Anon. (2006) 'Firestarter: the girl in the fireplace', Tachyon TV special edn
      (November), p.5.

35    Dave Golder (2007) 'Boom Town', SFX Collection special edn 28, Future
      Network, Bath, p.59.

36    See, for example, Pegg: 'Saturday night, Sunday morning', p.46.

37    Joe McKee (2005) 'The age of wonders: overview', Shockeye's Kitchen,
      16th Course, p.5.

38    See Dave Golder (2007) 'Pure Golder: everyone's a critic', available online
      at http://scifi.co.uk/oracle/puregolder_critic.asp, accessed 22 May 2007.

39    Hunt: 'The importance of trivia'.

40    Parkin: 'The incredible week', p.26.

41    Ibid., p.27.

42    Jancovich and Hunt: 'The mainstream, distinction, and cult TV'.

43    Jonathan Lomas in David May (ed.) (2007) Views From Behind the Sofa,
      Lulu, Raleigh, North Carolina, p.254.

44    Ash Stewart in May: Views From Behind the Sofa, p.258 (my italics); see
      also McKee: 'The age of wonders', p.4.

45    Jancovich and Hunt: 'The mainstream, distinction, and cult TV', p.28.

46   Tom Spilsbury (2008) 'Letter from the editor', *Doctor Who Magazine* 392, p.3.

47   Cited in Matt Hills (2005) 'Flat earthers write back', *Doctor Who Junkie*, 26 March souvenir issue, Cardiff, p.22.

48   Davies in Benjamin Cook (2008) 'In the midnight hour', *Doctor Who Magazine* 400, Panini Comics, Tunbridge Wells, p.34.

49   Johnson: *Telefantasy*, p.143.

50   In ibid., p.141.

51   In ibid., p.134.

52   Ibid., pp.136–7.

53   Ibid., p.143.

54   In Matt Hills (2003) '*Star Wars* in fandom, film theory, and the museum: the cultural status of the cult blockbuster', in Julian Stringer (ed.) *Movie Blockbusters*, Routledge, London and New York, p.185.

55   See Sharon Marie Ross (2008) *Beyond the Box: Television and the Internet*, Blackwell Publishing, Malden and Oxford.

56   Martin Belam (2007) '"The Tardis and multiplatform" – Julie Gardner talks about *Doctor Who*'s multi-media incarnations', 28 September, available online at *http://www.currybet.net/cbet_blog/2007/09/the_tardis_and_multi platform.php*.

57   Steve O'Brien and Nick Setchfield (2005) 'Russell spouts' in *SFX Collection: Doctor Who Special*, Future Network, Bath, p.38.

58   For another example of 'cult' versus 'mythology' discourse see Lynnette Porter and David Lavery (2007) on *Lost* (ABC, 2004– ) fandom (*Unlocking the Meaning of Lost*, Sourcebooks, Naperville, IL, p.268); however, Bruce Isaacs (2008) argues interestingly that cult status and mythic narrative are discursively linked rather than opposed (*Toward a New Film Aesthetic*, Continuum, New York and London, p.122).

59   Cited in Perryman: '*Doctor Who* and the convergence of media', p.26.

60   Ben Dowell (2008) 'Amy Winehouse would be a great Doctor', *Guardian*, 7 July, available online at *http://www.guardian.co.uk/media/2008/jul/07/ television.bbc*.

61   Hollows: 'The masculinity of cult'.

62   Davies in Nick Setchfield (2008) 'We have a twenty year plan...', in *SFX* 168, Future Network, Bath, p.46.

63   On the creation of SF neologisms, see Peter Stockwell (2000) *The Poetics of Science Fiction*, Longman, Harlow, p.124.

64   Interviewed for website 'Unreality SF' (2008), Davies sought to distance himself from the term 'ming-mong', saying 'I'm trying to clamp down on [it] ... I don't like it.' ('Russell T Davies and Benjamin Cook', available at *http://unreality-sf.net/interviews/thewriterstale.html*). This was after he'd been quoted using the phrase to attack sections of fandom, however.

65   Moffat in David Bailey (2008) 'Script doctors: Steven Moffat', *Doctor Who Magazine* 394, Panini Comics, Tunbridge Wells, p.46.

66   Moffat in Silas Lesnick (2008) 'SDCC Exclusive Interview: Steven Moffat on *Doctor Who*', available online at *http://www.comingsoon.net/news/ tvnews.php?id=47147*.

67   Tulloch and Jenkins: *Science Fiction Audiences*, p.145.

68   Ibid.

69   Ibid.

70   See ibid., p.161.

71   See Golder: 'Pure Golder'.

72   Johnson: 'Fan-tagonism', p.295.

73   Johnson: 'Inviting audiences in', p.76.

74   J. Shaun Lyon (2006) *Second Flight*, Telos Press, Tolworth, p.297.

75   See Andrew Rilstone (2008) 'The 50 greatest moments of *Doctor Who*', *Sci Fi Now* 19, Imagine, London, pp.56–60.

76   An 'Easter egg' is a short sequence of content hidden on a DVD by virtue of not being included in menu options. Viewers have to hunt for this 'Easter egg' content, hence its name.

77   Matt Hills (2008) 'The question of genre in cult film and fandom: between contract and discourse', in James Donald and Michael Renov (eds) *The Sage Handbook of Film Studies*, Sage, London, p.446.

78   See Matt Hills (2004) '*Dawson's Creek*: "quality teen TV" and "mainstream cult"?', in Glyn Davis and Kay Dickinson (eds) *Teen TV*, BFI Publishing, London, pp.54–67, and his (2006) 'Realising the cult blockbuster: *The Lord of the Rings* fandom and residual/emergent cult status in "the mainstream"', in Ernest Mathijs (ed.) *The Lord of the Rings: Popular Culture in Global Context*, Wallflower Press, London and New York, pp.160–71.

79   Tryon: 'TV Time Lords', p.310.

80   See Perryman: '*Doctor Who* and the convergence of media', p.31, 38 n.27.

81   Matt Hills (2002) *Fan Cultures*, Routledge, London and New York; Johnson: 'Inviting audiences in', p.73.

82   Ross: *Beyond the Box*, p.214.

83   Ibid., p.182.

84   Ibid., pp.13–14.

85   See Belam: 'The Tardis and multiplatform'.

86   Ross: *Beyond the Box*, p.13.

87   David Eick in ibid., p.185.

88   Russell T. Davies (2005) 'Pitch perfect', in *The* Doctor Who *Companion: Series One*, Panini Comics, Tunbridge Wells, p.43.

89   Justin Wyatt (1994) *High Concept: Movies and Marketing in Hollywood*, University of Texas Press, Austin, p.8.

90   Ibid., p.55.

91   See Matt Hills (2007) '"Gothic" body parts in a "postmodern" body of work? The Hinchcliffe/Holmes era of *Doctor Who* (1975–77)', *Intensities: The Journal of Cult Media* 4, available online at http://intensities.org/Issues/Intensities_Four.htm.

92   Chapman: *Inside the TARDIS*, p.98.

93   Philip Hinchcliffe in Charles Norton (2008) 'Evolution of a monster hit', *The Stage*, 15 May, p.52.

94   Jason Mittell (2006) 'Narrative complexity in contemporary American television', *The Velvet Light Trap* 58 (Fall), p.35.

95   Ibid., pp.35–6.

96   Ibid., p.35.

97    Ibid., p.31.
98    Ibid., p.35.
99    Ibid.
100   Anon.: 'Firestarter', p.5.
101   Mittell: 'Narrative complexity', p.35.
102   Ibid., p.38.
103   Ibid., p.33.
104   Ross: *Beyond the Box*, p.182.
105   Hardstaffe: 'Watching them watching *Who*', p.10; see also Jonathan Big-
      nell and Andrew O'Day (2004) *Terry Nation*, Manchester University Press,
      Manchester and New York, p.102.
106   John Ellis (1982) *Visible Fictions*, Routledge and Kegan Paul, London.
107   Russell T. Davies in Nick Setchfield and Steve O'Brien (2006) 'The Lord of
      Time', *SFX Collection* special edn 24, Future Network, Bath, p.6.
108   Stockwell: *The Poetics of Science Fiction*, p.117–18; see also Tulloch and
      Alvarado: Doctor Who: *The Unfolding Text*, pp.103–4.
109   Davies: 'Pitch perfect', p.42.
110   Adam McGechan (2005) 'Through rose-tinted glasses: old fans, new se-
      ries and one leaked episode', *Time Space Visualiser: The Journal of the New
      Zealand* Doctor Who *Fan Club* 71, pp.25–6.
111   In ibid., p.26.
112   Jack Graham (2006) 'Is 2006 the new 2005? The power of cool', *Shock-
      eye's Kitchen*, 17th course, p.11.
113   Ibid.
114   See the Shooting Script of 4.13 'Journey's End' (Russell T. Davies, 2008,
      available online at *http://www.thewriterstale.com/scr.html*).
115   Ross: *Beyond the Box*, pp.8–9.
116   See Jancovich and Hunt: 'The mainstream, distinction, and cult TV'; the
      same is also true of 'quality', given the range of differential quality TV
      discourses.
117   Johnson: *Telefantasy.*
118   Jancovich and Hunt: 'The mainstream, distinction, and cult TV'; Sand-
      voss: *Fans*; Thornton: *Club Cultures.*
119   Jenkins: *Convergence Culture*; Ross: *Beyond the Box.*
120   Chapman: *Inside the TARDIS*, p.viii.

# BIBLIOGRAPHY

Abercrombie, Nicholas and Brian Longhurst (1998) *Audiences*, Sage, London.
Adorno, Theodor and Hanns Eisler (1994 [1947]) *Composing for the Films*, Athlone Press, London and Atlantic Highlands.
Aldridge, Mark and Andy Murray (2008) *T Is For Television: The Small Screen Adventures of Russell T. Davies*, Reynolds and Hearn, Surrey.
Altman, Rick (1999) *Film/Genre*, BFI Publishing, London.
Amy-Chinn, Dee (2008) 'Rose Tyler: the ethics of care and the limit of agency', *Science Fiction Film and Television* 1.2, pp.231–47.
Ang, Ien (1985) *Watching Dallas*, Routledge, London and New York.
Anon. (2006) 'Firestarter: the girl in the fireplace', *Tachyon TV* special edn (November), p.5.
—— (2008) 'Dreamers in the night', in Josef Steiff and Tristan D. Tamplin (eds) *Battlestar Galactica and Philosophy: Mission Accomplished or Mission Frakked Up?* Open Court, Chicago and La Salle, IL, pp.359–67.
Arnopp, Jason (2007) 'Worlds apart', *Doctor Who Magazine* 383, Panini Comics, Tunbridge Wells, pp.12–19.
—— (2008) 'Master of the macabre', *Doctor Who Magazine* 397, Panini Comics, Tunbridge Wells, pp.26–34.
Bailey, David (2008) 'Script doctors: Steven Moffat', *Doctor Who Magazine* 394, Panini Comics, Tunbridge Wells, pp.46–50.
Bakhtin, M.M. (1981) *The Dialogic Imagination: Four Essays*, University of Texas Press, Austin.
Barlow, David, Philip Mitchell and Tom O'Malley (2005) *The Media in Wales: Voices of a Small Nation*, University of Wales Press, Cardiff.
Barthes, Roland (1981) *Camera Lucida*, Hill and Wang, New York.
BBC (2005) 'TV moments', available online at *http://www.bbc.co.uk/tvmoments/vote/*, accessed 22 August 2007.
—— (2006) *Annual Report and Accounts 2005/2006*, Broadcasting House, London.
—— (2006) 'BBC reorganises for an on-demand creative future', press release, 19 July, available online at *http://www.bbc.co.uk/pressoffice/pressreleases/stories/2006/07_july/19/future.shtml*, accessed 3 September 2008.

BBC (2008) *Doctor Who* website, series four episode commentaries, available on line at *http://www.bbc.co.uk/doctorwho/s4/misc/commentaries.shtml*, accessed 27 September 2008.

BBC News (2007) 'Billie Piper to return to *Dr Who*', available online at *http://news.bbc.co.uk/1/hi/entertainment/7114699.stm*, 27 November, accessed 27 September 2008.

—— (2008) 'Dr Who fan in knitted puppet row', available online at *http://news.bbc.co.uk/1/hi/entertainment/7400268.stm*, 14 May, accessed 25 August 2008.

Belam, Martin (2007) '"The Tardis and multiplatform" – Julie Gardner talks about *Doctor Who's* multi-media incarnations', 28 September, available online at *http://www.currybet.net/cbet_blog/2007/09/the_tardis_and_multiplatform.php*, accessed 3 September 2008.

Bell, Matt (2007) 'Doctor's notes – Murray Gold: composing for *Doctor Who*', *Sound on Sound* (June), pp.40–6.

Benshoff, Harry M. (1997) *Monsters in the Closet: Homosexuality and the Horror Film*, Manchester University Press, Manchester.

Berger, Richard (2008) 'GINO or dialogic: what does 're-imagined' really mean?', in Josef Steiff and Trista D. Tamplin (eds) Battlestar Galactica *and Philosophy: Mission Accomplished or Mission Frakked Up?* Open Court, Chicago and La Salle, IL, pp.317–28.

Berriman, Ian (2007) 'Writing *Who*', *SFX Collection*, special edn 28, Future Network, Bath, pp.11–12.

Bielby, Matt (2008) 'The *Death Ray* interview: Steven Moffat', *Death Ray* 15, Blackfish Publishing, Bath, pp.68–77.

—— (2008) 'Fly, lonely angel', *Death Ray* 12, Blackfish, Bath, pp.43–8.

Bignell, Jonathan (2004) 'Another time, another space: modernity, subjectivity and *The Time Machine*', in Sean Redmond (ed.) *Liquid Metal: The Science Fiction Film Reader*, Wallflower Press, London, pp.136–44.

—— (2004) *An Introduction to Television Studies*, Routledge, London and New York.

—— (2005) 'Space for "quality": negotiating with the Daleks', in Jonathan Bignell and Stephen Lacey (eds) *Popular Television Drama*, Manchester University Press, Manchester and New York, pp.76–92.

—— (2007) 'The child as addressee, viewer and consumer in mid-1960s *Doctor Who*', in David Butler (ed.) *Time and Relative Dissertations in Space: Critical Perspectives on Doctor Who*, Manchester University Press, Manchester, pp.43–55.

—— and Andrew O'Day (2004) *Terry Nation*, Manchester University Press, Manchester and New York.

Bird, S. Elizabeth (2003) *The Audience in Everyday Life*, Routledge, London and New York.

Bishop, Vanessa (2007) 'Original television soundtrack', *Doctor Who Magazine* 379, p.65.

—— (2007) 'Original television soundtrack: series three', *Doctor Who Magazine* 390, p.66.

Black, David A. (2004) 'Charactor; or, the strange case of Uma Peel', in Sara Gwenllian-Jones and Roberta E. Pearson (eds) *Cult Television*, University of Minnesota Press, Minneapolis, pp.99–114.

Blandford, Steve (2005) 'BBC drama at the margins: the contrasting fortunes of Northern Irish, Scottish and Welsh television drama in the 1990s', in Jonathan Bignell and Stephen Lacey (eds) *Popular Television Drama: Critical Perspectives*, Manchester University Press, Manchester and New York, pp.166–82.

Blum, Jonathan (2002) '50 essential questions: TV', *Doctor Who Magazine* 312, Panini Comics, Tunbridge Wells, pp.4–7.

Bodle, Andy (2004) 'Who dares, wins', *Guardian: G2*, 23 March, p.4.

Born, Georgina (2000) 'Inside television: television studies and the sociology of culture', *Screen* xli/4, pp.404–24.

Bould, Mark (2008) 'Science fiction television in the United Kingdom', in J.P. Telotte (ed.) *The Essential Science Fiction Television Reader*, University Press of Kentucky, Kentucky, pp.209–30.

Brabazon, Tara (2008) 'Christmas and the media', in Sheila Whiteley (ed.) *Christmas, Ideology and Popular Culture*, Edinburgh University Press, Edinburgh, pp.149–63.

Briggs, Caroline (2008) 'Doctor Who signing ban at *Hamlet*', available online at *http://news.bbc.co.uk/1/hi/entertainment/7523210.stm*, accessed 4 August 2008.

Bristol, Michael D. (1996) *Big-Time Shakespeare*, Routledge, London and New York.

Britton, Piers D. and Simon J. Barker (2003) *Reading Between Designs: Visual Imagery and the Generation of Meaning in The Avengers, The Prisoner, and Doctor Who*, University of Texas Press, Austin.

Brook, Stephen (2005) 'BBC apologises to Eccleston over *Doctor Who* spin', *Media Guardian*, 5 April, available online at *http://www.guardian.co.uk/media/2005/apr/05/broadcasting.bbc*, accessed 4 August 2008.

Brooker, Charlie (2007) *Charlie Brooker's Dawn of the Dumb*, Faber and Faber, London.

Brooker, Will (2002) *Using the Force: Creativity, Community and Star Wars Fans*, Continuum, New York and London.

Brown, Dan (2003) *The Da Vinci Code*, Doubleday, New York.

Brunsdon, Charlotte (1997) *Screen Tastes*, Routledge, London and New York.

Bukatman, Scott (1995) 'The artificial infinite: on special effects and the sublime', in Lynne Cooke and Peter Wollen (eds) *Visual Display: Culture Beyond Appearances*, Bay, Seattle, pp.254–89.

Burling, William J. (2006) 'Reading time: the ideology of time travel in science fiction', *KronoScope* vi/1, pp.5–30.

Burnand, David and Miguel Mera (2004) 'Fast and cheap? The film music of John Carpenter', in Ian Conrich and David Woods (eds) *The Cinema of John Carpenter: The Technique of Terror*, Wallflower Press, London, pp.49–65.

Burt, Richard (1998) *Unspeakable ShaXXXspeares: Queer Theory and American Kiddie Culture*, Macmillan, London.

Butler, David (2007) 'How to pilot a TARDIS: audiences, science fiction and the fantastic in *Doctor Who*', in David Butler (ed.) *Time and Relative Dissertations in Space: Critical Perspectives on Doctor Who*, Manchester University Press, Manchester, pp.19–42.

Camford, Vic (1999) 'If you tolerate this, your children will be next', *Doctor Who Magazine* 284, Marvel Comics, London, pp. 8–14.

Cardwell, Sarah (2002) *Adaptation Revisited: Television and the Classic Novel*, Manchester University Press, Manchester and New York.

—— (2005) 'The representation of youth in the twenty-something serial', in Michael Hammond and Lucy Mazdon (eds) *The Contemporary Television Series*, Edinburgh Press, Edinburgh, pp.123–38.

—— (2006) 'Television aesthetics', *Critical Studies in Television*, i/1, pp.72–80.

—— (2007) 'Is quality television any good? Generic distinctions, evaluations and the troubling matter of critical judgement', in Janet McCabe and Kim Akass (eds) *Quality TV: Contemporary American Television and Beyond*, I.B.Tauris, London and New York, pp.19–34.

Carroll, Noel (1990) *The Philosophy of Horror*, Routledge, New York and London.

Cartmel, Andrew (2005) *Script Doctor: The Inside Story of* Doctor Who *1986–89*, Reynolds and Hearn, London.

—— (2005) *Through Time: An Unauthorised and Unofficial History of* Doctor Who, Continuum, New York and London.

Caughie, John (2000) *Television Drama: Realism, Modernism, and British Culture*, Oxford University Press, Oxford and New York.

—— (2000) 'What do actors do when they act?', in Jonathan Bignell, Stephen Lacey and Madeleine Macmurraugh-Kavanagh (eds) *British Television Drama: Past, Present and Future*, Palgrave, Basingstoke, pp.162–74.

—— (2007) *Edge of Darkness*, BFI Publishing, London.

Cavendish, Dominic (2008) 'Look who's playing Hamlet', *Daily Telegraph*, 23 July, p.27.

Chapman, James (2006) *Inside the TARDIS: The Worlds of* Doctor Who, I.B.Tauris, London and New York.

Charles, Alec (2007) 'The ideology of anachronism: television, history and the nature of time', in David Butler (ed.) *Time and Relative Dissertations in Space: Critical Perspectives on* Doctor Who, Manchester University Press, Manchester, pp.108–22.

Chion, Michel (1994) *Audio-Vision: Sound on Screen*, Columbia University Press, New York.

Church Gibson, Pamela (2000) 'Fewer weddings and more funerals: changes in the heritage film', in Robert Murphy (ed.) *British Cinema of the 90s*, BFI, London, pp.115–24.

Cochran, Tanya R. (2008) 'The browncoats are coming! Firefly, serenity and fan activism', in Rhonda V. Wilcox and Tanya R. Cochran (eds) *Investigating Firefly and Serenity: Science Fiction on the Frontier*, I.B.Tauris, London and New York, pp.239–49.

Cole, Stephen (1998) 'The Caves of Androzani: hatred and heroism', *Doctor Who Magazine* 265, Marvel Comics, London, pp.22–3.

Collins, Jim (1992) 'Television and postmodernism', in Robert C. Allen (ed.) *Channels of Discourse, Reassembled*, Routledge, London, pp.327–53.

Cook, Benjamin (2005) 'Gardner's world', *Doctor Who Magazine* 354, Panini Comics, Tunbridge Wells, pp.12–19.

—— (2005) 'New series preview: Boom Town', *Doctor Who Magazine* 357, Panini Comics, Tunbridge Wells, p.27.

—— (2005) 'Tooth and claw: the Russell T. Davies interview', *Doctor Who Magazine* 360, Panini Comics, Tunbridge Wells, pp.12–19.

—— (2007) 'Favourite worst nightmares!', *Doctor Who Magazine* 384, Panini Comics, Tunbridge Wells, pp.44–50.

—— (2007) 'Leader of the gang', *Doctor Who Magazine* 386, Panini Comics, Tunbridge Wells, pp.12–20.

—— (2007) 'There's no way we want to let her go', *Doctor Who Magazine* 385, Panini Comics, Tunbridge Wells, p.18.

—— (2008) 'Everybody's Talkin'', *Doctor Who Magazine* 398, Panini Comics, Tunbridge Wells, pp.16–8.

—— (2008) 'In the midnight hour', *Doctor Who Magazine* 400, Panini Comics, Tunbridge Wells, pp.30–7.

Cooke, Lez (2005) 'The new social realism of *Clocking Off*', in Jonathan Bignell and Stephen Lacey (eds) *Popular Television Drama*, Manchester University Press, Manchester and New York, pp.183–97.

Coombe, Rosemary J. (1998) *The Cultural Life of Intellectual Properties: Authorship, Appropriation, and the Law*, Duke University Press, Durham and London.

Coppa, Francesca (2006) 'A brief history of media fandom', in Karen Hellekson and Kristina Busse (eds) *Fan Fiction and Fan Communities in the Age of the Internet*, McFarland, Jefferson, pp.41–59.

Cornea, Christine (2007) *Science Fiction Cinema: Between Fantasy and Reality*, Edinburgh University Press, Edinburgh.

Cornell, Paul (1995) *Human Nature*, Virgin, London.

—— (ed.) (1997) *Licence Denied: Rumblings from the Doctor Who Underground*, Virgin Books, London.

—— (2005) 'Father's Day', in *The Shooting Scripts*, BBC Books, London, pp.280–311.

—— (2007) 'Adapting the novel for the screen', available online at *http://www.bbc.co.uk/doctorwho/classic/ebooks/human_nature/adaptation.shtml*, accessed 18 July 2007.

Corner, John (1999) *Critical Ideas in Television Studies*, Oxford University Press, Oxford.

Costello, Victor and Barbara Moore (2007) 'Cultural outlaws: an examination of audience activity and online television fandom', *Television and New Media* viii/2, pp.124–43.

Couch, Steve, Tony Watkins and Peter S. Williams (2005) *Back in Time: A Thinking Fan's Guide to* Doctor Who, Damaris Books, Milton Keynes.

Crawford, Gary (2004) *Consuming Sport: Fans, Sport and Culture*, Routledge, London and New York.

Creeber, Glen (ed) (2004) *Fifty Key Television Programmes*, Arnold, London.

—— (2004) *Serial Television: Big Drama on the Small Screen*, BFI Publishing, London.

Creed, Barbara (2005) *Phallic Panic: Film, Horror and the Primal Uncanny*, Melbourne University Press, Melbourne.

Cregeen, Peter (1989) 'Reply to *Radio Times* letter', *Radio Times*, 25 November–1 December, available online at *http://www.cuttingsarchive.org.uk/radiotim/cs-s24-26/season26/letters.htm*, accessed 4 October 2008.

Cull, Nicholas J. (2001) 'Bigger on the inside ... *Doctor Who* as British cultural history', in Graham Roberts and Philip M. Taylor (eds) *The Historian, Television and Television History*, University of Luton Press, Luton, pp.95–111.

Cull, Nicholas J. (2006) 'Tardis at the OK Corral: *Doctor Who* and the USA', in John R. Cook and Peter Wright (eds) *British Science Fiction Television*, I.B.Tauris, London and New York, pp.52–70.

D'Acci, Julie (1994) *Defining Women: Television and the Case of Cagney and Lacey*, University of North Carolina Press, Chapel Hill and London.

Darlington, David (2005) 'Murray Gold: incidental hits', *Doctor Who Magazine* 362, pp.34–42.

—— (2006) 'Gold bars', *Doctor Who Magazine* 373, pp.50–7.

—— (2006) 'Murray Gold', in Doctor Who: *A Celebration*, BBC Wales, Cardiff, pp.5–6.

—— (2007) 'Script doctors: Steven Moffat – "I had to change the entire script just because of the title"', *Doctor Who Magazine* 383, Panini Comics, Tunbridge Wells, pp.22–6.

—— (2008) 'Music to your spheres', *Doctor Who Magazine* 399, Panini Comics, Tunbridge Wells, pp.36–9.

Davidhazi, Peter (1998) *The Romantic Cult of Shakespeare*, Macmillan, London.

Davies, Caroline and David Smith (2009) 'Dr Who? Big names lose out to Matt Smith', available at *http://www.guardian.co.uk/media/2009/jan/03/doctor-who-matt-smith*, accessed 5 January 2009.

Davies, Russell T. (1991) *Dark Season*, BBC Books, London.

—— (1996) *Damaged Goods*, Virgin, London.

—— (2002) 'Spearhead from space: back home', in *The Complete Third Doctor: Doctor Who Magazine* special edn 2, Panini Comics, Tunbridge Wells, p.15.

—— (2003) 'Fury from the deep: classical gas', in *The Complete Second Doctor: Doctor Who Magazine* special edn 4, Panini Comics, Tunbridge Wells, p.48.

—— (2004) '100,000 BC: how do you do it?', in *The Complete First Doctor: Doctor Who Magazine* special edn 7, Panini Comics, Tunbridge Wells, p.22.

—— (2004) 'The stones of blood: super nature', in *The Complete Fourth Doctor, Volume Two: Doctor Who Magazine* special edn 9, Panini Comics, Tunbridge Wells, p.21.

—— (2005) 'Aliens of London/World War Three', in *The Shooting Scripts*, BBC Books, London, pp.126–99.

—— (2005) 'Bad Wolf/The Parting of the Ways', in *The Shooting Scripts*, BBC Books, London, pp.430–511.

—— (2005) 'The End of the World', in *The Shooting Scripts*, BBC Books, London, pp.48–89.

—— (2005) 'Have a Russell T. Davies TV festival', *Guardian*, 1 January, available online at *http://www.guardian.co.uk/theguardian/2005/jan/01/weekend7.weekend4*, accessed 19 August 2008.

—— (2005) 'The long game', in *The Shooting Scripts*, BBC Books, London, pp.236–77.

—— (2005) 'Pitch perfect', in *The* Doctor Who *Companion: Series One*, Panini Comics, Tunbridge Wells, pp.40–9.

—— (2005) 'Rose', in *The Shooting Scripts*, BBC Books, London, pp.12–47.

—— (2006) 'Production notes: magic moments', *Doctor Who Magazine* 365, Panini Comics, Tunbridge Wells, p.66.

—— (2006) 'Production notes: Phil's space' in *Doctor Who Magazine* 366, Panini Comics, Tunbridge Wells, p.66.

—— (2006) 'Second Sight', *The* Doctor Who *Companion: Series Two*, Panini Comics, Tunbridge Wells, pp.4–10.

—— (2007) 'Production notes: between the lines', *Doctor Who Magazine* 388, Panini Comics, Tunbridge Wells, p.66.

—— (2007) 'Production notes: the Doctor calls', *Doctor Who Magazine* 387, Panini Comics, Tunbridge Wells, p.66.

—— (2007) 'Three-volution', in *The* Doctor Who *Companion: Series Three*, Panini Comics, Tunbridge Wells, pp.4–7.

—— (2008) 'Introduction' in *Doctor Who Magazine Special Edition: The* Doctor Who *Companion – Series Four*, Panini Magazines, Tunbridge Wells, p.5.

—— (2008) 'Journey's End', *The Shooting Scripts*, available online at *http://www.thewriterstale.com/scr.html*, accessed 7 October 2008.

—— (2008) 'Russell T. Davies introduces "Music of the Spheres"', in *Doctor Who Prom Programme*, BBC, p.15.

—— and Benjamin Cook (2008) *The Writer's Tale*, BBC Books, London.

Davis, Glyn (2007) *BFI TV Classics:* Queer as Folk, BFI, London.

de Certeau, Michel (1988) *The Practice of Everyday Life*, University of California Press, Berkeley and London.

De Vries, Kim (2007) 'The scholarship of *Doctor Who*, or, how cult TV gained street cred in the academy', available online at *http://www.sequentialtart.com/article.php?id=527*, 1 June, accessed 12 July 2007.

Dionne, Craig (2002) 'The Shatnerification of Shakespeare: *Star Trek* and the commonplace tradition', in Richard Burt (ed.) *Shakespeare After Mass Media*, Palgrave, London, pp.173–91.

Dobson, Nichola (2006) 'The regeneration of *Doctor Who*: the ninth Doctor and the influence of the slayer', *Flow* iv/4, available online at *http://flowtv.org/?p=227*, accessed 2 May 2006.

*Doctor Who Confidential* (2007) 'Do you remember the first time?', David Tennant (dir.), broadcast 9 June 2007, BBC3.

—— (2007) 'Untitled', executive producer: Mark Cossey, series producer: Gillane Seaborne, broadcast 25 December 2007, BBC3.

Donnelly, K.J. (1998) 'The classical film score forever? *Batman, Batman Returns* and post-classical film music', in Steve Neale and Murray Smith (eds) *Contemporary Hollywood Cinema*, Routledge, London and New York, pp.142–55.

—— (2005) *The Spectre of Sound: Music in Film and Television*, BFI, London.

—— (2007) 'Between prosaic functionalism and sublime experimentation: *Doctor Who* and musical sound design', in David Butler (ed.) *Time and Relative Dissertations in Space: Critical Perspectives on* Doctor Who, Manchester University Press, Manchester and New York, pp.190–203.

Dowell, Ben (2008) 'Amy Winehouse would be a great Doctor', *Guardian*, 7 July, available online at *http://www.guardian.co.uk/media/2008/jul/07/television.bbc*, accessed 7 August 2008.

Eagleton, Terry (1987) 'Awakening from modernity', *Times Literary Supplement*, 20 February.

—— (1988) 'Afterword', in Graham Holderness (ed.) *The Shakespeare Myth*, Manchester University Press, Manchester, pp.203–8.

Eaton, Michael (2005) *BFI TV Classics:* Our Friends in the North, BFI Publishing, London.

Eco, Umberto (1995) *Faith in Fakes: Travels in Hyperreality*, Minerva, London.

Elam, Keir (1980) *The Semiotics of Theatre and Drama*, Methuen, London.

Ellis, John (1982) *Visible Fictions*, Routledge and Kegan Paul, London.

Ellis, John (2000) *Seeing Things: Television in the Age of Uncertainty*, I.B.Tauris, London and New York.

Farley, Rebecca (2003) 'From Fred and Wilma to Ren and Stimpy: what makes a cartoon "prime time"?', in Carol A. Stabile and Mark Harrison (eds) *Prime Time Animation*, Routledge London and New York, pp.147–64.

Feuer, Jane (2007) 'HBO and the concept of quality TV', in Janet McCabe and Kim Akass (eds) *Quality TV: Contemporary American Television and Beyond*, I.B.Tauris, London and New York, pp.145–57.

Fischer, Bob (2008) *Wiffle Lever to Full: Daleks, Death Stars and Dreamy-Eyed Nostalgia at the Strangest Sci-Fi Conventions*, Hodder and Stoughton, London.

Fiske, John (1984) 'Popularity and ideology: a structuralist reading of *Doctor Who*', in William. D. Rowland and Bruce Watkins (eds) *Interpreting Television: Current Research Perspectives*, Sage, Beverly Hills, pp.58–73.

Fleming, Dan (1996) *Powerplay: Toys as Popular Culture*, Manchester University Press, Manchester.

Flinn, Caryl (1992) *Strains of Utopia*, Princeton University Press, Princeton.

Foucault, Michel (1979) *Discipline and Punish: The Birth of the Prison*, Penguin, Harmondsworth.

—— (1979) 'What is an author?', *Screen* xx/1, pp.13–33.

—— (2002) *The Archaeology of Knowledge*, Routledge, London and New York.

Fountain, Nev (2006) *The Kingmaker*, Big Finish Audio, London.

Frow, John (1997) *Time and Commodity Culture: Essays in Cultural Theory and Postmodernity*, Clarendon Press, Oxford.

Geraghty, Christine (2003) 'Aesthetics and quality in popular television drama', *International Journal of Cultural Studies* vi/1, pp.25–45.

Geraint, John (2008) '"For Wales, see England": network television from "the Nations", 1996–2006', *Cyfrwng: Media Wales Journal* 5, pp.38–53.

Gerard, Simon (2004) '"Assault" at Temple at Peace?', *Starburst* 317, Visual Imagination, London, pp.6–7.

Giddens, Anthony (1991) *Modernity and Self-Identity: Self and Society in the Late Modern Age*, Polity, Cambridge.

Gillatt, Gary (1996) 'First impressions', *Doctor Who Magazine* 235, Marvel Magazines, London, pp.4–9.

—— (1996) 'Second sight', *Doctor Who Magazine* 242, Marvel Magazines, London, pp.6–11.

—— (1998) 'The *DWM* Awards', *Doctor Who Magazine* 265, Marvel Comics, London, pp.4–7.

—— (1999) 'We're gonna be bigger than *Star Wars*!', *Doctor Who Magazine* 279, Marvel Comics, London, pp.8–12.

—— (2008) 'The sheer brilliance of *Doctor Who*', *Doctor Who Magazine* 400, Panini Comics, Tunbridge Wells, pp.16–26.

Gold, Murray (2006) 'Music notes' on the inlay card for *Doctor Who: Original Television Soundtrack*, BBC, Silva Screen Records.

—— (2007) Liner notes for *Doctor Who: Series 3 Music*, BBC National Orchestra of Wales, conducted by Ben Foster, BBC, Silva Screen Records.

Golder, Dave (2007) 'Boom Town', *SFX Collection* special edn 28, Future Network, Bath, pp.58–9.

—— (2007) 'Father's Day', *SFX Collection* special edn 28, Future Network, Bath, pp.52–3.

—— (2007) 'Pure Golder: everyone's a critic', available online at *http://scifi.
co.uk/oracle/puregolder_critic.asp*, accessed 22 May 2007.

—— (2008) 'Midnight', Doctor Who: *The Special FX*, with *SFX Collection* special
edn 35, Future Network, Bath, pp.20–1.

Gorbman, Claudia (1987) *Unheard Melodies: Narrative Film Music*, BFI Publishing, London.

Gordon, Andrew (2004) '*Back to the Future*: Oedipus as time traveller', in Sean
Redmond (ed.) *Liquid Metal: The Science Fiction Film Reader*, Wallflower
Press, London, pp.116–25.

Gorton, Kristyn (2006) 'A sentimental journey: television, meaning and emotion', *Journal of British Cinema and Television* iii/1, pp.72–81.

Graham, Jack (2006) 'Is 2006 the new 2005? The power of cool', *Shockeye's
Kitchen*, 17th course, pp.9–11.

—— (2008) 'Not all unconvincing giant stag beetles sit on the back: reflections
on "Turn Left"', available online at *http://www.freewebs.com/shabogan-
graffiti/turnleft.htm*, accessed 27 September 2008.

Grainge, Paul (2008) *Brand Hollywood: Selling Entertainment in a Global Media
Age*, Routledge, London and New York.

Gray, Jonathan (2006) *Watching with* The Simpsons: *Television, Parody and Intertextuality*, Routledge, New York and London.

—— (2008) *Television Entertainment*, Routledge, New York and London.

Gregory, Chris (2000) Star Trek: *Parallel Narratives*, Macmillan, Basingstoke.

Griffiths, Nick (2006) '*Doctor Who* watch: talk of the devil', *Radio Times*, 10–16
June, p.10.

—— (2007) *Dalek I Loved You: A Memoir*, Orion Publishing, London.

—— (2008) *Who Goes There: Travels Through Strangest Britain In Search of the
Doctor*, Legend Press, London.

Grutchfield, Ian (2005) 'Brand Aid!', *Doctor Who Magazine* 364, Panini Comics,
Tunbridge Wells, p.39.

*Guardian* (2005) 'Pass notes 2,608: Bad Wolf', 15 June, available online at *http://
www.guardian.co.uk/theguardian/2005/jun/15/features11.g2*, accessed
27 September 2008.

Gwenllian Jones, Sara (2000) 'Starring Lucy Lawless?', *Continuum: Journal of
Media and Cultural Studies* xiv/1, pp.9–22.

—— (2002) 'The sex lives of cult television characters', *Screen* xliii/1, pp.79–
90.

—— (2004) 'Virtual reality and cult television', in Sara Gwenllian-Jones and
Roberta E. Pearson (eds) *Cult Television*, University of Minnesota Press, Minneapolis and London, pp.83–97.

Hardstaffe, Andrew (2002) 'Watching them watching *Who*', *Doctor's Recorder*
30, pp.4–10.

—— (2005) 'Watch with others', *Doctor's Recorder* 43, pp.10–18, 27.

Harper, Graeme with Adrian Rigelsford (2007) *Calling the Shots: Directing the
New Series of Doctor Who'*, Reynolds and Hearn, London.

Hellekson, Karen (1996) 'Poaching *Doctor Who*', available online at *http://www.
frontiernet.net/~mumvideo/analysis.htm*, accessed 27 September 2008.

—— (2008) 'Fandom wank and history', available online at *http://khellekson.
wordpress.com/2008/03/30/fandom-wank-and-history/*, accessed 2 October 2008.

Hellekson, Karen and Kristina Busse (eds) (2006) *Fan Fiction and Fan Communities in the Age of the Internet*, McFarland, Jefferson and London.

Herman, Sarah (2008) 'Lleoliad, lleoliad, lleoliad!', *Torchwood: The Official Magazine* 8, Titan Magazines, London, pp.16–25.

Hermes, Joke (2005) *Re-reading Popular Culture*, Blackwell Publishing, Malden and Oxford.

Heuman, Josh and Richard Burt (2002) 'Suggested for mature readers? Deconstructing Shakespearean value in comic books', in Richard Burt (ed.) *Shakespeare After Mass Media*, Palgrave, London, pp.151–71.

Hewison, Robert (1987) *The Heritage Industry*, Methuen, London.

Hickman, Clayton (2004) 'Revolution number 9: the Christopher Eccleston interview', *Doctor Who Magazine* 343, Panini Comics, Tunbridge Wells, pp.10–13.

—— (2005) 'Perfect ten: the David Tennant interview', *Doctor Who Magazine* 359, Panini Comics, Tunbridge Wells, pp.12–18.

Hills, Matt (2002) *Fan Cultures*, Routledge, London and New York.

—— (2003) '*Star Wars* in fandom, film theory, and the museum: the cultural status of the cult blockbuster', in Julian Stringer (ed.) *Movie Blockbusters*, Routledge, London and New York, pp.178–89.

—— (2004) '*Dawson's Creek*: "quality teen TV" and "mainstream cult"?', in Glyn Davis and Kay Dickinson (eds) *Teen TV*, BFI Publishing, London, pp.54–67.

—— (2004) '*Doctor Who*', in Glen Creeber (ed.) *Fifty Key Television Programmes*, Arnold, London, pp.75–9.

—— (2005) 'Flat earthers write back', *Doctor Who Junkie*, 26 March Souvenir Issue, Cardiff.

—— (2005) *How to Do Things with Cultural Theory*, Hodder-Arnold, London.

—— (2005) *The Pleasures of Horror*, Continuum, London and New York.

—— (2005) 'Who wants to be a fan of *Who Wants to Be A Millionaire*?', in Catherine Johnson and Rob Turnock (eds) *ITV Cultures*, Open University Press, Milton Keynes, pp.177–95.

—— (2006) 'Realising the cult blockbuster: *The Lord of the Rings* fandom and residual/emergent cult status in "the mainstream"', in Ernest Mathijs (ed.) *The Lord of the Rings: Popular Culture in Global Context*, Wallflower Press, London and New York, pp.160–71.

—— (2006) 'Triumph of a Time Lord (Part One): an interview with Matt Hills', available online at 'Confessions of an Aca-Fan: the official weblog of Henry Jenkins', *http://www.henryjenkins.org/2006/09/triumph_of_a_time_lord_part_on.html*, 28 September, accessed 3 September 2008.

—— (2007) 'From the box in the corner to the box set on the shelf: "TV III" and the cultural/textual valorisations of DVD', *New Review of Film and Television Studies* v/1, pp.41–60.

—— (2007) '"Gothic" body parts in a "postmodern" body of work? The Hinchcliffe/Holmes era of *Doctor Who* (1975–77)', *Intensities: The Journal of Cult Media* 4, available online at *http://intensities.org/Issues/Intensities_Four.htm*.

—— (2007) 'Televisuality without television? The Big Finish audios and discourses of "tele-centric" *Doctor Who*', in David Butler (ed.) *Time and Relative Dissertations in Space*, Manchester University Press, Manchester and New York, pp.280–95.

—— (2008) 'The dispersible television text: theorising moments of the new *Doctor Who*', *Science Fiction Film and Television* i/1, pp.25–44.

—— (2008) 'The question of genre in cult film and fandom: between contract and discourse', in James Donald and Michael Renov (eds) *The Sage Handbook of Film Studies*, Sage, London, pp.436–53.

—— and Amy Luther (2007) 'Investigating "CSI television fandom": fans' textual paths through the franchise', in Michael Allen (ed.) *Reading CSI: Crime TV Under the Microscope*, I B Tauris, London and New York, pp.208–21.

—— and Rebecca Williams (2005) '*Angel*'s monstrous mothers and vampires with souls: investigating the abject in "television horror"', in Stacey Abbott (ed.) *Reading Angel: The TV Spin-Off with a Soul*, I.B.Tauris, London and New York, pp.203–17.

Hinton, Craig (2002) 'Dripping with camp menace', available online at *http://www.shockeye.org.uk/Freezer/Griller/Hinton/Hinton.html*, accessed 9 July 2007.

—— (2003) 'Live chat with Craig Hinton, *Doctor Who* Online, 14 May, 8pm–9pm', available online at *www.drwho-online.co.uk/chat-craighinton.doc*, accessed 26 August 2008.

Hodgdon, Barbara (2007) 'Shakespearean stars: stagings of desire', in Robert Shaughnessy (ed.) *The Cambridge Companion to Shakespeare and Popular Culture*, Cambridge University Press, Cambridge, pp.46–66.

Hollows, Joanne (2003) 'The masculinity of cult', in Mark Jancovich, Antonio Lázaro Reboll, Julian Stringer and Andy Willis (eds) *Defining Cult Movies*, Manchester University Press, Manchester, pp.35–53.

Hornby, Nick (1992) *Fever Pitch: A Fan's Life*, Gollancz, London.

Howarth, Chris and Steve Lyons (2006) *Doctor Who: The Completely Unofficial Encyclopedia*, Mad Norwegian Press, Des Moines, IA.

Howe, David J. and Arnold T. Blumberg (2006) *Howe's Transcendental Toybox Update No. 2: The Complete Guide to 2004–2005 Doctor Who Merchandise*, Telos, Tolworth.

Hugo, Simon (2008) 'Executive decisions', *Torchwood: The Official Magazine* 8, Titan Magazines, London, pp.8–14.

Hunt, Nathan (2003) 'The importance of trivia: ownership, exclusion and authority in science fiction fandom', in Mark Jancovich, Antonio Lázaro Reboll, Julian Stringer and Andy Willis (eds) *Defining Cult Movies*, Manchester University Press, Manchester and New York, pp.185–201.

Hutchings, Peter (2004) *The Horror Film*, Pearson Education, Harlow.

Hutchinson, Thom and Matt Bielby (2008) 'The gay agenda', *Death Ray* 15, September, Blackfish, Bath, p.59.

—— —— (2008) 'Love & Monsters', *Death Ray* 15, Blackfish, Bath, pp.56–9.

Isaacs, Bruce (2008) *Toward a New Film Aesthetic*, Continuum, New York and London.

Jacobs, Jason (2001) 'Issues of judgement and value in television studies', *International Journal of Cultural Studies* iv/4, pp.427–47.

—— (2006) 'Television aesthetics: an infantile disorder', *Journal of British Cinema and Television* iii/1, pp.19–33.

無

Jameson, Fredric (1991) *Postmodernism, or, The Cultural Logic of Late Capitalism*, Verso, London and New York.

Jancovich, Mark and Nathan Hunt (2004) 'The mainstream, distinction, and cult TV', in Sara Gwenllian-Jones and Roberta E. Pearson (eds) *Cult Television*, University of Minnesota Press, Minneapolis, pp.27–44.

—— and James Lyons (eds) (2003) *Quality Popular Television*, BFI Publishing, London.

Jenkins, Henry (1992) *Textual Poachers*, Routledge, New York and London.

—— (1995) '"Do you enjoy making the rest of us feel stupid?": alt.tv.twinpeaks, the trickster author and viewer mastery', in David Lavery (ed.) *Full of Secrets: Critical Approaches to* Twin Peaks, Wayne State University Press, Detroit, pp.51–69.

—— (2006) *Convergence Culture*, New York University Press, New York and London.

Johnson, Catherine (2005) *Telefantasy*, BFI Publishing, London.

—— (2007) 'Tele-branding in TVIII: the network as brand and the programme as brand', *New Review of Film and Television Studies* v/1, pp.5–24.

Johnson, Derek (2007) 'Fan-tagonism: factions, institutions, and constitutive hegemonies of fandom', in Jonathan Gray, Cornel Sandvoss and C. Lee Harrington (eds) *Fandom: Identities and Communities in a Mediated World*, New York University, New York and London, pp.285–300.

—— (2007) 'Inviting audiences in: the spatial reorganization of production and consumption in "TVIII"', *New Review of Film and Television Studies* v/1, pp.61–80.

Johnson-Smith, Jan (2005) *American Science Fiction TV: Star Trek, Stargate and Beyond*, I.B.Tauris, London and New York.

Jones, Matthew (1996) 'Fluid links: that's what I like', *Doctor Who Magazine* 238, Marvel Comics, London, p.20.

Kalinak, Kathryn (1995) '"Disturbing the guests with this racket": music and *Twin Peaks*', in David Lavery (ed.) *Full of Secrets: Critical Approaches to* Twin Peaks, Wayne State University Press, Detroit, pp.82–92.

Kane, Pat (2005) 'Doctoring the Corporation', available online at *http://theplayethic.typepad.com/play_journal/2005/03/index.html*, accessed 4 August 2008.

Kaveney, Roz (2005) *From Alien to the Matrix: Reading Science Fiction Film*, I.B.Tauris, London and New York.

Kilburn, Matthew (2007) 'Bargains of necessity? *Doctor Who*, Culloden and fictionalising history at the BBC in the 1960s', in David Butler (ed.) *Time and Relative Dissertations in Space: Critical Perspectives on* Doctor Who, Manchester University Press, Manchester, pp.68–85.

Kramer, Peter and Alan Lovell (1999) 'Introduction', in Alan Lovell and Peter Kramer (eds) *Screen Acting*, Routledge, London and New York, pp.1–9.

Lambess, Neil (2006) 'Errant nonsense', *Time Space Visualiser* 73, pp.67–9.

Landon, Brooks (2002) *Science Fiction After 1900: From the Steam Man to the Stars*, Routledge, London and New York.

Lavery, David (2002) 'Afterword: the genius of Joss Whedon', in Rhonda V. Wilcox and David Lavery (eds) *Fighting the Forces: What's at Stake in* Buffy the Vampire Slayer, Rowman and Littlefield, Maryland, pp.251–6.

Lem, Stanislaw (1991) 'The time-travel story and related matters of science-fiction structuring', *Microworlds*, Mandarin, London, pp.136–60.

Lennon, John and Malcolm Foley (2000) *Dark Tourism: The Attraction of Death and Disaster*, Continuum, London and New York.

Lesnick, Silas (2008) 'SDCC exclusive interview: Steven Moffat on *Doctor Who*', available online at *http://www.comingsoon.net/news/tvnews.php?id=47147*, accessed 7 August 2008.

Letts, Quentin (2008) 'Who's the greatest?', *Daily Mail*, 4 July, available online at *http://www.dailymail.co.uk/tvshowbiz/article-1031715/Whos-greatest.html*, accessed 28 August 2008.

Levy, Pierre (1997) *Collective Intelligence*, Perseus Books, Cambridge, MA.

Longhurst, Brian (2007) *Cultural Change and Ordinary Life*, Open University Press, Maidenhead and New York.

Lury, Karen (2007) '*CSI* and sound', in Michael Allen (ed.) *Reading CSI*, I.B.Tauris, London and New York, pp.107–21.

Lyon, J. Shaun (2005) *Back to the Vortex*, Telos Press, Tolworth.

—— (2006) *Second Flight*, Telos Press, Tolworth.

Lyons, Steve (2004) 'All our Christmases', in Paul Cornell (ed.) *Short Trips: A Christmas Treasury*, Big Finish, Maidenhead, pp.185–94.

Macdonald, Myra (2003) *Exploring Media Discourse*, Arnold, London.

Magrs, Paul (2007) 'Afterword: my adventures', in David Butler (ed.) *Time and Relative Dissertations in Space*, Manchester University Press, Manchester and New York, pp.296–309.

May, David (ed.) (2007) *Views From Behind the Sofa*, Lulu, Raleigh, NC.

McDougall, Julian (2008) *OCR Media Studies for AS*, 3rd edn, Hodder Education, London.

McGechan, Adam (2005) 'Through rose-tinted glasses: old fans, new series and one leaked episode', *Time Space Visualiser: The Journal of the New Zealand Doctor Who Fan Club* 71, pp.24–7.

McKee, Alan (2001) *Australian Television: A Genealogy of Great Moments*, Oxford University Press, Oxford and New York.

—— (2001) 'Which is the best *Doctor Who* story? A case study in value judgements outside the academy', *Intensities: The Journal of Cult Media*, available at *http://intensities.org/Essays/McKee.pdf*, accessed 26 August 2008.

—— (2002) 'Interview with Russell T. Davies', *Continuum: Journal of Media and Cultural Studies* xvi/2, pp.235–44.

—— (2003) *Textual Analysis: A Beginner's Guide*, Sage, London.

—— (2004) 'How to tell the difference between production and consumption: a case study in *Doctor Who* fandom', in Sara Gwenllian Jones and Roberta E. Pearson (eds) *Cult Television*, University of Minnesota Press, Minneapolis and London, pp.167–85.

—— (2004) 'Is *Doctor Who* political?', *European Journal of Cultural Studies* vii/2, pp.201–17.

—— (ed.) (2007) *Beautiful Things in Popular Culture*, Blackwell Publishing, Malden and Oxford.

—— (2007) 'Why is "City of Death" the best *Doctor Who* story?', in David Butler (ed.) *Time and Relative Dissertations in Space: Critical Perspectives on Doctor Who*, Manchester University Press, Manchester and New York, pp.233–45.

McKee, Joe (2005) 'The age of wonders: overview', *Shockeye's Kitchen*, 16th Course, pp.4–7, 30–5.

McKee, Robert (1999) *Story*, Methuen, London.

Messenger Davies, Maire (2007) 'Quality and creativity in TV: the work of television storytellers', in Janet McCabe and Kim Akass (eds) *Quality TV: Contemporary American Television and Beyond*, I.B.Tauris, London and New York, pp.171–84.

Miles, Lawrence (2005) 'Doctor Who, season X 1: "Rose": a review of the series, and the twenty-first century, so far', available online at *http://www. beasthouse.fsnet.co.uk/who01.htm*, accessed 2 September 2008.

—— (2007) 'Secs sell', available online at *http://Beasthouse.LM2.blogspot.com*, 29 November, accessed 29 November 2007.

—— (2008) '*Doctor Who* 2008, week two: the past is another country ... it's full of bloody tourists', cited in *Doctor Who* Forum posting 5, 'At last the Lawrence Miles show', 13 April, available at *http://lawrencemiles.blogspot. com/2008/04/fires-of-pompeii.html*.

—— and Tat Wood (2004) *About Time 3: 1970–74*, Mad Norwegian Press, Des Moines, IA.

—— —— (2004) *About Time 4: 1975–79*, Mad Norwegian Press, Des Moines, IA.

—— —— (2005) *About Time 5: 1980–84* Mad Norwegian Press, Des Moines, IA.

Mittell, Jason (2004) *Genre and Television*, Routledge, New York and London.

—— (2006) 'Narrative complexity in contemporary American television', *The Velvet Light Trap* 58 (Fall), pp.29–40.

Moffat, Steven (1996) 'Afterword', in Andy Lane and Justin Richards (eds) Doctor Who: *Decalog 3*, Virgin Publishing, London, pp. 304.

—— (1996) 'Continuity errors', in Andy Lane and Justin Richards (eds) Doctor Who: *Decalog 3*, Virgin Publishing, London, pp.214–39.

—— (2005) 'What I did on my Christmas holidays by Sally Sparrow', in Clayton Hickman (ed.) *Doctor Who Annual 2006*, Panini Books, Tunbridge Wells, pp.53–9.

—— (2008) 'A letter from the Doctor' in *Doctor Who Storybook 2009* Panini Books, Tunbridge Wells: p. 5.

—— (2008) 'Production notes' in *Doctor Who Magazine* 397 Panini Comics, Tunbridge Wells: pp. 4–5.

Moran, Albert (1998) *Copycat TV: Globalisation, Program Formats and Cultural Identity*, University of Luton Press, Luton.

Moran, Joe (1999) *Star Authors*, Pluto Press, London.

*Moths Ate My Doctor Who Scarf* (2007), writer: Toby Hadoke, producer: Paul Hardy, BBC Audio, London.

Muir, John Kenneth (1999) *A Critical History of* Doctor Who *on Television*, McFarland, Jefferson and London.

Mulvey, Laura (1999) 'Visual pleasure and narrative cinema', in Sue Thornham (ed.) *Feminist Film Theory*, Edinburgh University Press, Edinburgh, pp.58–69.

Murray, Andy (2007) 'The talons of Robert Holmes', in David Butler (ed.) *Time and Relative Dissertations in Space: Critical Perspectives on* Doctor Who, Manchester University Press, Manchester and New York, pp.217–32.

Nathan, Sarah (2003) 'Duckie Who: Time Lord has gay show writer', *The Sun*, 27 September, p.33, available online at *http://www.cuttingsarchive.org.uk/ news_mag/2000s/cuttings/ukls/duckie.htm*, accessed 28 August 2008.

Nelson, Jenny (1990) 'The dislocation of time: a phenomenology of television reruns', *Quarterly Review of Film and Video* xii/3, pp.79–92.

Nelson, Robin (1997) *TV Drama in Transition*, Macmillan, Basingstoke.

—— (2007) *State of Play: Contemporary 'High-End' TV Drama*, Manchester University Press, Manchester and New York.

Newman, Kim (1996) '*Doctor Who*', in Kim Newman (ed.) *The BFI Companion to Horror*, Cassell, London, pp.95–6.

—— (2005) *BFI TV Classics:* Doctor Who, BFI Publishing, London.

Niebur, Louis (2007) 'The music of machines: "special sound" as music in *Doctor Who*', in David Butler (ed.) *Time and Relative Dissertations in Space: Critical Perspectives on* Doctor Who, Manchester University Press, Manchester and New York, pp.204–14.

Norton, Charles (2008) 'Evolution of a monster hit', *The Stage*, 15 May, pp.52–3.

O'Brien, Daniel (2000) *SF: UK, How British Science Fiction Changed the World*, Reynolds and Hearn, London.

O'Brien, Steve and Nick Setchfield (2005) 'Russell spouts', in *SFX Collection:* Doctor Who *Special*, Future Network, Bath, pp.36–40.

O'Mahony, Daniel (2007) '"Now how is that wolf able to impersonate a grandmother?" History, pseudo-history and genre in *Doctor Who*', in David Butler (ed.) *Time and Relative Dissertations in Space: Critical Perspectives on* Doctor Who, Manchester University Press, Manchester and New York, pp.56–67.

Osgerby, Bill, Anna Gough-Yates and Marianne Wells (2001) 'The business of action: television history and the development of the action TV series', in Bill Osgerby and Anna Gough-Yates (eds) *Action TV*, Routledge, London and New York, pp.13–31.

O'Shaughnessy, Michael (1999) *Media and Society*, Oxford University Press, Oxford and New York.

Osmond, Andrew (2005) 'Sexing up the Tardis', *Sight & Sound* (December), p.88.

Owen, Dave (2007) 'The Lazarus experiment', *Doctor Who Magazine* 384, Panini Comics, Tunbridge Wells, p.60.

—— (2008) 'Turn Left/The Stolen Earth/Journey's End', *Doctor Who Magazine* 399, Panini Comics, Tunbridge Wells, pp.59–61.

Parkin, Lance (2005) 'The incredible week', *Enlightenment: The Official Fanzine of the* Doctor Who *Information Network* (June/July), pp.26–7.

—— (2007) 'Canonicity matters: defining the *Doctor Who* canon', in David Butler (ed.) *Time and Relative Dissertations in Space: Critical Perspectives on* Doctor Who, Manchester University Press, Manchester and New York, pp.246–62.

—— (2007) 'Re: *Time and Relative Dissertations in Space*', 18 December, 7:29pm, available online at *http://www.doctorwhoforum.com*.

Parks, Lisa (2003) 'Brave new *Buffy*: rethinking "TV violence"', in Mark Jancovich and James Lyons (eds) *Quality Popular Television*, BFI Publishing, London, pp.118–33.

Pearson, Roberta E. (1992) *Eloquent Gestures*, University of California Press, Berkeley, Los Angeles and Oxford.

—— (2004) '"Bright particular star": Patrick Stewart, Jean-Luc Picard and cult television', in Sara Gwenllian-Jones and Roberta E. Pearson (eds) *Cult Television*, University of Minnesota Press, Minneapolis, pp.61–80.

Peel, John (2007) *I Am the Doctor: The Unauthorised Diaries of a Time Lord*, Zone, London.

Pegg, Alistair (2005) 'Saturday night, Sunday morning', *Black Scrolls* 8 (winter), pp.45–6.

Penley, Constance (1990) 'Time travel, primal scene and the critical dystopia', in Annette Kuhn (ed.) *Alien Zone*, Verso, London, pp.116–27.

—— (1997) *Nasa/Trek*, Verso, London.

Perryman, Neil (2008) '*Doctor Who* and the convergence of media: a case study in "transmedia storytelling"', *Convergence: The International Journal of Research into New Media Technologies* xiv/1, pp.21–39.

Pierson, Michele (2002) *Special Effects: Still In Search of Wonder*, Columbia University Press, New York.

Pixley, Andrew (2005) 'Fact file: Aliens of London/World War Three', *Doctor Who Magazine Special Edition: The* Doctor Who *Companion – Series One*, Panini Comics, Tunbridge Wells, pp.32–5.

—— (2006) *Doctor Who Magazine Special Edition: The* Doctor Who *Companion – Series Two*, Panini Comics, Tunbridge Wells.

—— (2007) *Doctor Who Magazine Special Edition: The* Doctor Who *Companion – Series Three*, Panini Comics, Tunbridge Wells.

—— (2008) *Doctor Who Magazine Special Edition: The* Doctor Who *Companion – Series Four*, Panini Comics, Tunbridge Wells.

Porter, Lynnette and David Lavery (2007) *Unlocking the Meaning of* Lost, Sourcebooks, Naperville, IL.

*Project: Who?* (2005) BBC Audio, London.

Pryor, Cathy (2006) 'Russell T Davies: one of Britain's foremost television writers', *Independent*, 22 October, available online at *http://www.independent.co.uk/news/people/russell-t-davies-one-of-britains-foremost-television-writers-421182.html*, accessed 5 August 2008.

Redhead, Steve (1997) *Post-Fandom and the Millennial Blues*, Routledge, London and New York.

Richards, Barry (1994) *Disciplines of Delight: The Psychoanalysis of Popular Culture*, Free Association Press, London.

Richards, Justin (2002) *The Time of the Daleks*, Big Finish Audio, London.

—— (2005) Doctor Who: *Monsters and Villains*, BBC Books, London.

Richardson, David (2004) 'Russell T. Davies', *TV Zone Special 56*, Visual Imagination, London, pp.70–1, 74–5, 78–9.

Rilstone, Andrew (2008) 'The 50 greatest moments of *Doctor Who*', *Sci Fi Now* 19, Imagine, London, pp.56–60.

Rixon, Paul (2008) '*Star Trek*: popular discourses – the role of broadcasters and critics', in Lincoln Geraghty (ed.) *The Influence of* Star Trek *on Television, Film and Culture*, McFarland, Jefferson and London, pp.153–69.

Roberts, Gareth (2005) 'Guess Who?', *Doctor Who Magazine Special Edition: The* Doctor Who *Companion – Series One*, Panini Comics, Tunbridge Wells, pp.6–13.

—— (2006) 'A groatsworth of wit', in *The Ninth Doctor Collected Comics*, Panini Comics, Tunbridge Wells, pp.87–104.

—— (2006) *I Am a Dalek*, BBC Books, London.

Robins, Tim (2003) 'Sutekh's gift', *In-Vision* 109, Cybermark Services, Borehamwood, p.28.

Robins, Tim and Paul Mount (2004) 'Lights, camera, legal action!', *Starburst* 317, Visual Imagination, London, p.12.

Rodowick, D.N. (1997) *Gilles Deleuze's Time Machine*, Duke University Press, Durham and London.

Rolinson, Dave (2007) '"Who done it": discourses of authorship during the John Nathan-Turner era', in David Butler (ed.) *Time and Relative Dissertations in Space: Critical Perspectives on* Doctor Who, Manchester University Press, Manchester and New York, pp.176–89.

Rollings, Grant (2009) 'Who are ya', available at *http://www.thesun.co.uk/sol/homepage/showbiz/tv/article2094236.ece*, accessed 5 January 2009.

Ross, Sharon Marie (2008) *Beyond the Box: Television and the Internet*, Blackwell Publishing, Malden and Oxford.

Rubin, Martin (1999) *Thrillers*, Cambridge University Press, Cambridge.

Russell, Gary (2006) Doctor Who: *The Inside Story*, BBC Books, London.

Sandvoss, Cornel (2005) *Fans: The Mirror of Consumption*, Polity Press, Cambridge.

Schuster, Marc and Tom Powers (2007) *The Greatest Show in the Galaxy: The Discerning Fan's Guide to* Doctor Who, McFarland, Jefferson and London.

Scott, Suzanne (2008) 'Authorized resistance: is fan production frakked?', in Tiffany Potter and C.W. Marshall (eds) *Cylons in America: Critical Studies in Battlestar Galactica*, Continuum, New York and London, pp.210–23.

Setchfield, Nick (2007) 'When Russell met Verity: the outtakes', *SFX Collection* special edn 28, Future Network, Bath, pp.120–4.

—— (2008) 'We have a twenty year plan...', *SFX* 168, Future Network, Bath, pp.44–51.

—— and Steve O'Brien (2006) 'The Lord of Time', *SFX Collection* special edn 24, Future Network, Bath, pp.6–9.

—— —— (2006) 'When Russell met Verity', *SFX* 150, Future Network, Bath, pp.54–8.

Slusser, George and Danielle Chatelain (1995) 'Spacetime geometries: time travel and the modern geometrical narrative', *Science Fiction Studies* xxii/2, pp.161–86.

Smith, Dale (2007) 'Broader and deeper: the lineage and impact of the Timewyrm series', in David Butler (ed.) *Time and Relative Dissertations in Space*, Manchester University Press, Manchester and New York, pp.263–79.

Smith, Greg. M. (1999) '"To waste more time, please click here again": Monty Python and the quest for film/CD-ROM adaptation', in Greg M. Smith (ed.) *On A Silver Platter*, New York University Press, New York and London, pp.58–86.

Smith, Jeff (1998) *The Sounds of Commerce: Marketing Popular Film Music*, Columbia University Press, New York.

Spigel, Lynn and Henry Jenkins (1991) 'Same Bat Channel, different Bat Times: mass culture and popular memory', in Roberta E. Pearson and William

Uricchio (eds) *The Many Lives of the Batman*, Routledge/BFI, London and New York, pp.117–48.

Spilsbury, Tom (2008) 'Letter from the editor', *Doctor Who Magazine* 392, p.3.

Staiger, Janet (2003) 'Authorship approaches', in David A. Gerstner and Janet Staiger (eds) *Authorship and Film*, Routledge, New York and London, pp.27–57.

Stanton, James (2004) 'Will the new *Doctor Who* TV series be any good?', *Dreamwatch* 117, pp.46–50.

Stevens, Alan and Fiona Moore (2005) '*Doctor Who*: the unquiet dead', available online at *http://www.kaldorcity.com/features/articles/unquiet.html*, accessed 27 September 2008.

Stilwell, Robynn J. (2001) 'Sound and empathy: subjectivity, gender and the cinematic soundscape', in K.J. Donnelly (ed.) *Film Music: Critical Approaches*, Edinburgh University Press, Edinburgh, pp.167–87.

Stockwell, Peter (2000) *The Poetics of Science Fiction*, Longman, Harlow.

Storey, John (2006) *Cultural Theory and Popular Culture: An Introduction*, 4th edn, Pearson, Harlow.

*Sun* (2008) 'Billie is gunning for the Daleks', available online at *http://www.thesun.co.uk/sol/homepage/showbiz/tv/article920788.ece*, 15 March, accessed 27 September 2008.

Suvin, Darko (1979) *Metamorphoses of Science Fiction*, Yale University Press, London.

Sweet, Matthew (2006) 'Inside the TARDIS, by James Chapman', *Independent*, available online at *http://www.independent.co.uk/arts-entertainment/books/reviews/inside-the-tardis-by-james-chapman-480122.html*, 28 May, accessed 1 June 2006.

Sweney, Mark (2008) 'Merlin: BBC cues up TV and cinema ads', 29 August, available online at *http://www.guardian.co.uk/media/2008/aug/29/bbc.television*, accessed 27 September 2008.

Talbot, Mary (2007) *Media Discourse*, Edinburgh University Press, Edinburgh.

Taylor, Jerome (2008) 'Daleks invade the proms (while earthlings pay £250 for a ticket)', *Independent*, 28 July, available online at *http://www.independent.co.uk/arts-entertainment/music/news/daleks-invade-the-proms-while-earthlings-pay-163250-for-a-ticket-878691.html*.

Taylor Herring Public Relations (2008) 'Case study: *Doctor Who*', available online at *http://www.taylorherring.com/doctorwho_case.html*, accessed 2 October 2008.

Tennant, David (2006) 'My Time Lord is now', *Telegraph Magazine*, 8 April, pp.36–9.

Thacker, Anthony (2006) *Behind the Sofa: A Closer Look at* Doctor Who, Kingsway Publications, Eastbourne.

Thompson, Kristin (2003) *Storytelling in Film and Television*, Harvard University Press, Cambridge and London.

Thornham, Sue and Tony Purvis (2005) *Television Drama: Theories and Identities*, Palgrave-Macmillan, Basingstoke and New York.

Thornton, Sarah (1995) *Club Cultures*, Polity Press, Cambridge.

Todd, Matthew (2006) 'Any queries? Where you ask the questions – John Barrowman', *Attitude* 152 (December), pp.34–9.

Todorov, Tzvetan (1975) *The Fantastic*, Cornell University Press, Ithaca.

Topping, Keith (2006) 'Craig Hinton', available online at *http://keithtopping. blogspot.com/2006/12/craig-hinton.html*, 6 December, accessed 3 September 2008.

Tryon, Charles (2008) 'TV Time Lords: fan cultures, narrative complexity, and the future of science fiction television', in J.P. Telotte (ed.) *The Essential Science Fiction Television Reader*, University Press of Kentucky, Kentucky, pp.301–14.

Tulloch, John (1999) *Performing Culture*, Sage, London.

—— (2000) 'Multiple authorship in TV drama' in Jonathan Bignell, Stephen Lacey and Madeleine Macmurraugh-Kavanagh (eds) *British Television Drama: Past, Present and Future*, Palgrave, Basingstoke, pp.175–84.

—— (2005) *Shakespeare and Chekhov in Production and Reception: Theatrical Events and their Audiences*, University of Iowa Press, Iowa City.

—— (2007) 'Fans of Chekhov: re-approaching "High Culture"', in Jonathan Gray, Cornel Sandvoss and C. Lee Harrington (eds) *Fandom: Identities and Communities in a Mediated World*, New York University Press, New York and London, pp.110–22.

—— and Alvarado, Manuel (1983) Doctor Who: *The Unfolding Text*, Macmillan, London.

—— and Jenkins, Henry (1995) *Science Fiction Audiences: Watching* Doctor Who *and* Star Trek, Routledge, London and New York.

Turnbull, Sue (2005) 'Moments of inspiration: performing Spike', *European Journal of Cultural Studies* viii/3, pp.367–73.

Turner, Graeme (2001) 'Genre, format and "live" television', in Glen Creeber (ed.) *The Television Genre Book*, BFI Publishing, London, pp.6–7.

Tushnet, Rebecca (2007) 'Copyright law, fan practices, and the rights of the author', in Jonathan Gray, Cornel Sandvoss and C. Lee Harrington (eds) *Fandom: Identities and Communities in a Mediated World*, New York University Press, New York and London, pp.60–71.

Unreality SF (2008) 'Russell T Davies and Benjamin Cook', available at *http://unreality-sf.net/interviews/thewriterstale.html*, accessed 5 January 2009.

Urry, John (1990) *The Tourist Gaze*, Sage, London.

van Zoonen, Liesbet (2005) *Entertaining the Citizen: When Politics and Popular Culture Converge*, Rowman and Littlefield, Lanham, MD.

Wachhorst, Wyn (1984) 'Time-travel romance on film', in *Extrapolation 25*, pp.340–59.

Walker, Jesse (2004) '*Doctor Who* and the fandom of fear: what happens when fans take over a franchise?', in *Reason Online*, available at *http://www.reason.com/news/show/33494.html*, accessed 21 September 2008.

Walker, Stephen James (1999) 'Surprised? You should be...', *Doctor Who Magazine 277*, Marvel Comics, London, pp.6–11.

—— (2007) *Third Dimension*, Telos Press, Tolworth.

Warf, Barney (2002) 'The way it wasn't: alternative histories, contingent geographies', in Rob Kitchin and James Kneale (eds) *Lost in Space: Geographies of Science Fiction*, Continuum, London and New York, pp.17–38.

West, Matt (2005) 'Kids today: when even getting kids to watch TV is a struggle', *Time Space Visualiser: The Journal of the New Zealand Doctor Who Fan Club 71*, pp.22–3.

Wheatley, Helen (2006) *Gothic Television*, Manchester University Press, Manchester.

Whotopia (2006) '*Doctor Who* adventures number 3 review', available online at *http://newdoctorwhostuff.blogspot.com/2006/05/doctor-who-adventures-3-review.html*, accessed 6 June 2006.

Williams, John (2008) 'Whose fanwank is it anyway?', available online at *http://www.behindthesofa.org.uk/2008/07/whose-fanwank-i.html*, 4 July, accessed 3 September 2008.

Williams, Kevin (2006) 'An uncertain era: Welsh television, broadcasting policy and the National Assembly in a multimedia world', *Contemporary Wales: An Annual Review of Economic, Political and Social Research*, vol. xviii, University of Wales Press, Cardiff, pp.214–35.

—— (2008) 'Broadcasting and the National Assembly: the future of broadcasting policy in Wales', *Cyfrwng: Media Wales Journal 5*, pp.94–110.

Williams, Linda (1996) 'When the woman looks', in Barry Keith Grant (ed.) *The Dread of Difference: Gender and the Horror Film*, University of Texas Press, Austin, pp.15–34.

Williams, Linda Ruth (2005) '*Twin Peaks*: David Lynch and the serial-thriller soap', in Michael Hammond and Lucy Mazdon (eds) *The Contemporary Television Series*, Edinburgh University Press, Edinburgh, pp.37–56.

Williamson, David (2008) 'BBC Wales won't depend on *Doctor Who*', *Western Mail*, 10 June, available online at *http://www.walesonline.co.uk/news/politics-news/2008/06/10/bbc-wales-won-t-depend-on-doctor-who-91466-21047606/*, accessed 18 September 2009.

Wood, Robin (1986) *Hollywood from Vietnam to Reagan*, Columbia University Press, New York.

Wood, Tat (2007) *About Time 6: The Unauthorized Guide to* Doctor Who *1985–1989*, Mad Norwegian Press, Des Moines, IA.

Wood, Tat and Lawrence Miles (2006) *About Time 1: 1963–66*, Mad Norwegian Press, Des Moines, IA.

—— —— (2006) *About Time 2: 1966–69*, Mad Norwegian Press, Des Moines, IA.

Wright, Peter (1999) 'The shared world of *Doctor Who*', *Foundation: The International Review of Science Fiction*, xxviii/75, pp.78–96.

Wyatt, Justin (1994) *High Concept: Movies and Marketing in Hollywood*, University of Texas Press, Austin.

Wyman, Mark (2005) 'Class of 2005', *Doctor Who Magazine 361*, Panini Comics, Tunbridge Wells, pp.12–21.

Zizek, Slavoj (1989) *The Sublime Object of Ideology*, Verso, London.

# INDEX